SLICK SPINS
and FRACTURED FACTS

SLICK SPINS
and FRACTURED FACTS

How Cultural Myths Distort the News

Caryl Rivers

Columbia University Press New York

Columbia University Press
New York   Chichester, West Sussex
Copyright © 1996 Caryl Rivers

Library of Congress Cataloging-in-Publication Data

Rivers, Caryl.
  Slick spins and fractured facts : how cultural myths distort the
news / Caryl Rivers.
    p. cm.
  Includes bibliographical references (p.) and index
  ISBN 0–231–10152–X
    1. Journalism—Objectivity.   2. Mass media—Objectivity.
3. Journalistic ethics.   4. Mass media—Moral and ethical aspects.
I. Title.
PN4784.024R58   1996
302.23—dc20

Casebound editions of Columbia University Press books are printed on permanent
and durable acid-free paper.

Printed in the United States of America

c 10 9 8 7 6 5 4 3 2 1

CONTENTS

ACKNOWLEDGMENTS

❂

I wish to thank Ann Miller at Columbia University Press for being a thoughtful and insightful editor and Polly Kummel for an excellent job of copy editing. It's a delight to work with real pros. I'm indebted to the Massachusetts Foundation for the Humanities for the grant that helped make this book possible. Thanks as well to Dean Brent Baker and David Anable of Boston University College of Communication for helping with support for the research. And I want to thank my husband, Alan Lupo, for his support, help, and advice—and his insights on the profession we share.

INTRODUCTION:
THE INSIDER-OUTSIDER

By the time I was a freshman in high school, I knew I wanted to be a journalist.

I wanted to belong to a group that was allowed to pry into life's secrets. Journalists—unlike nice little Catholic girls—had permission to go anywhere. I could already see, as I began the metamorphosis from gritty little tomboy to young woman, that there were fences and walls, whole areas of life roped off and marked FOR MEN ONLY. It never occurred to me that the walls would crumble, as if before Joshua's trumpets. The world was as it was—solid, unbending. But walls had cracks, and with grit and cunning, I might slip through them.

Audacity was called for. My best friend, Clare Josephine Wootten—a year older than I, with a sharp eye for the openings—inspired me. It was she who dragged me off on one of my most bizarre journalistic adventures. We stood, wearing our parochial school uniforms (I was gripping a camera) on the steps of Pumphrey's Funeral Home, next to St. Michael's church. When the large white door opened, a man in sepulchral black peered out to see the odd duo on the steps.

"We're journalists," Clare said, "and we want to take pictures of the dead people."

The door closed decisively in our faces. I was a bit relieved. It was not my idea of a story; sports was my field of interest. I was on *my* turf on one of our next forays, a trip to Griffith Stadium to interview a Washington Senators pitcher of remarkable longevity named Bobo Newsom. Clare, untutored in Senators lore—but audacious—was ready as Bobo entered the clubhouse. She stuck out her hand and said, "Glad to meet you, Mister Bosom."

Journalism, it seemed to me then, was like the magic carpet at which I had marveled in the color picture book of the *Arabian Nights* much beloved in my childhood. It could carry me over the walls and fences; everything would stretch out like the landscape beneath for my inspection. And in truth it has proved to be so. I have been in many places I never expected to be. I remember once, standing in the White House Rose Garden, watching then-president Lyndon Johnson handing out some forgettable award to a Future Farmer of America, and a thought flashed into my mind. *Holy Shit! I am here! I, Caryl Ann Theresa (for St. Theresa, the Little Flower) Rivers, former editor of the* Silver Quill *of the Academy of the Holy Names in Silver Spring, Maryland, am in the White House. I am in the* goddamn *White House.*

And paid to be there, to boot.

For a long time I was simply grateful to be let into the game. I believe that men from good families, with pedigrees and high expectations, simply can't understand how thrilling it is for some people just to be admitted to the arena—be it journalism or politics or law or business. The kid from the ghetto, the barrio, the blue-collar neighborhood—or the girl from the parochial school—often feels that stab of amazement. *Holy Shit. I'm here!*

The cold thrill of anxiety often follows. *Do I belong here? Will I ever?* Will a Secret Service agent stride resolutely across the Rose Garden, grip my arm, and announce in steely tones: "We know who you are! You are not a real reporter. You're just the editor of the *Silver Quill.* Come with me!"

Pride in your achievement is always accompanied by the sense that you are an impostor, a fraud. In this situation you have to be a quick study. You watch closely to pick up clues to how to behave. You glance edgily out of the corner of your eye, like an untutored dinner guest trying to figure out the spoons. It's not so hard once you get the hang of it, but your very success induces a kind of schizophrenia. A crust forms over your true self that is as fragile as pond ice on a spring day. It convinces casual observers, but you know it could give way at any minute. You know that the surface conceals something quite different and not entirely legitimate. You learn to "stifle yourself," as Archie Bunker admonished Edith. Spontaneous reactions can be dangerous. You know this, because at times they have crept out and you've seen other people looking at you as if you were a Martian.

You find you have several choices. One is to simply try to convince yourself that you are just like them, to let the frozen surface gradually creep into your whole being, to become an imitation man, or white, or WASP. I've seen people who have become rather expert at this, but they are never totally at ease with it, not the real McCoy. There is always some part that doesn't get frozen, that stays mushy and soft, never to be trusted.

Or you can become a rebel and simply opt out of the game, hurling rocks—or invective—from outside. Sometimes you can even achieve a modicum of power that way, particularly if longevity runs in your genes. When some rebels age, they become beloved curmudgeons, honored by the very institutions they have long assaulted. But most are completely ignored, their howls curling up and out into emptiness.

But if you have no taste for being a chameleon or an outcast, you have a third alternative: hanging in, walking on that tenuous edge between the inner and outer world. Balancing, always balancing.

But this enterprise drains much of your energy. You do not want to go plunging like a Flying Wallenda, head down into chaos. And the longer you do it, the more precarious it gets, because as you get older, the small voice inside tends to get louder, more insistent. If you are wise, you listen.

The voice may say, *What are you doing up on that tightrope anyhow, dummy?* It may prompt you to wonder who wrote the rules you so readily obey. You are so busy playing the game that you have not wondered about the game itself. Whose is it? Why do things operate as they do? Who guards the guardians? And then comes the subversive thought: why couldn't things be different?

From that germ of dissent follow all sorts of dark and untidy notions. *They* aren't any smarter than I am. Who elected *them*? Could I do it better? I *could* do it better. From such mutterings revolutions are born.

The amazing thing to me is that I have heard Joshua's trumpet call. The solid, immobile, white male world I perceived as unshakable has shifted, cracked, opened. It is not Gibraltar. It is just a structure. New wings can be added, old space remodeled. As James Baldwin said, "Everything is in question. One has to forge a new language to deal with it."

Women are among those seeking that new language, trying to redefine a world that has been presented heretofore only in male terms. With them has come a flood of energy; new structures are going up faster than downtown condos. It is an energy that on the whole is constructive rather than destructive. Women by and large do not want to smash in the old houses and raze them from the earth. "Bomb them back to the Stone Age" is not something women usually say. But we are demanding to add our voices to those who define what it is to be human—or to be male or female or political or powerful or rational. We no longer want to inhabit a world we had no part in making.

Men sometimes blanch when the words *feminist* and *critic* are mentioned in the same breath. This is partly because men fear women's anger and partly because in our hypercompetitive society, men don't always feel like such winners. The temptation is to shut out all those voices—the women, the blacks, the gays, the Hispanics—the whole chorus that, once silent, now sounds like an overpowering roar. But this is not a zero-sum game. White men do not lose because others win. There is world enough and time for all of us, and journalists especially gain from seeing the world through an unexpected prism.

But for me this is a fairly newfound perspective. For many years being a woman in journalism meant being an Outsider—even as you fancied yourself an Insider, privy to the secrets. It is as if you have a third eye, seeing things invisible to those around you. Your first impulse is to doubt the legitimacy of your vision. You wonder whether it is *you* who are crazy. But gradually you begin to understand that it is your angle of vision that is different. It is that which gives you the extra orb.

Being an Insider-Outsider tends to make you acutely aware of the nature of the beast to which you have devoted your working life. Seeing things other people don't gets to be a habit. Maybe it is that you are less completely integrated than others in the system of rewards and punishments, of fiats and the conventional wisdom and this-is-how-we-do-it routines.

For me, writing about the behavioral sciences helped me start to get a handle on my peculiar status. It heightened my tendency to ask questions. I began to wonder why certain stories vaulted into the headlines, whereas others quietly died. I wondered about the persistence of certain ideas and theories that seemed to sprout like malevolent weeds, especially about people who were nonwhite, nonmale, nonstraight, non-Western. The more I read of people whose job it is to probe our motivations and our actions, the more I began to understand. Elizabeth Janeway's *Man's World, Woman's Place* was especially germane to the business in which I have spent three decades. She explains how a society invents myths about itself, how the storytellers are drawn from among the elite groups who weave tales to their own design. The power to *define* is perhaps the essential power; from that everything else flows. And we in journalism too rarely wonder about the origins of our worldview. Our business is "facts"; we have little time to question the assumptions on which those facts are based. Usually, we are so busy minding other people's business that we have little truck with our own.

Journalism has been called "literature under pressure," and *pressure* is the operative word. It is a business of deadlines and crises. When the shells are going off overhead (and they always are, metaphorically), you don't have much time to look at what you do. You think you are a pro, that you are *objective*. Often you don't realize that decisions about what is—or is not—"news" grow out of a lifetime of experiences. Class, race, sex—all these have a profound influence. So does the tangle of myth that makes up the collective tapestry of what kind of a people we think we are. Cultural mythology has a power and logic all its own. In time it becomes impossible to separate it from truth. Plato wrote of a group of cave dwellers inhabiting a world of darkness who saw their shadows on the wall in the firelight and thought it was the shadows that were real. Those twisted figures dancing in the firelight became, to them, as solid as flesh.

As an Insider-Outsider it is these shadows I want to probe. Perhaps I see them more clearly because of my divided self, my feeling of being kin both to those who have power and to those who have not—more viscerally to the have-nots. My gut instinct is to side with those who storm the battlements, not its defenders. The myths of which I write pertain especially to gender, race, and class in America, because those are areas in which the new power struggles are increasingly being waged.

Because the media have become so powerful in our society, so capable of shaping thought and enforcing prejudice, I want to pierce through the cultural myths that can cripple those of us who do not fit in the pictures painted by powerful others. I want to say that the status quo is not all that can be. Alternative realities exist and to imagine them is to begin to create them. I want that task to be easier for a younger generation of journalists than it has been for me.

I have admired many critiques of the media by my male colleagues, although I usually find them rather different from mine. We do not always see the same things in the firelight and the shadows. It has taken me a while—half a lifetime—to understand that my vision is real, my instincts legitimate. As Harvard psychologist Carol Gilligan puts it, my speaking in a different voice does not mean I should be silent.

We are heading into a century in which the old gods will certainly continue to crumble. As a nation we can no longer simply see ourselves as shades of pale. The new century will be in living color, and it may often speak in languages that are unfamiliar to our ears. Women will walk fully out of the shadows of men's dreams. If we wish to build a new world, we will have to understand the way that worlds are made and how ideas can freeze into dogma.

Make no mistake: there will be much resistance to change. Already the cannons are being dragged to the barricades, and shots are being fired. We hear that women are destroying their families and their society as well by venturing too far beyond home and hearth; that freedom is making them sick. We hear that blacks are taking away jobs from honest, hard-working white folk, that Asians are pushing whites out of deserved places in our universities, that Hispanics are destroying our language and our cherished Anglo culture, that gays are rotting the moral fiber of our God-fearing Christian nation. And although some left-wing zealots may indeed try to push their brand of orthodoxy in colleges and universities, the threat is overstated by some people clinging desperately to power and privilege. They brand as "political correctness" and a violation of some freedom or other any move to broaden a curriculum to include more than a white European male perspective. Some people seem to believe that the only America that works is a carbon copy of a 1940s America, when women knew their place, blacks were kept at arm's length by "separate but equal," gays stayed in the closet, Hispanics appeared only as cringing bad guys in Western movies, and Asians were represented either by Charlie Chan with his pidgin English or by the sadistic Japanese officer in John Wayne movies.

Powerful retrograde forces at work today oppose any change, especially any move toward a truly multicultural society. "Cultural nationalists" on all sides of the political spectrum preach their own orthodoxy. The late Allan Bloom (*The Closing of the American Mind*) seemed to think that if one Anglican British poet gets cut out of the curriculum anywhere, anyplace (and Toni Morrison gets *in*), the entire structure of Western civilization will fall into a vast crumpled heap, probably right next to a classroom in which a women's studies course is being taught. Some Afrocentrists preach a peculiar doctrine about "peoples of the sun" whose melanin supply makes them more intelligent than white folks and a lot nicer than cold-hearted pale people who grow up in cooler climes. But it is the defenders of the white male European faith—those who want not just a share of the culture but a stranglehold on its soul—who are the most to be feared, because they are accustomed to power and do not want to give it up.

However, we are mistaken if we imagine only cabals or conspiracies. The real enemies of constructive change may be the ideas that lodge inside our heads. Well-meaning men and women often have no notion of the tired old stories that play inside their skulls, distorting their view of the world. Like Plato's cave dwellers, they don't look beyond the dancing shadows. And it is the shadows and their power that we must understand if we are to escape them and walk into the sunlight.

SLICK SPINS
and FRACTURED FACTS

1. TOTEM AND TABOO

The Culture of the News Media

The best way to understand journalists and their culture is to see yourself as an anthropologist, trekking off in search of some little-known exotic tribe—a group camped on an ice floe somewhere north of the Arctic Circle, for example, or a brace of hunter-gatherers in the desert. You would observe such people with a fresh eye and a sense of wonder, noting their habits and their rituals, their gods and their totems, with no familiarity to blunt your perceptions, no annoying context to prejudice your judgments.

Viewed in this way, the members of the news clan can be seen to have a set of tribal ways that sets them apart from their neighbors. Oh, they may look like Uncle Fred or Cousin Julie, or nice Mister So-and-So from down the street, but that is not how you must think of them. Understanding the culture of members of the news media is important to deciphering their behavior, as is the culture of any tribe.

The artifacts of the clan also are crucial to understanding that culture and how it affects its members. We should think of newspeople as a group of hunter-gatherers. Instead of studying pots and shards and arrowheads, we can look at the nature of the game they are hunting: news, most of it bad.

When the tribal drums sound across the veldt, reverberating from bush to hillock to bush again, the messages are of some uncommon happening. They do not say: *Attention! The son of the chief was* not *eaten by the lion today.* You may ride for years on a New York subway car, and only when someone enters and begins taking potshots at other riders with an automatic pistol will reporters arrive; only if your house is flooded by the Mississippi, or scorched by a forest fire, or knocked flat by a hurricane will you see the news media.

This phenomenon has a different effect on different types of people. If the bad news is about some malefactor who is disturbing the civic tranquillity, it will stir—as if from primordial ooze—fears, judgments, and subterranean myths in the mind of the readers or viewers. The more marginal the group from which the malefactor comes, the more the news will affect members of that group who did *not* shoot up a subway, blow up the World Trade Center, or pillage and loot.

Psychologist Jean Baker Miller, author of *Toward a New Psychology of Women*, identifies two groups in society—the dominants and subordinates. The dominants know little about the subordinates, but the reverse is not true. Women, for example, know more about men than men do about women. Few men buy books on the psychology of women. But books about how men behave, relate, think, and communicate are snatched up by women. Likewise, whites usually know little about black life, culture, mores, daily life. But blacks know a great deal about whites; they have to, to survive.

When a white person—especially a white Protestant man—does an evil deed, it does not arouse great fear in the majority. When white guys saunter down the street, people do not cross to the other side because Charles Manson and Jeffrey Dahmer had pale skins. But when a group of Arabs was indicted in the bombing of the World Trade Center, perfectly innocent shopkeepers and pedestrians of Arab descent were kicked and harassed in such places as Detroit. The Arab becomes the terrorist. The black man becomes the rapist or the mugger. A black journalist I know bought his young son a bicycle and tied it to the back of his car to get it home. He was stopped by white police officers and made to "spread 'em" against the side of the car, even though his son was with him and he had a bill of sale for the bicycle. When your group is continually identified to the majority only in the framework of crime, you become suspect.

Any group considered marginal or not conforming with society's rules can suffer this effect: welfare mothers, young black males, single parents, Hispanics, Haitian immigrants, Asians, even working women. Moreover, members of such groups can internalize the message. One psychological study asked a group of women to describe characteristics of the typical mother, the typical wife, and the typical working woman. The women described the mother and the wife in similar complimentary ways. But they described the working woman as somewhat unfeminine and not very maternal—and the women who took part in the study were themselves full-time working women.

The news media are usually thought of as agents for change, and sometimes this is true. The intense coverage of the civil rights movement, with images of southern sheriffs setting dogs on nonviolent protesters, shocked and shamed the nation and helped get new antidiscrimination laws enacted. But just as often the staccato of bad news bolsters the status quo and a conservative agenda. Why? Because people tend to believe that the world was once more orderly and just, especially when today seems chaotic and disordered. It's easy to think that if we could only return to some vanished Eden, all would be well again. If only we could make the world like it used to be, by restoring family values or throwing more people in jail, we'd all be better off. But the past was rarely as good as we thought it was nor the present so bad.

Bad news can in fact persuade people that the world is much more dangerous than it is. George Gerbner of the Annenberg School of Communication at the University of Pennsylvania finds that people who watch a lot of television see the world as much more threatening and filled with menace than those who watch less do.[1] James Alan Fox, dean of the College of Criminal Justice at Northeastern University in Boston, says that fears about crime have less to do with actual crime rates than with the perception of crime we get from the news. "The technology of reporting has changed dramatically in the past fifteen years," he says. "With live mini-cams and satellites, it is possible for any local news outlet to lead every night's newscast with a crime story, including good video."[2] He calls the 11 P.M. report "Crimetime News." Bad news can create panic and distort the public agenda. A case in point: in the spring of 1994 polls showed that the number one issue on the minds of Americans was crime, whereas only a few months earlier it had been health care. Was this change in concern warranted?

Not according to the statistics. Crime had in fact been decreasing in recent years; Americans were less likely than a few years earlier to be the victims of violence. Why were they suddenly terrified? Because the media coverage of crime had intensified. Several shocking high-profile crimes had made the national news—the aforementioned subway shooter and the killings of tourists in Florida—and coverage of gang violence in the inner city was incessant. The rise in popularity of tabloid journalism—in print or on the many sensational TV shows—also helped to fuel the concern about crime. But the irony is that the profitability of the drug trade—and the involvement of so many inner city gangs in its bloody pursuit—made it *less* likely that the average American was going to be mugged on a city thoroughfare. The gangs had turned inner cities into scenes of carnage, and for the inhabitants of those areas it was a tragedy, but few Americans in other areas were menaced by drive-by shootings. In fact, we are far more likely to be killed by someone we know than by a homeboy with an AK-47. But bad news can reshape the world in unfamiliar and frightening contours.

The bad news syndrome is linked to another characteristic of the news media tribe—its exclusive focus on the present and its tendency to ignore the past. The news media are by definition ahistorical. They have a tendency to reinvent the wheel. Some member of the tribe will come up with a shiny new spherical object, and peers will gather 'round, oohing and ahhing at its marvelous shape, its surprising ability to roll along the ground, while in the cave just behind them are dozens and dozens of wheels in all sizes and shapes, fashioned by other members of the tribe in the months and years that have just passed. I am often astonished not only by simple errors of fact that show up in news stories but by the total lack of context. Journalists make flat statements about welfare, about history, about science, about women, about almost everything, that reflect a total ignorance beyond what some expert or some politician has just said.

This tendency has been heightened in recent years because older people—who could supply such context just by having lived for a while—are fast disappearing from newsrooms. The anchorman you see on the evening news may have touches of gray in his hair, but the assignment editor is probably a twenty-three-year-old who doesn't even know who the mayor *was* ten years ago, much less what his policies were. And it is the assignment editor who's deciding what's on the news. Newspapers are offering buyouts to older and more expensive employees in favor of inexpensive, young, energetic talent. If you look around many newsrooms today, you will find hardly a soul who was there twenty years ago. The young journalists often mistake the handy conventional wisdom, or the latest intellectual fad or pronouncement from a media-anointed guru, as actual fact.

I did it when I was a cub reporter. Wisdom, perspective—these come only with time. Without them you get uncritical acceptance of such ahistoric ideas as the notion that welfare *created* illegitimacy, to mention a currently popular shibboleth repeated often in the media as if it were so. But one-third of births in pre–Revolutionary War Concord were illegitimate, and our founding mothers were not on food stamps.

Combine the bad news of today with the news media's inability to grasp much beyond the recent past, and it's clear why people believe in a golden past that really didn't exist. You want crime? Try the nineteenth century, when the police were terrified to even set foot in some neighborhoods, and roving bands of violent young men terrorized the populace at will. Worried about how kids are behaving? You may think the fifties were happy days, but in fact the media at the time were filled with stories of unmanageable "juvenile delinquents."

Every era has its problems, but thinking that only *we* are in dire straits, that no people have ever grappled with our problems before, can lead to foolish actions. Fifty years from now, because the news media filled us with terror about crime, will we be straining to pay the bills for housing criminals we sent to jail for life at twenty and are now the most expensive segment of our elderly population? The media drumbeat about drugs a few years back helped create mandatory sentences that filled the jails with dealers. It turned out that we had to let murderers and rapists out to keep the small-fry drug dealers in.

In any event, take what you read and hear in the media with a grain of salt. We tend to believe what is spread before us, because the media have such an air of authority. Television news comes with the cadence of urgent-sounding music, sets of bright colors, and words like *Action News* flashing across the screen; the stentorian tones of the anchors can make a late-day snow storm sound like Armageddon. Newspapers have thick black type and pious editorials and labels that announce *Commentary* in commanding tones on their op-ed pages. All this is the wrapping, and it's easy to provide if you have a good deep voice or a throbbing theme song or a computer that makes nice graphics. But try to ignore all this and remember: it may not really be the gray-haired anchorman who chose the news he brings us today but somebody who is still using acne medicine.

The news media clan, like tribes who live in forests or by rude streams, has its own "anointed ones," Those-Who-Speak-with-Gods. Now we all know that the guys (I use the word advisedly) who speak with gods have a good deal of power in the tribe. But the anointed ones—be they sources or columnists or Big Foot reporters—tend to be much alike. They are nearly always upper-middle-class white males whose worldview is remarkably similar. Even if they didn't start out as upper class, years of being part of a privileged elite have usually dimmed the sense of what it is like for the rest of us, who live less elevated lives. Whom do you see on *Crossfire*, on *Meet the Press*, on the *McLaughlin Group*, on the evening news, on the op-ed pages of newspapers? The same guys, over and over. A few women, only a handful of blacks and a couple of Hispanics are in this group.

The result is that the national debate tends, day after day, to focus on the interests and experiences of these people. It was not surprising that in the 1992 presidential election the problems of cities and the issues of poverty were barely mentioned, and instead a middle-class tax cut was debated roundly. The Clinton camp didn't want to talk about poor people or blacks, because blacks weren't going to vote Republican, and Clinton knew the election lay with the middle class. George Bush wasn't about to dwell on poverty. The boys (and girls) on the bus didn't push the issues. They grew up for the most part in suburbia and had no memory of being poor or working class. When I criticized the lack of media coverage of such issues, a Washington reporter said to me, "The president who deals with the issues of the cities will be the next president—of Common Cause." That may be good campaign strategy, but reporters should be holding the candidates' feet to the fire on precisely the issues they want to avoid. They didn't, because the press was bored with poverty, which had no personal effect on them. Nobody got off the press plane and drove home to Bedford-Stuyvesant.

Working-class voices—not to mention those of poor people—are rarely heard on op-ed pages. The exotic minutiae of foreign policy, the endless inside-the-beltway battles, are the stuff that interests elite journalists. Rarely do such people face layoffs or downsizing, whereas millions of Americans are facing an economic crisis as companies get meaner and leaner, young people can't get jobs, and older workers are being laid off. Couples trying desperately to juggle home and work are struggling to find affordable day care. Yet these issues hardly dominate coverage and comment. Whitewater, however, with its hints of insider intrigue and power players, becomes a megastory.

Because the media tend to be fascinated with games men play—politics, war, sports—and the reader is generally assumed to be male, you get an overabundance of news of interest to white men and surprisingly little that is of interest to others. Also, white guys tend to assume white males are individual voices, whereas blacks, women, Hispanics, and others always speak for the entire group. Thus you may see fifteen columns on Bosnia or Whitewater on op-ed pages—sometimes two on the same subject on the same day—but one piece by an African American journalist on a "black issue" is assumed to have covered the subject fully. The same goes for women. How often do you see two pieces on day care by two women on the same op-ed page? Editors will say, about a "women's issue" piece, "Oh, Ellen Goodman did that already." But day after day, page after page, white men pontificate on Bosnia or the arms race or crime, and no one says the subjects have already been done.

Like all groups, the news media clan has its traditions and rituals that it assumes are shared by one and all. They have been written down by Those-Who-Speak-with-Gods. But they tend to exclude many of the not-so-elite, which is why many of us do not strongly identify with what we see or read. For instance, newspapers are losing female readers. Perhaps it is because women do not see themselves when they open their morning newspaper. Studies show that since 1985 women have been disappearing from the front pages of newspapers[3]—and their appearances there were never terribly frequent. A female point of view is even rarer.

In our society maleness is the norm and whiteness is the "norm." The set of viewpoints, ideas, and attitudes that often comes with being male or being white is seen as neutral and unbiased. At the same time people with a different set of attitudes are nearly always seen as being biased or as being "advocates." This sense is pervasive in the news media, despite the inroads that women and members of minority groups are making. I was fascinated by a conversation I had with a male reporter from a major East Coast newspaper. He complained that his paper had been taken over by women and blacks and that white men were afraid to speak out. He also complained that he didn't like to speak at colleges because students got angry at him when he said that blacks and women didn't really have it so bad anymore and that it was white men who were being discriminated against. He was clearly a man who had strong emotions on the subject.

I asked him about the ways in which women had too much influence over the news at his paper, and he cited the story about a study claiming that teachers in school were biased against girls. He remarked that he thought it absurd to think that in this day and age girls still faced such discrimination, and he said he thought the story was overplayed.

As it happened, this was a story I was quite familiar with, having reviewed much of the research for a book I had written and having fairly recently looked at the newer studies. I found the research to be compelling, because the findings were replicated time and again—found in more than one study, a good indication that bias against girls is a real phenomenon. I had seen videos in which female teachers, unaware of their behavior, ignored the waving hands of little girls in the front row time and again to call on boys in the back. I knew about all this prior research. I judged from the reporter's remarks that he did not.

So I told him that I had looked at the research and found it compelling, and he impatiently brushed me off. He said that of course I was not reliable on that issue because I had a feminist agenda.

I am perfectly willing to admit to being a feminist, but that fact certainly did not make me unable to look at research and evaluate it with some degree of impartiality. But he seemed unable to recognize that he had an agenda, being quite angry about the whole issue. And *he* hadn't looked at the data. None of that mattered. He was the objective, impartial one, and I was not to be trusted. In much the same way black journalists complain that editors don't want to send them to Africa because they will be somehow "biased" because they are black. But no editors refuse to send a white man to Poland or to England because he is white. If you are a white man, you are assumed to be free of bias. I've faced this dilemma again and again in my own writing career. I've been asked to prove or substantiate my point of view to a degree that white males are not. Black, gay, and Latino journalists have the same complaint.

This same attitude emerges in the coverage of "political correctness" (PC), which I'll deal with in some depth later. Programs in women's studies, black history, Asian history, Hispanic studies, and the like are often routinely described in news stories or columns as "special," or as peripheral, as if the history of whites was the real history, and the other stuff was just Scotch-taped on. Advocates of such courses are often described as having an agenda, and this makes them—as I was to that reporter—unreliable. At the same time a history that deals only with white men and ignores what is happening to all other groups is not seen as biased.

Of course, the proverbial Man from Mars looking at such an argument would find it absurd. He would find that all camps had their own particular views of history, and all are partly right, partly wrong. White men wrote about and recorded what was important to them and ignored what was not. Perfectly understandable—but incomplete.

The PC issue is a good example of the way in which stories that touch the lives of upper-middle class white males get major attention in the media. In the current news file (roughly two years, 1993–1995) of one major data base (NEXIS) are 9,724 stories about political correctness and 7,526 stories about sexism. Now what is the level of influence of political correctness on most people's lives? For the most part pressure to conform to a certain point of view may make people uncomfortable and irritated; they may hesitate to speak up on certain issues on their jobs for fear of disapproval. Academia certainly sees some bitter battles over issues like free speech, tenure, and the like. Important issues, of course, but in fact political correctness is a minor issue for most people. Sexism, however, has a deep and abiding effect on every aspect of a woman's life—her job, her self-image, her relationships with men, her eating habits, her sexuality. Why so many more stories about political correctness? Because charges of insensitivity are often directed at white males, and these are the people who control the media to a great extent. I'm not suggesting a conspiracy here; it is just that human beings feel more connected to—or threatened by—things that directly touch their lives. The massive coverage of political correctness is directly tied to the gender and the social class of those who have the most power in the media.

That the reporter from the big paper was not familiar with the research on girls and school systems was not unusual. I am always surprised— although I shouldn't be—that male journalists who are well read on many major issues can know nothing at all about matters of vital interest to women. Most have never even heard of the major theorists, don't know about the research—even when it has sometimes been on the front pages of major papers—and are totally out of touch with the battles raging about gender issues. I often wonder how they could be *alive* and still have missed them. It gets back to Jean Baker Miller's observation: these men don't know about what's of concern to women because they don't feel they *have* to know. Most men were raised with the notion that women are not important people in areas other than intimate relations. They are not in the habit of listening to women. A woman on the editorial board of a major newspaper told me of a peculiar dynamic she observed in meetings. It was as if, she said, a tape was running, and the men were engaged and active when men spoke, but when a woman spoke, the tape stopped. The men sat quietly, and there was little reaction. Then the tape started again. The group reacted only when a man made the same point that a woman had made earlier. The women's words seemed simply to be inaudible. A lot of men grew up learning to "tune out" women, and it still goes on in newsrooms across the country.

Members of the media often say—rather piously, as if citing a passage from Scripture—that they merely hold "a mirror up to the world." Nonsense. The news media have the power to frame the news, and the frame makes all the difference. As media scholar Erna Smith of San Francisco State University says, "News coverage of the same event can communicate different underlying meanings by elevating some facts and downplaying others. Thus, news frames are as important a component of news as the facts themselves."[4] What you choose to look at often decides what you will see. Here is a question that runs all through this book: Who decided what the story on the poor *really* is about? Or about women? About blacks? About immigration? About mothers?

It's also important to understand that the allocation of resources, rather than the ideal of "holding a mirror up to the world," can determine what is news and what isn't. Holding a mirror up to reality—if that's what you think you are doing—costs money. No one wants to come up empty-handed. Back to the metaphor of the tribe. Let's say a hunting party is sent out to bring back tiger meat. Members stalk through the bushes, emitting tiger calls, but no tiger appears. In the end they spear a rather bedraggled brown rabbit. Do they say, "It is a lousy rabbit, it will hardly feed a child for an evening meal, let us toss it back into the bushes"?

They do not. They march proudly back into the village, proclaiming it to be the most magnificent rabbit that ever trod the earth. Skeptical villagers who say, "Weren't you looking for a tiger?" are silenced by withering stares as the hunters sing and dance proudly around the trophy.

The news media do much the same dance. If reporters have been sent off to chase a story for six months, rarely do their editors look at what they have snared and say, "Small game. Let's put it on page twenty-seven under a car ad." No indeed—all those hours and all that money have to pay off. The resulting story is often blazoned across page one, and its very positioning and length signal the reader that something important has happened. When the *Wall Street Journal* sent reporters off in search of mob ties in Geraldine Ferraro's background when she was the Democratic vice presidential candidate, they returned with a pittance. But the *Journal* ran a story on the editorial page saying that her father-in-law's pistol permit had been revoked twenty-five years earlier because he had once provided a character reference for a man who was the brother of an organized crime figure. That item, and other innuendo, was included in a four-column story labeled, REP. FERRARO AND A PAINFUL LEGACY?[5]

But there was no legacy. *Newsweek*'s media critic, Jonathan Alter, asked, "Short of hard evidence that Ferraro and [her husband] Zaccaro associated regularly with mobsters—which the press has not come close to finding—was there anything worth printing at all?"[6] The stories created a media flurry that was at base about nothing. But the notion that Ferraro was somehow connected to organized crime stuck. A friend of mine was conversing with her seatmate on an airliner, and when Ferraro's name came up, the woman said, "Oh, but she's connected with the Mafia!"

Similarly, when the *New York Times* and other papers sent reporters to Little Rock to look into Hillary Clinton's commodities trading, they could find nothing illegal and hardly a hint of anything improper. But the Hillary trades, which should have been a one-day story, became big news, thanks to the thumping of Republicans and the effort devoted to the story. When a story is that big, it must be important—right? If the media come after you with all their guns blazing, you will not escape—even if there is no story at all.

All tribes, whether they use bronze arrowheads or laptop computers, have ritual incantations, words they repeat often and ceremoniously. For the news media one such word, muttered reverently in the council halls and the hunting lodges where the tribe gathers (called Hilton or Sheraton), is *objectivity.*

It is a serious word, but one that is not quite appropriate for this particular tribe, despite its scientific ring. It has taken me quite a few years to come to terms with this fact.

When I was seventeen, I had a summer job as a copy girl in the Washington bureau of the *New York Daily News.* One front-page photograph the *Daily News* ran that summer stays with me to this day. A terrible auto crash had occurred in New York—teenagers driving too fast. The auto had hit something with such force that one young man had been hurled up onto the limb of a tree; his body hung draped across the limb like one of the watches in a Salvador Dali painting. His shirt had been ripped from his back. He was about my age; the thought of a young life so precipitously destroyed gave me intimations of my own mortality.

I remember knowing in my gut—a sensation of dread someplace inside me—that the picture was so terrible that it never should have been used. I thought of that young man's family—that image seared into their memories. At my still-tender age I could barely imagine the horror of that, but I could feel enough of it to be certain my judgment was right. But I had no language in which to put forth that proposition. I remember the discussions in the office. People argued that the picture would perhaps have a salutary effect—maybe other young people would see it and would temper their behavior. I felt that the presumed good that might come from this photograph was like a night fog, floating, diaphanous—you were not certain it was really there. But the pain was so immediate, so searing, that its intensity could power a hundred cities. But that was the arithmetic of my emotions, and how could it be argued? (One other point—the young man was black and the editors white. I am certain that played a part in why the picture ran.)

Today I do have the words to argue what I felt. But for many years I wrestled with the notion of what journalism told me I was supposed to be: objective. It had a cold hard ring to it. I wondered then, doesn't *truth* have more to it than that? Now I know. Yes, it does. A good deal more.

Journalists give a number of explanations for their tradition of "objectivity." The invention of the telegraph, which dictated the need for a short terse form; the creation of the wire services, which had to send the same information to many outlets, so the information had to be bled dry of what might seem an ideological bent. I also think something else was at work. As journalism moved upscale, as journalists came to see themselves not as lower-class scribblers with a press pass in their hat and a predilection for purple prose but as professionals, they sought respectability. Near at hand was Science, replacing the Trinity as the new deity.

Objective is the language of science. It has the ring of facts weighed and measured, as precise as molecules, free from the taint of unreliable emotion. What does this have to do with journalism? Not much. But it *sounds* so scientific and thus reassuring. Stanford journalism professor Theodore L. Glasser calls objectivity a set of beliefs that are rooted in "an enduring commitment to the supremacy of observable and retrievable facts."[7] But *whose* facts? This is the central question.

Mathematician Evelyn Fox Keller of Northeastern University has thought a lot about objectivity. She sees—growing like a cancer—a concept of science as artificially separated from much of what is natural. She sees it cast as a tool for dominion over all that is natural, and that, she thinks, is ominous. Such a view "serves to foster the growth of a civilization that stakes its future on the development of a science and a technology [and I'd add *a journalism*] in which the hopes, loves, and fears of ordinary human beings are regarded as distractions, as irrelevant to the pursuit of important matters, as wastes of energy. The world of everyday life, or, as Einstein puts it, 'The narrow confines of swirling personal experience,' is something to be overcome, to be transcended."[8]

But "the swirl of personal experience" was the thing that drew me to journalism; in fact I think it's what draws most journalists, male or female. We are at heart storytellers, not scientists. Journalism is more art than science, and the notion that we are androids, collecting, weighing, and measuring "facts" that are as fixed and intractable as moon rocks, is a chilling one.

Transcending personal experience is an impossible goal at any rate. Among those who argued in the 1920s for a new scientific journalism was Walter Lippmann. He called for journalists to remain clear and free of their irrational and unexamined biases. Lippmann, a German Jew who was so assimilated that he hardly remembered he was Jewish, wrote hardly at all about the Holocaust, one of the great tragedies of the twentieth century. Could he not face the vulnerability of a group to which he belonged, however marginally? You have to suspect that the omission had nothing at all to do with "scientific journalism" and everything to do with the swirl of personal experience.

The consequences of the reporter as android are many; Theodore Glasser sums them up this way:

> Objectivity is biased in favor of the status quo; it is inherently conservative to the extent that it encourages reporters to rely on what sociologist Alvin Gouldner describes as "the managers of the status quo"—the prominent and the elite. Second, objective reporting is biased against independent thinking. It emasculates the intellect by treating it as a disinterested spectator. Finally, objective reporting is biased against the very idea of responsibility—the day's news is viewed as something journalists are compelled to report, not something they are responsible for creating.[9]

The idea of objectivity can combine with the white male norm to keep the parameters of what is considered legitimate opinion quite narrow. Objectivity often does not mean a hard examination of all "facts" but only of those that the gatekeeper suspects. Once I was doing an article for a newspaper in which I used as my major sources a black academician and a female professor. But an editor asked me to add another source, a white male professor who had no history of research in the area. Clearly, the editor simply did not have confidence in the "facts" offered by the woman and the black, believing—probably subconsciously—that they were somehow suspect. When my source was a white male, I have never been asked to go and find a woman or a black to bolster the credibility of the information, but the reverse has often been true.

The canon of objectivity is one reason that the voices of blacks and women are not quite trusted. They are suspected of either special pleading or of fuzzy emotionalism. Several women journalists I know have heard editors make remarks indicating that women, although able to turn a nice phrase, are just not as objective in their way of thinking as men.

Objectivity fosters another illusion: that the journalist has no connection to—or, as Glasser says, responsibility for—the subjects of his or her inquiry. Pressure to achieve that detachment is one reason journalists drink too much. We are often put in difficult situations regarding other human beings. We criticize them. We sometimes reveal that they are doing things that are wrong. We invade their private worlds in times of pain. Our job— to find and report the truth as best we can—may indeed result in harm to others. We ought not to pretend that all we feel is the buzz and clang of electronic gears when this happens. We ought to agonize over that. It will keep us honest—and human. We can try to be unbiased; we can try to be fair. But we will never really be *objective*. And we should not dodge moral responsibility in the name of this impossible goal.

And last is another sacred assumption I would like to address in this look at the rituals of the news media—the myth of the liberal press. It was always overdone. When I came into the business during the Kennedy era, the press bus did stop at many places it no longer goes. Many reporters came from working or lower-middle-class backgrounds and identified at a gut level with the underdog. Although publishers and newspaper owners tended to be staunchly conservative, the rank-and-file did not identify with wealth or privilege. During the Kennedy era liberal ideas often drove public policy initiatives. Michael Harrington's *The Other America*, read by Kennedy, was the wellspring of what became Lyndon Johnson's War on Poverty.

That has changed dramatically during my years as a journalist. Today, as I've noted, journalists tend to lead upper-middle-class lives, often far removed from ordinary people. Indeed, Washington journalists today give speeches, star on TV panel shows, and are far more glamorous than many people they cover. As *Washington Post* media critic Howard Kurtz points out, the pundits of both right and left warmly embraced the North American Free Trade Agreement, almost off-handedly dismissing fears of working-class Americans who felt their jobs were threatened. Kurtz says, "What was striking to me was how casually many journalists dismissed these concerns, comfortably secure in a business that is not among those threatened by foreign competition."[10]

I have seen the political winds shift significantly from left to right, and journalists have swung with them. The media always go where the power goes. Today policy is driven by an energetic and powerful right funded by well-financed think tanks. When I covered the Goldwater convention as a young reporter, it seemed to many reporters that what we witnessed there was a strange and radical force that was alien to us. Today those ideas are in the mainstream, and it is the liberal ideas that often seem alien. In fact, much of the domestic agenda of John F. Kennedy would today be considered quite radical. The darlings of the media today are black conservatives, not the civil rights activists who were at center stage when I was a young reporter.

The political climate in America can only be called stunningly different from my early days in journalism. As sociologist Herbert Gans says, one of the great victories of the Reagan years was the creation of "a cadre of ideologically driven right-wing social scientists and intellectuals. Even now, the cadre's highly vocal presence helps keep liberals out of the media. For example, the so-called liberal position on media op edit pages and television panels is usually occupied by a moderate Democrat."[11]

Consider the case of Charles Murray, the co-author of *The Bell Curve*, now a media superstar, a frequent guest on talk shows, quoted by newsmagazines, asked to speak for considerable fees. Murray argues for the compete abolition of welfare, and his success, as historian Michael Katz points out, "illustrates the role of big money in the marketplace of ideas."[12] William Hammet, president of the Manhattan Institute, read a pamphlet by Murray he liked and supported him for two years while Murray wrote his welfare book, *Losing Ground*. Hammet then invested in the production and promotion of the book, spending some $15,000 to send more than seven hundred free copies to power brokers and journalists, and paid a public relations specialist to manage Murray, booking him on TV shows and the lecture circuit. The institute held a seminar on the book to which it invited journalists and intellectuals to participate, offering honoraria of $500 to $1,500. It was not Murray's brilliance that earned him entrée to the marketplace of ideas but the power of money and influence.[13]

A more affluent press corps identifies more easily with the attitudes and instincts of such a cadre, traditionally associated in America with the wealthy upper classes. Journalists no longer afflict the comfortable and comfort the afflicted. We *are* the comfortable.

There is a lot I don't miss from the days when I was a cub reporter—the provincialism, the tendency to play ball with elected officials, the high levels of alcoholism, the male chauvinism, the near-total absence of minority reporters, the lousy pay, to mention a few. But I do believe journalism was a more compassionate business when I entered it, if only because more journalists came from the working classes. I worry that journalists have become too comfortable, too far removed from the daily struggles and the little terrors of getting by that so many people experience. I'm not sure we should be supping so casually at the tables of wealth and ease. It's too easy to forget what it was like out there, beyond the warmth of the fire where we always used to stand with the hired help, rubbing our hands and cursing, saying that if *we* were inside, surely we would do things differently.

Today's conventional wisdom in the media is created by a comfortable suburban press corps on whose ears the arguments of the right may fall with a pleasing ring. But what my thirty years as a journalist have taught me is that everything changes. When I stood inside the Cow Palace in San Francisco listening to the Goldwater minions roar, I could not have imagined that the political landscape would change so radically. It was chic to believe in those days that conservatism had died along with Bob Taft and the America Firsters and would never be seen again in our lifetime. It's chic in media circles today to embrace the neoconservative creed, and journalists often write that liberal ideas are dated and shopworn. But today's shopworn goods can become tomorrow's haute couture. You never know.

Throughout this book the culture of the news media will play a background theme—like Muzak in an elevator—to the discussion of wider cultural myths that create journalistic distortions. Careful, thoughtful journalists can often avoid the pull of mythology and the conventional wisdom. Indeed, I quote a number of them in this book. The problem is that the nuanced, careful piece too often simply gets drowned out by the clamor of the chic trend stories of the moment, and misinformation and half-truth blare from headlines and TV sound bites and nest in "background" paragraphs of otherwise competent stories. Most often the biases I discuss are subconscious and unintentional. I believe most journalists are conscientious and want to do a good job. That their thinking has been shaped by forces and ideas they do not realize they possess is no more an indictment of journalists than it is of all Americans—except that what journalists write and say is so important. "The first rough draft of history," as journalism has been called, needs to be corrected.

2. PUT THE BLAME ON EVE, BOYS

The Devil Made Her Do It–
Or Maybe It Was Just Her Tiny Brain

The wonderful thing about myths is that they don't have to be logical; often two of them operate side by side, even though they are polar opposites. That's exactly what happens with two of the most potent—the Myth of Female Weakness and the Myth of Female Strength. In one, a woman is a sniveling, small-brained, hormone-wracked creature so filled with anxieties and chemical twitches it seems a miracle she can get out of bed in the morning. In the other, she's Wonder Woman and Medusa, all wrapped up in one, able to reduce men to irrational behavior, making them desert their senses and become besotted fools. And media coverage of women often bounces from one to the other like bumper cars gone mad.

Mythology about women pervades our culture, and feminist scholars have spent the last two decades trying to unravel it. Simone de Beauvoir, in her brilliant critique of women's place, *The Second Sex*, fired the first shot in the current era of what was to become a barrage of female inquiry and scholarship. Yet the myths still stand, like battlements on a hill, exerting a tremendous power over our media, our politics, our culture, our imaginations.

Beauvoir pointed out how women's physiology, which is more involved in the processes of giving birth and nurturing life than men's, is devalued by that very fact. Anthropologist Sherry Ortner says,

> Woman's body seems to doom her to mere reproduction of life; the male, in contrast, lacking natural creative functions, must (or has the opportunity to) assert his creativity externally, "artificially" through the medium of technology and symbols. In doing so he creates relatively lasting, eternal, transcendent objects, while the woman creates only perishables—human beings.
>
> This formulation opens up a number of important insights. It speaks, for example, to the great puzzle of why male activities involving the destruction of life (hunting and warfare) are often given more prestige than the female's ability to give birth, create life. Within De Beauvoir's framework, we realize it is not the killing that is the relevant and valued aspect of hunting and warfare, rather it is the transcendental (social and cultural) nature of these activities, as opposed to the naturalness of the process of birth. For it is not in giving life but in risking life that man is raised above the animal; that is why superiority has been accorded in humanity not to the sex that brings forth but that which kills.[1]

If woman in her essence is seen as nature, in her sexuality she is seen once again through the prism of the male imagination. Vivian Gornick writes,

> Deeply interwoven in the fabric of this cultural cloak is the image of woman: woman the temptress, woman the slut, woman the heartless bitch—luring men eternally towards spiritual death, making them come up against what they most fear and hate in themselves, pulling them down, down into the pit of themselves. Sensuous Circe luring Ulysses onto the rocks of his worst self, sluttish Mildred in *Of Human Bondage* mangling crippled Philip still further, heartless Marlene Dietrich casually destroying the weak, decent professor in *The Blue Angel*—the list is endless and the lesson is always the same. Woman herself is not locked in this profound struggle with the self; she is only the catalyst for the man's struggle with himself. It is never certain that the woman has any self at all. What is certain is that

onto woman is projected all that is worst in man's view of himself, all that is primitive, immature and degrading.[2]

Or, conversely, woman becomes another mirror image: the idea of goodness—the noblest, the best, the most loved. If she is not the temptress, she is the goddess, the mother, the angel of mercy, the pure golden-haired heroine of Victorian fiction. Norman Mailer once said that women were either sloppy beasts or goddesses—quite a choice. Can you imagine those as the only choices given to men—gods or slobs? Either way, woman is not whole, a true complex person.

"I am not real to my civilization," Gornick writes, "I am not real to the culture that has spawned me and made use of me. I am only a collection of myths. I am an existential stand-in. The *idea* of me is real: the temptress, the goddess, the child, the mother—but *I* am not real. The mythic proportions of women are recognizable and real; it is only the human dimensions that are patently false and will be denied to the death; our death."[3]

To be denied humanity, to be reassembled as a collection of myths, also means to be silenced. As scholar Deborah Cameron has pointed out, "The silence of woman is above all an absence of female voices and concerns from high culture."[4] Women have always been allowed to talk to their children, to gossip, to tell stories, to write in their diaries—but these are only private means of communication. Women's public speech has been silenced by law, by tradition, and by taboo. The strictures against women's speech in public go back to primitive societies that had rules forbidding women to speak outside the house—in the tribal council, in the town meeting—and are seen as well in the long-standing tradition in Western culture that women be barred from universities; they linger today in a ban on women in the priesthood and the absence of women in legislative bodies. In 1992 it was still considered an unusual event when two women won Senate seats from the state of California.

Feminist scholars have pointed out that women throughout history have been defined as mad when they were overtly sexual or assertive, that they were burned at the stake as witches when they threatened the social status quo or gained too much wealth, that at the same time that they were worshiped as sexless ministering angels in upper-class society in the Victorian era, they were physically mutilated when they displayed what was seen as excessive sexuality. Weak or strong, woman is to be feared. And when journalists take up their pens or march to their word processors, these myths linger in their subconscious, and *woman weak/woman strong* are two archetypes that resonate still.

The news media sensation of the decade, the Clarence Thomas–Anita Hill duel that took place before the eyes of millions of viewers, exemplified this mythological paradox with stunning clarity. Watching Anita Hill, many people saw a poised, coolly professional black woman talk about the sexual invitations and suggestive talk of a man who was her employer in the federal government. But if you stayed tuned, as the Senate Republicans came down like a wolf on the fold and the news media watched it all, you would have seen sketches of two separate portraits of Professor Hill, two myths in operation:

The Myth of Female Weakness: Alas, poor Anita. Perhaps she was simply a pawn in the scheming designs of those (read: liberal Democrats) who wanted to see Clarence Thomas defeated for the Supreme Court. Naïve, foolish, willing to be used as a pawn in the plans of powerful men, she was a silly woman embroiled in something she could not understand. (Or perhaps she was simply a prisoner of her hormones. Judge Thomas's wife—picking up the lead of the senators—suggested in a *People* magazine cover piece that Hill was a poor, love-besotted girl, a pathetic creature who fantasized a relationship with a powerful man.)[5] *Poor thing*, clucked some of the Senate Republicans, seduced by Democrats or bewitched by her fantasies, she should be an object of pity.

Unless . . .

Unless she was the embodiment of the *Myth of Female Strength*, that witch, that temptress, that Medusa whose pleasure lies in destroying men. In this reincarnation she was, Senator Arlen Specter suggested again and again in his prosecutorial tones, the scorned woman, lying in wait for revenge, and hell hath no fury et cetera, et cetera. According to Specter, Hill apparently spent her time prowling through old copies of *The Exorcist*, looking for obscure references to pubic hairs, or doing a little light reading of Oklahoma obscenity cases to come across the porno star Long Dong Silver. (Just what a woman from a Baptist family does on her weekends.) Or maybe she was just a pathological liar, like the heroine of *Fatal Attraction*, a career woman whose barren life and biological clock led her to terrible dark deeds. Or perhaps she was a steely-eyed Joan of Arc eager to become a feminist martyr.

This chapter and the next deal with the first myth, the Myth of Female Weakness, which may have begun as far back as Eve, who, according to Scripture, couldn't resist taking a bite out of the apple and thus got the

First Couple kicked out of Eden. I was a parochial school student and remember that—as soon as we were old enough to understand kissing—the nuns interpreted Eve's noshing as having to do with lust. But long before sex reared its ugly head, I found myself identifying with Eve. Biting into the apple seemed to me to be the first example of intellectual curiosity in recorded history. Adam, the lout, just wanted to sit around Paradise, fat, dumb, and happy, but Eve, an achiever, wanted to know something of what God knew.

Male biblical sages did not render this interpretation, however. They often wailed about how all afflictions were the curse of Eve; her weakness brought on everything from the Babylonian captivity to the pains of childbirth, a punishment for her curiosity. In medieval times church fathers seriously discussed whether women had a soul. The preponderance of evidence was negative, as I recall.

As we move closer to our own time, the tradition of blaming Eve does not abate. The debate over the soul shifts to a more easily located place: her brain. Oh, she has one, but how big is it? Women and blacks seem to be the subjects of most brain-size inquiries. In the early nineteenth century Louis Agassiz, a well-respected Harvard zoologist, declaimed that the brain casing of blacks was smaller than that of whites, and too much education would expand the brain size beyond the capacity of the skull, causing serious brain damage or death. (Kids have tried to use a similar argument as an excuse to avoid homework, but it rarely works.) Later on, as biologist Stephen Jay Gould has pointed out in his book *The Mismeasure of Man*, such measurement "dominated the human sciences for much of the 19th century and remained popular until intelligence testing replaced skull measurement as a favorite device for making invidious comparisons among classes, races and sexes."[6]

Craniologist Paul Broca suggested that women could never reach the intellectual heights of men, because their brains were smaller. And one of Broca's disciples suggested that giving women equal education with men would be a "dangerous chimera."[7]

If tiny weak brains weren't enough to keep women away from the halls of learning, some people decided to focus on a lower area of the anatomy. It was accepted medical belief in much of the nineteenth century that women's brains and reproductive organs could not develop at the same time. That's why women's education consisted of a little knitting, a little French, nothing too heavy; those all-important ovaries needed all of a woman's energy.

"Woman is less under the influence of the brain than the uterine system," Dr. J. G. Mulligan, a prominent physician, wrote in 1848. And G.
Stanley Hall, president of Clark University, warned in 1906 that "over-
activity of the brain during the critical period of the middle and late teens
will interfere with the full development of mammary power and of the
functions essential for the full transmission of life generally."[8]

Early in the century surgical removal of the clitoris was a favored remedy for all forms of mental illness, including depression, and later medical
science turned to lobotomies. Even when nineteenth-century science
found that women did something better than men did, it managed to turn
that information into further proof of women's weakness. When one
researcher found that women could read faster and more accurately than
men, two esteemed scientists of the era decreed that the ability to read well
is linked with the ability to lie, and women are better liars than men.[9]

Another theory—proposed by none other than Charles Darwin himself—was that of morphological infantilism—the notion that women,
being smaller than men, are *morphologically*—that is, physically—more
like babies or children than men. As psychologists Paula Caplan and
Jeremy Caplan explain,

> Some Victorian theorists speculated that, therefore, women are less intelli-
> gent than men but more intelligent than infants and children. This is equiv-
> alent to saying that men must be more like gorillas than are women, because
> men are hairier. It might even be valid, but what reason is there to believe
> it? . . . The Social Darwinists who promoted morphological infantilism as
> applied to women used the same notion to keep whites in power over
> blacks. Black people, they argued, are more similar to apes than are white
> people and are therefore, less intelligent.[10]

But this is ancient history—is it not?—the stuff of Gothic novels or history courses but having nothing to do with today. Would that that were
true. In intellectual—and family—history, 1906 was only yesterday. Our
grandparents or great-grandparents lived in a world that accepted these
beliefs.

Many deep-seated cultural myths have the abilities of chameleons—
they shed the Victorian garb of yesteryear and emerge in wash-and-wear
Spandex: the same old thing, decked in modern dress. Women's brains are
still regarded with suspicion. Anita Hill may have been a graduate of Yale

Law, but that did not stop the esteemed gentlemen of the Senate from picturing her as the embodiment of female irrationality or the media from echoing that scenario. No matter what women achieve, that fatal flaw—located someplace in the cerebellum or the ovaries—is going to crop up sooner or later.

Women's strengths rarely become the focus of media attention, except in a distorted way—as when women are seen as *too* strong. When tests show that on average women are better than men at something, this fact is mentioned sotto voce. Footnote, page 242, women have generally tested better than men on verbal ability. Do we get headlines like ARE MEN BORN TO BE ILLITERATE? or DO WOMEN HAVE A WRITING GENE MISSING IN MEN? You see those about as often as you see a unicorn in your driveway. But let a test apparently show that men do something better than women do, and it's bring out the banners.

MATH AND SEX; ARE GIRLS BORN WITH LESS ABILITY? headlined *Science* magazine, on a story in the early eighties about a study done by two Johns Hopkins University psychologists of Scholastic Aptitude Tests (SATs) of 9,927 gifted seventh- and eighth-grade boys and girls. The girls did less well than the boys on the math test, especially in mathematical reasoning. The researchers concluded—in the most controversial section of their report—that the difference could not be explained by environmental factors, so it had to be genetic. The most chilling aspect of their report was the suggestion that maybe girls just shouldn't *try* to be good at math. One researcher likened the girls' situation to that of a short boy's thinking he should make the basketball team.[11]

Voilà! the math gene leapt into the headlines.

DO MALES HAVE A MATH GENE? asked *Newsweek*, and the story wondered, "Can girls do math as well as boys? All sorts of recent tests have shown that they cannot." The *Washington Post* headlined, AT MATHEMATICAL THINKING, BOYS OUTPERFORM GIRLS. *Time* looked at THE GENDER FACTOR IN MATH. The *New York Times* asked, ARE BOYS BETTER AT MATH?[12]

Why were the media so eager to believe in the math gene? Why did this particular piece of scientific research—from among the veritable torrent of such studies that researchers produce every year—receive such widespread attention? Because it was a modern incarnation of the idea that something is wrong with women's brains. But how conclusive was the research? Not very, said a lot of critics. For one thing the researchers invited ten thousand junior-high-school–aged children to take the SAT. "But what does it mean to give a seventh or eighth grader college level tests?" asked mathematician

Edith H. Luchins. "How are we to interpret the results? We scarcely know what the test scores mean when they are made by high school students. Many educators now question the ability of the SAT to test mathematical reasoning, problem-solving and spatial ability."[13]

But the main problem was that the researchers, Camilla Benbow and Julian Stanley, had made a whopping assumption when they said that these boys and girls at their stage of schooling probably had the same training in—and attitudes about—math. Their entire thesis rested on the assumption that because boys and girls often shared classrooms, their experiences were the same. Had they forgotten that they were talking about children in the seventh grade?

The Seventh Grade. You were considered a dork if you had even half a brain. You fell in love with rock stars and scribbled their names across your algebra texts. In the seventh grade, if everybody else had pink hair and green lipstick, *you* had pink hair and green lipstick. And math? That's for the geeky boys who haven't hit puberty yet, whose skin is the shade of flounder bellies because they sit in their basement rec rooms all day hacking with their computers. Math. Ugh. Will guys make out in the back seat with a girl who likes *math?* Peer pressure at this age is at its most intense, and it is also the age, as Harvard's Carol Gilligan found in her studies of girls at puberty, that sturdy independent little girls begin to suffer a loss of self-esteem as they first encounter the tremendous pressure to please males above all else. Boys generally do not suffer the same loss of self-esteem as they hit puberty.[14] To assume that girls and boys at this age have the same experiences is to ignore the reality of adolescence in America.

As Professor Alice Schafer of Wellesley College, chair of the Women in Math Committee of the American Mathematical Society, says, "Just because seventh-grade boys and girls sat the same number of hours in the same classroom doesn't mean they get the same mathematical education."[15]

Research showed she was right, in particular about the youngsters who were part of the Hopkins test. Another Hopkins scientist, Lynn Fox, interviewed the kids who took part in the test. She found that boys' parents noticed their sons' talents at an early age, encouraged them by buying math books, and talked about math careers. Girls' parents generally didn't notice.[16] Studies have shown that nearly half of girls interested in math careers have reported being discouraged by high-school guidance counselors from taking advanced math courses. And when Edith Luchins gave a talk at a local high school career day, a guidance counselor told her, "I'll be honest with you; I don't encourage girls to go into math. They wouldn't be good at it, and in any case, what would they do with it?"[17] Sadly, that is an attitude reflected in many American schools.

Science writer K. C. Cole, whose specialty is physics, writes about a friend who won a Bronx-wide mathematics competition in the second grade: "Her friends—both boys and girls—warned her that she shouldn't be good in math. 'You'll never find a boy who likes you.' The girl nevertheless went on to win a number of awards at Bronx High School of Science, but after a year as a science major at Harvard, she switched her major to English. She had been discouraged, she said, by the macho mores of science, and besides, what was the payoff for sticking with it? 'You'd be considered a freak.'"[18]

It's exactly this sort of experience the Hopkins researchers ignored. The math gene argument doesn't account for the sudden precipitous drop in girls' math ability at puberty—exactly when stereotypes about correct female behavior kick in. A number of studies show that girls score evenly with boys until about the first year of high school—and that only 18 percent of girls—compared with 64 percent of boys—taking high school physics and calculus classes plan to major in science or engineering in college.[19]

Could the math gene just disappear in girls when they get their first bra? "Unless nature selected for smart girls and dumb women, something goes very wrong at the middle school level," writes critic Barbara Ehrenreich. "Maybe it's teachers who call on and encourage boys more. Or maybe it's high school politics that equate good grades with terminal geekdom. Even more important than teachers, though, is girls' growing realization that straight A's aren't necessarily the fastest way to point B (for boyfriend)."[20]

Ehrenreich's hunches were borne out by research. The girls who took part in the tests told researchers that they didn't want to take part in accelerated math classes. They thought that other kids would regard them as "different," and they thought that the classes were dull and the boys in them "little creeps."[21]

Evelyn Fox Keller, the author of *Reflections on Gender and Science*, notes that the roots of viewing science as male go deep into our cultural soil. "The linguistic rooting of this stereotype is not lost among children. . . . From strikingly early ages, even in the presence of non-stereotypic role models, children learn to identify mathematics as male. 'Science,' my five-year-old son declared, confidently bypassing that fact that his mother was a scientist, 'is for men!'"[22]

Researchers also say that instructors tend to teach to the learning style of boys—which favors getting the right answer, whereas girls enjoy the *process* as much as they enjoy getting the answer—and girls do better in cooperative situations. And studies of children in the United States, Japan, and China show that when girls are in the first grade, they and their mothers assume that boys are better at math. The result of that self-fulfilling prophecy starts to show up around the third grade.[23]

But none of this got into the headlines. MATH GENE swept the national media. Anne Fausto-Sterling, a Brown University biologist, writes of an urgent call from a friend whose ten-year-old daughter had read that girls simply shouldn't try to do higher math and was devastated.

"Daddy," she said, "I always wanted to be a math professor just like you. Does that mean I can't do it?"

Fausto-Sterling remembered the cartoon she had seen in *Time* a few days earlier. A puzzled little girl and a toothy smiling boy stood in front of a blackboard with a multiplication problem on it. Obviously, the little girl didn't know the answer, and the boy did. "Interpreting the image does not require a degree in art history, and the aftershocks from the *Science* article and subsequent press coverage still rumble beneath our feet," she says.[24]

The father who made the panicked phone call was not alone. Psychologist Jackie Eccles, in a longitudinal study, found that mothers who read the news reports had lower expectations of their daughters' math abilities than they did before.[25] Here then was an example of the media's reporting uncritically a questionable scientific assumption and the mass media coverage's reinforcing the low expectations that could keep girls from doing well in math. Another exercise in self-fulfilling prophecy.

Wading further into muddy waters, Camilla Benbow and her husband Robert Benbow claimed that hormones accounted for boys' "greater" ability in math. Hormones are really sexy these days. Psychologists Paula and Jeremy Caplan say,

> Naturally, the media eagerly reported the story. What they did not mention was that hormonal levels of the students in their study were never measured, thus making the Benbows' claim entirely unjustified. This is a particularly important issue, since, when there is, or seems to be, a biologically based and innate difference such as a hormonal one, people are likely to assume that little or nothing can be done to reduce the supposed inferiority of one sex.[26]

The Caplans explain that the hormonal argument is convoluted and presents problems every step of the way. Two researchers had previously reported that left-handed people are more likely than righties to suffer from immune disorders, learning disabilities, and migraines, hypothesizing that this was the result of high levels of the male hormone testosterone. (This claim was vigorously criticized and not supported by other research.) If testosterone slows down the development of the left hemisphere of the brain so that the right side compensates by growing stronger, the mathematical abilities *might* improve in the possessor of this brain. So good math students ought to be left-handed and have more immune problems than the rest of the population. Indeed good math students include more left-handers and more people who have allergies than the general population. "However," the Caplans point out, "as every introductory psychology student learns, left-handers are more common in a wide range of unusual populations, including prisoners and students at Harvard University. Math genius may be rampant in Harvard Yard, but is it at Sing Sing?"

If you are still following this complex and convoluted reasoning, the Benbows went on to speculate that some good math students might have been exposed before birth to high testosterone levels. They had no proof of this, but they claimed that these students were more likely than other students to have been born during months that have more than twelve hours a day of light, and "daylight affects pineal gland secretion, altering the level of melanin, which in turn has an inhibitory effect on reproductive hormones."

The Caplans say,

> Aside from the sheer length of this unproved explanation about how top math students might have been exposed to high levels of testosterone, their reasoning is simply wrong. If more daylight is supposed to reduce the reproductive hormones, then these students should have had less testosterone, not more, than most students. And according to the Benbows' own (unsupported) line of reasoning, lower testosterone levels should lead to *poorer* mathematical abilities.[27]

If all this makes the old how-many-angels-can-you-fit-on-the-head-of-a-pin argument seem positively straightforward, it is but an example of the complex realm of hormones, genes, and behavior. In this case a tortured train of highly questionable assumptions led to the math gene stories. The Caplans note, "If you look at the headlines . . . it may seem surprising that the public could be presented such claims when they are based on highly speculative theories, research on extreme groups of people and just plain poor reasoning. However, such presentation is not uncommon. When some journalists hear what seems to be a 'hot' story, they do not stop to learn whether or not there is any scientific basis for it."

Of course, most people are not fascinated with the intricate details of left-brain, right-brain functions and daylight actions of hormones, and all they remember is the headline. The Caplans note that "many scientists and lay people, and today, the media, become intensely interested in an issue, believe in a report of some bit of research about the issue, and then lose interest in it. If, later on, the research they had read about is discredited, they may have become so accustomed to believing in the early research they do not invest the mental and emotional energy necessary to revise that belief."[28]

In other words, many people do not want the facts to confuse them.

Add to that the tendency for the media to repeat old information even after it is moribund, and you understand why the math gene might well be immortal.

But since the math gene was trumpeted in the early eighties, a surprising thing has happened: gender differences in math and verbal abilities on tests have begun to disappear. In recent years all the things that used to show up on the standardized tests, and that we have come to believe—such as girls' superior verbal abilities and boys' math superiority—have been knocked into a cocked hat. When researcher Alan Feingold studied national tests given since 1947, he noted that girls' edge in verbal ability had become tiny, and boys' edge in spatial relations had shrunk by half.[29] In 1989 Berkeley psychologist Marcia C. Linn reported that she had looked at results of the SATs and the PSATs and differences had virtually disappeared.[30] Recent meta-analyses—very sophisticated studies—confirm this.

Girls outperform boys on language and spelling tests only by a small margin. (Why are boys doing better than they used to with verbal skills? Perhaps old notions about writing and literature being "sissified" have declined in a competitive society in which only the brightest and best-prepared student will get ahead. The "gentleman's *C*" is a thing of the past.)

On math tests, in verbal reasoning, using analogies, abstract reasoning, and numerical ability, the girls have caught up with the boys. Boys still do better in spatial relations—the ability to manipulate objects in three dimensions, although the girls are gaining here as well. Feingold told *Newsweek*, "Biological imperatives do not change in the space of a generation." He notes, "As women's roles change, so have the abilities encouraged by parents and teachers. . . . In a more egalitarian society, the sexes develop more similarly."[31]

The boys' edge in manipulating objects in three-dimensional space may be the result of boys' early games involving such skills as throwing and kicking balls. Games such as baseball and football give a player a feeling for relationships of time, speed, and distance.[32] As more girls play Little League baseball and soccer, perhaps that gap will close more rapidly.

However, these findings will probably not make a dent in the conviction—thanks to the media—that a math gene really does exist. ABC's John Stossel completely missed the new science in a 1995 hour-long, primetime TV special, "Boys and Girls Are Different." He simply failed to report the shrinking sex differences in math and verbal abilities, giving the impression that huge gaps still exist. Not only was the show bad science, but it clearly implied that girls should be discouraged from entering such fields as architecture.

The media also love simple solutions to complex problems. A math gene fits neatly in a headline, and it seems easy to understand. But as Evelyn Fox Keller says, behavior is a complex phenomenon. You wouldn't look at your car and say that the carburetor makes it run, but that's the sort of reductionist thinking that too often goes on where women are concerned. There is a vast difference, Keller says, between genetic information and complex traits, be they physical or behavioral. Not only do genetically coded contributions act on each other, but "for human behavioral traits . . . the influence of the external, including cultural, environment becomes critical."[33] In other words, just as in a car's engine, it takes a number of parts, acting together, to produce the final result. However, this sort of complexity does not produce neat Bodoni bold, 48-point headlines.

Another intriguing thing about the math gene controversy was not what the media chose to put under their microscope but what they did *not* examine.

Professor Mary Gray, who heads the math department at American University, notes that the same SAT scores also showed that Asian-American males outscored white males. Where, she wondered, was the *Science* magazine headline that reported, ASIANS INNATELY SUPERIOR TO WHITES AT MATH? Why was this finding not trumpeted in headlines across the nation? It came from the same study. Why was it a nonstory, whereas the female "weakness" shot into the headlines?[34]

After all, Asian-American students often walk away with top math and science prizes, they are disproportionately represented in graduate programs, and the stereotype of today's MIT student is an Asian-American with a calculator. But where is the demand to study the brains of Asian-Americans to find the biological root of Asian superiority? Why aren't people suggesting that white guys just accept fate and not try to make the math team?

And, of course, if it turns out to be true that more males have superior math ability than females, so what? There will still be lots of women math whizzes out there. The fact that women for many years scored significantly higher than men on verbal abilities did not mean that Shakespeare, Faulkner, and even Stephen King did not exist. But massive coverage of real or perceived sex differences in which women come out the losers reinforces—and to some justifies—their second-class status. The coverage that created the math gene notion was not followed by the same bold headlines for the critics who carefully and convincingly deconstructed the idea. A good indicator of how deeply entrenched in the culture the math gene has become is that in 1992, a "talking Barbie" came onto the market, and one of the things she said was that she didn't like math.

From *Science* headlines to Barbie Dolls: the line of cultural transmission of a wrongheaded idea is complete.

3. UNRULY BODIES

Is It PMS, or Just the Wrong Side of Her Brain?

◈

Vive la différence! goes the old saying. It is usually assumed to be about romance, but it is at times a prayer fervently uttered by scientific researchers on the scent of a major grant or by members of the news media on the trail of a different commodity—a cover story or a five-minute segment or at the very least a snappy headline. Differences sell, no doubt about it, and if they are between men and women, so much the better. Difference between men and women is an appealing story; sameness is not.

Biology, as we all know, gives men and women both strengths and weaknesses. Men have superior upper-body strength and musculature—and they are prone to dropping dead of heart attacks at earlier ages than women. Women can endure certain kinds of stress better but can't run the marathon as fast as men or bench press four hundred pounds. Biology, however, always seems to be the albatross hung around *women's* necks. We humans are all simmering little cauldrons of hormones—but women's are the ones you have to worry about. The Myth of Female Weakness is awash in them.

Take, for example, PMS—premenstrual syndrome. It's surprising that nobody said Anita Hill was just off her hormonal tidal flow when she accused Clarence Thomas of sexual harassment. The Republican senators seemed to have used everything *but* PMS.

This is an affliction that in its severest forms affects only a minority of women. Many women may get grouchy or slightly bloated before their periods, but how many women do you know who have hacked their lovers to bits or run their cars over the next-door neighbor in a fit of pre-period rage? It's certainly important for women to know that the changing hormone levels in their bodies can affect their moods and to know medication is available if it's so severe it interferes with their lives. But why did PMS become a Darling Disease of the media? Female weakness again.

Media coverage of the syndrome was so prevalent—it even had its own thirty minutes on *Nightline*—that a visitor from Mars might have assumed it was a plague about to destroy the planet. For example, surfing through NEXIS for news stories of the past two years (roughly 1993–1995), I found 1,810 references to PMS and only twenty to pneumonia. How many more people does PMS kill each year than pneumonia? Colitis and hepatitis, both serious ailments, had only half as many citations as PMS.

Psychologist Carol Tavris, author of *The Mismeasure of Woman*, writes, "Today we are witnessing a rebirth in the belief in the unruly female body." She notes that a U.S. District judge, hearing a sex discrimination case in 1990, commented from the bench that "women have a monthly problem that upsets them emotionally, and we all know that." And, Tavris notes, "Most of the media today regard PMS as a clearly defined disorder that most, if not all women 'suffer.' For example, *Science News* called it 'The Monthly Menace' and the *Orange County Register* called it 'an internal earthquake.' An article in *Psychology Today* began: 'Premenstrual syndrome (PMS) remains as baffling to researchers as it is troubling to women.'"

But, Tavris asks, is it troubling "to *all* women, as implied? The article [in *Psychology Today*] turns out to be about a study of 188 nursing students and tea factory workers in China. *Suffered?* Overall, nearly 74 percent rated their symptoms as mild, 24 percent as moderate and 3 percent said they were severe. In other words, for 97 percent of the women the symptoms of this 'syndrome' were no big deal."[1]

No matter. Premenstrual syndrome has gotten so much coverage that it has become a part of the vernacular. I recently heard a man refer to a female colleague as having "permanent PMS."

PMS, it seems, causes just about every problem known to woman. The symptoms attributed to PMS include alcoholism, suicide, perceptual problems, glaucoma, epilepsy, allergies, headaches, depression, dizziness, and laziness.[2] PMS has been said to make women unable to get good grades, drive cars, operate machinery, serve in Congress, or do just about everything it is humanly possible for people to do. But much of the research on PMS has been fuzzy, poorly designed, or just so wide ranging it is almost impossible to categorize.

Some PMS research is based on what women remember about their moods. Women will often tell researchers, yes indeed, before their periods they did get weepy, grumpy, bitchy, and so on. Tavris notes that psychologists now see women internalizing the PMS notion and deciding after the fact that it *must* have caused their mood swings and other changes that they remember when they were about to get their periods.

But when women keep diaries of their mood changes, their actual moods don't match what they *remembered* their moods as having been. One study of groups of men and women showed an intriguing difference. The women who knew the study was about premenstrual mood swings reported a much higher level of negative feelings and physical complaints, such as headaches, than did the women who didn't know what the study was about—or the men. In other words, if you're paying close attention to every twitch and twinge of your body, it will seem more intense than when you are not. In the study the women who knew its focus reported a 76 percent increase in negative emotions and a 193 percent increase in physical complaints.

Interestingly enough, research shows that both women's and men's positive moods occur most frequently on weekends. "If you want to predict when a woman will feel happiest . . . you do better to know when it's a Saturday or Sunday than when she is ovulating," Tavris notes wryly. PMS research also often suffers from lack of a control group of men as a comparison. Studies have shown that if males are given a checklist of the same sorts of ailments that are characterized as PMS symptoms (excluding breast tenderness or menstrual cramps), men report as many of these symptoms as women do. However, if you *specifically* call them "menstrual symptoms," men report they don't have them.[3]

In other cases the media take a minute difference in male and female abilities based on a narrowly focused study and turn it into grist for the headlines. In 1988 the *New York Times* and the *Los Angeles Times* found a study of male and female "tasking ability" that resulted in this headline in the former: FEMALE SEX HORMONE IS TIED TO ABILITY TO PERFORM TASKS.[4]

What were these "tasks," readers might have wondered? designing new computer chips? doing differential calculus? brain surgery?

As it turned out, the study was of tongue twisters and precise hand movements. Tavris writes, "The newspaper editors must have thought these skills matter a great deal in real life, because women need to be able to say *Timothy it's time to transport the totally titanic ton of terrible trash* five times in a row quickly. . . . And perhaps women's skill at precise hand movements explains the predominance of females in needlepointing, although it cannot account for the predominance of males in neurosurgery."

By the way, the researchers hadn't actually measured men's or women's hormone levels. They just asked women to remember what phase of the menstrual cycle they were in, which, as we've just seen, is an unreliable method for assessing women's hormone levels.

So why the headlines? Tavris thinks it was not only a slow news period after the '88 presidential elections but also that "people have been trying for roughly eight billion years to find a link between women's hormones and their behavior, without success. When someone gets results, that's news."[5]

Even, I would add, if the science was sloppy, the subject was insignificant, and the conclusions unwarranted. But newspapers don't run headlines about the fact that *no* substantial research has linked women's abilities—or lack of them—with their hormonal flow. Tavris reports that when psychologist Sharon Gloub examined fifty years' worth of studies that have purported to link menstruation with all sorts of activity, from the most simple tasks to the most complicated intellectual endeavors, she found that "the menstrual cycle has no consistent demonstrable effect on cognitive tasks, work, or academic performance despite beliefs to the contrary that persist."[6]

And persist they do. It was undoubtedly the media maelstrom that led the American Psychiatric Association (APA) in 1993 to consider listing premenstrual dysphoric disorder (PMDD), a more severe form of PMS, as an official mental disorder. Supporters of the move said this would make it easier for women to avoid being dismissed by doctors when they were having real problems. Opponents thought that having another way of calling women nuts was not particularly helpful. "It's a lie, a bribe," psychologist Paula Caplan told the *Washington Post*. "The APA says, 'We'll believe what you women tell us about how you're feeling—but you've got to let us call you mentally ill.'"[7]

And once again some people wondered why it was only women's hormones that counted when it came to craziness. Female hormones, so it is believed, make women unstable, unpredictable, and unfit for everything from flying a plane to being president.

Men, however, are steady, stable, dependable—a veritable horde of Jimmy Stewarts. Of course, men never climb tall towers and pick off pedestrians with hunting rifles; they never wander into schoolyards and open up on children with an assault rifle—or mow down everybody in the McDonald's because the fries were cold. Anthropologist Melvin Konner, for one, has put the blame for male mayhem squarely on testosterone.[8] But does *Nightline* ever do a show on "Testosterone Poisoning"? Does anyone say, as handgun deaths soar, "Hey, should we let guys with all those chemicals sloshing around have *guns*?" Does anybody ask, about a presidential candidate, should we let a *man* be trusted with the button? Psychologist Paula Caplan has suggested a new category, delusional dominating personality disorder, characterized by such symptoms as "inability to identify and express a range of feelings" and the "delusion that physical force is the best method of solving interpersonal problems."[9] She finds it odd that *no* category at all addresses men's hormone-based mood swings, given the social chaos caused by male violence. As psychologist Harriet Lerner puts it, "Do you stay off the streets at night because you fear attack from uncontrolled, irrational women in the throes of their premenstrual syndrome? Probably not. We stay at home at night because we fear the violence of men."[10]

After all, research shows that in the hormone department the effects on men and women are about equal. Doreen Kimura of the University of Western Ontario reports that a man's level of cognitive ability is directly related to seasonal fluctuations of testosterone.[11]

However, in the case of men, aberrant behavior is seen merely as one man going out of his gourd in an act that has no connection with—or significance for—manhood in general. If woman or a member of a minority group behaves in what is seen as a peculiar way, it indicts the whole group. Patty Bowman, the woman in the Palm Beach rape trial, became Everywoman when she couldn't remember where she put her pantyhose. Ah ha, we *knew* they couldn't be trusted!

In addition, reports of men's hormones are often cast in a more favorable light than stories about female chemicals. James Dabbs Jr. and Robin

Morris of Georgia State University studied 4,262 male veterans and found a link between unusually high levels of testosterone and drug use, delinquency, abusiveness, promiscuity, and violence. Carol Tavris says,

> When the *New York Times* eventually published a report on these findings (in 1990) . . . the bad news of the link between testosterone and anti-social behavior was buried late in the story. The headline was AGGRESSION IN MEN: HORMONE LEVELS ARE A KEY with the subtitle TESTOSTERONE IS LINKED TO DOMINANCE AND COMPETITIVENESS. Aggression, dominance and competitiveness are considered desirable for men, of course. The implication of the title was that these qualities are hormonally determined. It is only halfway through the article that the writer cites Dabbs's study and quotes him as saying: "The overall picture among the high-testosterone men is one of delinquency, substance abuse and a tendency towards excess." This point, which is the real news, is not mentioned in the headlines.[12]

Of course, most men do not behave in the antisocial ways described, especially men of high social class who have other nonviolent ways to work off some urges that might be associated with testosterone. Going heli-skiing or getting into a fast game of squash are avenues open to affluent men that are not often available to poor men, who may also have to deal with terrible jobs, drug-riddled violent neighborhoods, and a range of modern urban ills. Anatomy is not destiny, for either men or women.

But we worry more about women.

Why, asks Tavris, is the *Wall Street Journal* "unruffled about the cost to the economy of men's hormones, while it features a story about the cost of women's?"[13]

Paula and Jeremy Caplan point to the highly political nature of sex difference research—and the media coverage of it: "Research on how women are controlled by their hormones fits with the prevailing social belief that women have less self-control than men. . . . Research that fits with widely accepted beliefs has historically been more likely to receive financial support, to receive moral support from the researcher's peers and to be accepted for publication in scholarly journals than research that goes against the grain."[14]

Suspicion about female hormones has a long history. In the first century A.D., Pliny the Elder reported the effects of menstruating women: "On approach of a woman in this state, grass withers away, garden plants are parched up, new wine becomes sour and the fruit will fall from the tree beneath which she sits."

Perhaps the sage in recent memory whose quote on women's hormones is best remembered is Dr. Edgar Berman's. He was the personal physician of Senator Hubert Humphrey and said flatly in 1970 that women were unfit for elected office because of their unstable natures. When Representative Patsy Mink, the Hawaii Democrat, got furious at him, Berman blandly commented that it was just her raging hormones going out of control: "Even a Congresswoman must defer to scientific truths. . . . There are just physical and psychological inhibitants that limit a female's potential. . . . I would still rather have a male John F. Kennedy make the Cuban missile crisis decisions than a female of the same age who could possibly be subject to the curious mental aberrations of that age group."[15]

Whether it's can she fly a plane, try a big case, or run for president, a woman is likely to be ambushed by a question that would not be asked of a man. Even when the question isn't asked out loud, it's implied. And massive media coverage of women's hormones only deepens the cultural suspicion that women are a witch's brew of chemicals sloshing around and ready to overflow at any minute.

If a woman's hormones aren't the problem, perhaps it's her brain. Chapter two enumerated the dreary legacy of ideas about the size of the brains of blacks and females. Tavris points out that "the history of brain research does not exactly reveal a noble and impartial quest for truth, especially on sensitive matters such as sex and race differences."[16]

Today we laugh at such nonsense as measuring women's brain mass like coffee grounds to prove their inferiority or saying blacks have brains like apes'. The new fad in the sciences is female-male brain difference. It's a notion tailor-made for the media; remember, difference is a story, but sameness is not. *Flash: men's and women's brains are pretty much the same* is not a cover line. There *is* no science of sex similarities, as the late Ruth Bleier, a professor of neurophysiology at the University of Wisconsin, pointed out.[17]

The big news in recent years has been left brain, right brain differences, with a special focus on the corpus callosum, the highway between them. Tavris says, "Today, many researchers are splitting brains instead of weighing them, but they are no less determined to find sex differences. Nevertheless, skeptical neuroscientists are showing that biases and values are just as embedded in current research—old prejudices and new technologies."[18]

The right brain, left brain split has drawn all sorts of speculations in recent years. The left brain is for language, the right brain for spatial perception; the left for thought, the right for feeling; the right nonlogical and creative, the left rational; the left Eastern, the right Western. Scientists Richard Lewontin, Steven Rose, and Leon Kamin note in their book *Not in Our Genes* that "one prominent Catholic neurophysicist has placed the seat of the soul in the left hemisphere. Hemispheric specialization has become a sort of trash can for all sorts of mystical speculation."[19]

And, I'd add, for all sorts of ideas about how the sexes differ.

One school of thought speculates that brain "lateralization" is the key to all sorts of gender differences—that males use their brains in more specialized ways than women do. Scientists Norman Geschwind and Peter Behan say that this sex difference begins in the womb, when the male hormone testosterone washes over the brains of fetuses that are beginning to develop as males. The hormone damages parts of the left hemisphere, briefly arresting its development, and the result is right hemisphere dominance in men. This, the scientists speculated—and *Science* reported—produces "superior right hemisphere talents, such as artistic, musical or mathematical talent."[20]

In the game of musical brains the right now seems to be winning out. Tavris says researchers have been constantly changing their minds about which side of the brain matters more. For a long time the left brain was supposed to be the seat of intelligence and reason, whereas the right side was

> the sick bad crazy side, the side of passion, instincts, criminality and irrationality. Guess which sex was thought to have the left-brain intellectual superiority? (Answer: Males.) In the 1960's and 70's, however, the right brain was resuscitated and brought back into the limelight. Scientists began to suspect that it was the source of genius and inspiration, creativity and imagination, mysticism and mathematical brilliance. Guess which sex was now thought to have the right-brain specialization? (Answer: Males.)[21]

But in fact all this is highly speculative. The brain is somewhat like a starship that has landed in a rather primitive society. Would the bush people of the Kalahari be able to understand *Star Trek*'s *Enterprise* if it landed in their midst? How little we know about the brain is proved by the British University student who has an IQ of 126, is socially perfectly normal, has first-class honors in mathematics, and yet has hardly any nerve cells in his cerebral cortex.[22] The brain is an amazing complex organ, and we are at the very dawn of understanding its functions. That doesn't stop the media from announcing speculative conclusions as fact.

Often the studies on which such conclusions are based are quite seriously flawed. For example, when Ruth Bleier took a close look at the data produced by Geschwind and Behan, she found contradictions. In one study of 507 fetal brains the scientists had stated they found no significant sex differences. If testosterone has such a powerful effect on the developing brain, it should have shown up in this sample. But the two scientists ignored this study as far as sex differences were concerned, citing it only in another context. Instead they looked at studies of rats' brains, which showed that areas of the cortex thought to process visual information were 3 percent thicker on the right than on the left.

Bleier found more holes in this argument than in the Swiss cheese that rats love to nibble on. No one knows, Bleier argued, "what the greater thickness in the male rat's cortex means for the rat, let alone what it means for human beings." Bleier fired off a letter to *Science*, offering a scholarly paper detailing her criticisms. Did *Science* publish it? No. Why not? One reviewer commented that Bleier "tends to err in the opposite direction from the researchers whose results and conclusions she criticizes" and also that "she argues very strongly for the predominant role of environmental influences." Bleier concluded that "one is allowed to err in only one direction if one wants to be published in *Science*."[23] Bleier also took issue with another article in the publication by two scientists who reported sex differences in the splenium—the posterior end of the corpus callosum. They wrote that "the female brain is less well lateralized, that is, manifests less hemispheric specialization—than the male brain for visiospatial functions." Tavris says, "Notice the language. The female brain is less specialized than—and by implication inferior to—the male brain. They did not say, as they might have, that the female brain was more integrated than the male's."

Once again Bleier looked at the research and once again found major problems that should have been fatal to its publication. The study was based on a sample of only fourteen brains, a tiny sample by any measure. The authors didn't describe their method of brain selection, so the brains could have been diseased. Most important, the sex differences in the brains were not statistically significant, and that is the basic standard in the sciences for validating data.

Once again Bleier sent a missive to *Science*. Once again *Science* ignored her.

This is not an unusual fate for those who argue against the conventional wisdom. As psychologist Naomi Weisstein writes, "It isn't necessarily conscious conspiracy. Rather, the new data are not acknowledged, or they are treated as trivial, or appropriate implications from them are overlooked. The data don't act to influence the theories, and so the theories remain the same."[24] This can be the fate of women scientists, who are too often not seen as being as authoritative as men, both by their peers and by the media. A co-author of mine, the late Grace Baruch, encountered one of the most striking examples of this phenomenon. She told me that when the *New York Times* Science section was about to feature her and her partner, Rosalind Barnett, as being among the scientists who were "re-drawing the map of women's psychology," she got a call from a reporter. He said he had been told by his editor that in order for the story to run, he had to get a quote from a male scientist saying her work was valid. There was no little irony in the fact that the scientist they used for this "validating" quote was a man whose doctoral thesis Baruch had supervised. A male brain is needed, it seems, to say that the product of the female one is up to snuff.

The stories of brain difference in the media show the writers often struggle to make difference the story, and the stories carry leads and headlines that the facts cited in the stories don't justify.

For example, a 1989 *New York Times* story said that "researchers who study the brain have discovered that it differs anatomically in men and women in ways that may underlie differences in mental abilities."

[*And then again it may* not *underlie differences in mental abilities. The negative is just as likely.*]

The story continued: "The findings, although based on small-scale studies and still very preliminary, are potentially of great significance."[25]

[*And then again may be of very little significance.*]

Theories about sex differences in the brain go in and out of fashion almost as fast as hemlines, so it is hard for journalists to keep up. Brown University biologist Anne Fausto-Sterling describes the merry-go-round:

- A 1962 theory that spatial ability is linked to the X chromosome and thus males show it more frequently than females—*clearly disproved*
- A 1966 theory that high levels of prenatal androgen may increase intelligence–*disproved*

- The 1968 idea that males are better at "restructuring" tasks because of lower levels of estrogen—*critiqued in the '70s; not cited in current literature*
- The 1972 theory that a sex-linked "spatial gene" is expressed only in the presence of testosterone—*clearly Disproved*
- The 1972 idea that female brains are more lateralized than male brains—*no evidence; not an important view* in the 1990s [26]

The opposite view, that male brains are more lateralized, hypothesized by Dr. Jerre Levy, is in vogue today. But the research is tentative, Fausto-Sterling points out: When psychologist Meredith Kimball reviewed the "small number of studies that might act as tests of Levy's supposition . . . she came up empty handed, concluding that there is no evidence to support the key assumption on which Levy builds her hypothesis."

Dr. Roger Sperry, who won the Nobel Prize for research on the functions of the brain, warns, "The left-right brain dichotomy . . . is an idea with which it is very easy to run wild."[27]

Running wild is something the media do very well. Sometimes they just skip all the nuances and announce theory as evidence. *Newsweek* asserted as fact in 1990 that "women's language and other skills are more evenly divided between left and right hemisphere; in men such functions are concentrated in the left brain."[28]

Sometimes publications just ignore recent findings. In 1992 the *Economist* flatly announced that nature had won out over nurture: "The failure of liberal reforms to deliver the Great Society has cast doubt on the proposition that better nurture can deliver better nature."

Because a few social programs didn't produce paradise, we are to believe that environment does not influence behavior?

"And a better understanding of how genes work has made it possible for liberals who still believe in the perfectibility of man to accept genetic explanations."

Had the Economist *simply not been listening to the rancorous debates about sociobiology, genes, and crime and the like in American society?*

And the *Economist* stated flat out that the "mathematical ability and spatial skills of boys are the product of their biology (genes and hormones), not their family," and that "the character-reading, verbal, linguistic and emotional interest and skills of girls are also biological."[29]

Hello! Don't you guys read the studies? Differences in math and verbal skills are disappearing rapidly. But hey don't let the facts get in the way of a good argument.

Too often the media not only report speculative conclusions but propose social policies that should be implemented on the basis of such research. For example, *Discover* in 1981 reported on new brain research at a time when the math gene was a hot item in the press. The article suggested that perhaps we ought to simply accept the fact that math is not important for certain jobs in order to help women, with their inferior math abilities, to advance: "For example, tests of mathematical competence have been used as criteria for admission to law school, where math is barely used. Tests of spatial ability have been used to screen people for all types of non-technical pursuits. If scientists can prove that such tests discriminate unnecessarily against women, hiring policies could be changed."[30]

This is essentially an argument for second-class citizenship for women. Imagine what sort of protests might be made—and lawsuits filed—if law schools had one set of admission standards for men and another for women. Or if in other fields women were seen as "math handicapped" but hired anyway. That would not only hurt their chances for advancement but would build resentment in men who would think their "superior" abilities were being ignored in the face of affirmative action. Mind you, all these policy recommendations were being suggested in an influential national magazine at a time when all the research was speculative. And they are unnecessary. We now know that the gender gap in math is shrinking—and when you remove the few male math prodigies from the mix, most men and women look identical on math abilities anyway.

But our fascination with the "sexy brain" will probably continue. Indeed some useful things may come out of this research. Even small anatomical differences could lead to different treatments for brain damage or other brain diseases, but this is a speculative projection indeed. It may turn out that sex differences are so small—and differences between individuals so great—that the notion of treating men and women in different medical modes is not realistic at all.

The danger is that the fascination of both scientists and the media with differences, and the media's tendency to make a big deal out of tentative research, will wind up making women feel their brains are somehow not as good as men's. And although it may not be politically correct to mention the inferior female brain out loud—as people used to do all the time—private decisions in universities, in corporations, in the Pentagon—will draw on such stereotypes.

In an era of diminishing resources, when men's wages are declining and good jobs at good wages are getting harder to find, you don't have to be paranoid to worry that the game of musical brains will be turned against women. Will women's brains once again be found to be suited for a little French, a little knitting—or today's equivalent of that argument? Will they be too lateralized for the executive suite? More suited to empathy than command? Will their callosums be too large—or too small?

Ruth Bleier wrote,

Such efforts directed at the Callosum (or any other particular structure in the brain, for that matter) are today's equivalent of 19th century craniology; if you can find a bigger bump here or a smaller one there on a person's skull, if you can find a more bulbous splenium here or a more slender one there . . . you will know something significant about their intelligence, their personality, their aspirations, their astrological sign, their gender and race and their status in society. We are still mired in the naive hope that we can find something that we can see and measure and it will explain everything. It is silly science and it serves us badly.[31]

4. DRAGON LADIES

Give Women Power,
and Who Knows What Will Happen

❂

Medusa is perhaps the most compelling reflection of male fear of female power. Her coiffure is not exactly Vidal Sassoon; her hair is a nest of snakes, and if she looks you in the eye, you turn to stone right on the spot.

The lady with the ultimate cold-eyed stare and the reptilian coiffure is only one legend of powerful women that emerges from the mists of our distant past. Coatilicue was the Aztec goddess who created time, and when two male gods fought her and sliced her in two, her top half became the sky, her bottom half the earth. She weeps at night, and the only thing that quiets her sobs is to be fed beating human hearts. The Amazons were a race of macho women who cut off a breast in order to get a better bead on you with their bows and arrows. The sirens of Homerian legend sat on a rock and sang so sweetly no man could resist their summons—but it led only to a watery grave. Myth and literature are filled with sirens, whores, temptresses, and vixens who in one way or another lure men to their doom—be it actual or psychological.

From many cultures, Eastern and Western, come myths of the powerful evil woman that, as Marilyn French writes in *Beyond Power*, transform the character of the female into something ugly, venomous, dark, and mysteriously threatening. Anita Hill becomes the avenging Woman Scorned, the career woman becomes the murderer of *Fatal Attraction*, Nancy Reagan turns from a vain woman who frets about the china into a dragon lady who is deciding the fate of the Republic. And Hillary Clinton—well, more of *her* in just a bit . . .

Throughout history this fear of women persists in patriarchal cultures. Cato warned in the second century B.C. that women must be strictly controlled or they will rise up and dominate men; so did John Knox in the sixteenth century. Around the twelfth century charges of witchcraft began to appear in Christendom and reached their high-water mark several centuries later. Confessions were usually obtained through torture, and no one knows exactly how many witches were burned at the stake or otherwise executed. Estimates range from one hundred thousand to several million. It was reported that in the city of Toulouse four hundred witches were burned in one day, and in the bishopric of Trier in the sixteenth century several villages were left with only one female inhabitant each after the burnings. In the sixteenth and seventeenth centuries witch burning was widespread throughout Europe.[1]

Some women accused were female healers, as men came to dominate the emerging science of medicine; some were indigent women, members of a class of former peasants forced off the lands—the homeless of the Middle Ages; some were members of religious sects considered heretical; some just ran afoul of a neighbor or relative who wanted to settle a grudge. Those accused of witchcraft were supposed to be in league with the Devil, who bestowed upon them evil and mysterious powers.

Power is the key word here; Delilah supposedly took Samson's strength when she cut his hair, and more recently Robert Bly warned in *Iron John* that women have destroyed the warrior in men. Why is it that so often the association of women and power is presented in so fearful an aspect? Edwin Schur, in *Labeling Women Deviant*, says that men have a tendency "to experience the very condition of femaleness as threatening. . . . If femaleness itself poses some kind of threat, then it becomes all the more important to keep it under control."[2]

One aspect of this threat is sexual; will the man be able to satisfy what Dorothy Dinnerstein, author of *The Mermaid and the Minotaur*, refers to as "the archetype of the insatiable female"?[3] Nineteenth-century American writings on women's sexuality reveal the notion that sex saps men's energy for dealing with the world. A man who gives in to a woman's demands would be "drained of his life's blood and enslaved by woman's appetite, and he would fail in business."[4]

If the female is not insatiable, she's deadly. From Medusa to Lady Macbeth the fatal female arouses more dread than a slew of male dictators, tyrants, and murderers. It's no coincidence that the "Year of the Woman," which saw two female senators elected from California, was also the Year of the Psychobitch in the popular media. You could hardly go to your local cinema without running into a deadly female. Madonna didn't have to use a weapon, she *was* one in *Body of Evidence*. She played a woman accused of killing a man through rough sex. In *Damage* Juliette Binoche destroyed all the males in sight, with some kinky sex along the way. Amy Fisher, the Long Island Lolita who shot her boyfriend's wife, was on all three television networks in the same week, an honor usually reserved for inaugurations or national disasters. Sharon Stone played a knife-wielding murderer in *Basic Instinct*, Rebecca de Mornay a murderous nanny in *The Hand That Rocks the Cradle*, Jennifer Jason Lee a crazed roommate from hell in *Single White Female*. The prototype of the genre was *Fatal Attraction*, in which the single career woman was portrayed as desperate and murderous. She was dispatched by the "good woman"—the faithful homemaker-wife.

The "good" homemaker and the "bad" career woman was also a theme of the 1992 Republican convention. Unfortunately, the GOP selected Marilyn Quayle as the Good Mother—as opposed to Hillary Clinton's "bad" Career Woman. The public of course did not buy it, because Marilyn Quayle is, if anything, more ambitious than Hillary Clinton. As *Time* magazine pointed out, as second lady Quayle spent so much time on the road that "almost any paying job, short of flight attendant, would give her more time at home with the kids."[5]

And of course, the Myth of Female Strength was in full sway as Lorena Bobbitt became one of the most celebrated women of the decade, slicing off her husband's penis after a history of abuse. The bizarre nature of the story—especially her tossing of the member from a car window, and the police search that ended in its recovery and reattachment—made it a headline story, as well as the subject of nervous jokes.

Usually, these freakish stories vanish from the public mind as quickly as they appear. The Bobbitt story had "legs." A male writer for Scripps Howard News Service, citing "a dozen women" as the source for his story, wrote that women relished the Bobbitt story in a fiendish way. "They cackle," he said. "Women love this story . . . it's a scary gender."

Writer Barbara Bonham dashed off a letter to the *Lawrence* (Massachusetts) *Eagle Tribune*, which had run the Scripps Howard piece, describing a conversation she overheard while out biking with her husband. As a group of twelve-year-old boys was riding by, one said, "'Did ja hear! What that woman did to her husband!'" Bonham wrote, "The adolescent listeners are enthralled because this is bloodier and scarier than any ghost story. 'Can you imagine if it happened to you?' one asked. And the male psyche spins, churning out all these fears of castrating, ball-busting women; that scary gender they have to share the world with—the mothers of their children, their coworkers in the office. At a tender age, these boys are learning to fear, distrust and dislike women."[6]

Few will forget Lorena Bobbitt, thanks to the massive coverage. But who remembers the names of the hundreds of thousands of women who are shot, beaten, maimed, and burned by their male partners each year? (Nicole Brown Simpson is remembered because she was married to a celebrity.) One woman takes out a knife, and her name is emblazoned in the media hall of fame. It sends shivers down the spines of adolescent boys—who have about the same chance of suffering Mr. Bobbitt's fate as they do of being hit by an asteroid. No matter. The powerful female is scary stuff.

If stories of fatal females terrify men, the memory of the loving but all-powerful mother also creates the perception of a threat. Women evoke, Dinnerstein writes, "the terror of falling back wholly into the helplessness of infancy."

And last—but not least—woman is seen to represent unpredictable nature and the body with all its frailties. Dinnerstein says that man has "magic feelings of awe and fear, sometimes disgust, towards all things that are mysterious, powerful and not himself."[7]

Western religion has a strong tradition of separating the natural world, including the body and all its rather messy juices and fluids, from the purer and higher realm of the spirit. Celibacy is seen as being of the spirit, sexuality of nature—and thus not only evil but a reminder that transcending the physical world is not always possible. St. John Chrysostom wrote that

"the passions are all dishonorable." St. Basil disapproved even of sex leading to procreation: "He who follows nature in these matters condemns
himself in that he has not completely conquered nature and is still ruled
by the flesh." Augustine—perhaps typical of the reformed libertine—was
humiliated by lack of control over the penis, which he deemed shameful.
"Women," writes Marilyn French, "reminded men that they were not
transcendent but were still part of nature."[8] (Did Clarence Thomas really
want to remember Long Dong Silver as he was about to enter the august
halls of justice?)

The Western nation-state from early on regarded control of nature as a
primary goal. When white colonials encountered the "Indians," who
believed that people must live in harmony with nature, not subdue and
destroy it, the Native Americans were branded as savages. Today it is science and civilization, not just religion, whose reach for omnipotence is tar-
nished by the very existence of women, because women are equated with
the natural world.

Whatever the complex reasons, our culture has a pervasive sense that
women are powerful creatures, and the idea of their getting *more* power
scares the pants off some men. John Adams voiced this fear openly, when
his wife Abigail asked him to "remember the ladies" in his revolution. That
was exactly what he had no intention of doing. "Depend on it," he wrote,
"We know better than to repeal our masculine systems. Although they are
in full force, you know they are little more than theory. . . . In practice, you
know we are the subjects. We have only the name of master, and rather than
give this up, which would completely subject us to the despotism of the
petticoat, I hope that general Washington and all our heroes would fight."[9]

Those "masculine systems" are still operating in today's media; the fear
that John Adams voiced openly is woven subtly through news stories and
columns about the subject of women and power. Centuries of male fear,
suspicion, and distrust of women have not vanished from the modern
world. But in the twentieth century the old fears are voiced more subtly.

As a young journalist I began to notice that the attitudes about—and
the language used to describe—women in the public arena was different
from that used for men. My mother had told me something of the way
Eleanor Roosevelt was mocked, reviled, and scorned because she took up
such causes as poverty and racism. Her dress, her girth, her slightly pro-
truding teeth were savagely ridiculed.

The more I observed the reaction to women in politics, the more I
sensed that although male power is treated as something normal and

expected, female power is approached with what can only be described as overtones of hysteria. For example, I was astonished at the reaction of seasoned political reporters during the 1984 political campaign when Walter Mondale, the Democratic candidate, was a speaker at the convention of the National Organization for Women (NOW). The group was actively lobbying for a female vice presidential candidate. Some delegates, carried away with enthusiasm for their cause, actually had the temerity to wave their signs and *yell* at Mondale, urging him to give them what they wanted.

Mind you, this is typical convention behavior. When the steelworkers or the surgeons or the airline pilots or the National Rifle Association devotees get together as one big happy family, yelling and waving a bit is considered good form, part of the electoral process. Unless people try to drown out the speaker, or completely disrupt the meeting, it is considered politics as usual. But when a few women did it—my god, the coverage was so hysterical you'd have thought they went after the nominee with drawn hat pins!

Several news stories used the word *witch* or *witchlike*; one columnist called the delegates a group of "Madame Defarges." Madame Defarge was the woman, you may remember, who knitted as people's heads were lopped off in *A Tale of Two Cities*. Isn't that image a bit extreme? If a burly steelworker hooted at a candidate, would anyone call him Robespierre? What if one of the NOW members had really gotten into it and stamped her foot? The psychic terror displayed by the press over a mild display of political enthusiasm by women told me more was going on than met the eye.[10]

When Geraldine Ferraro secured the second spot on the ticket, media gurus complained that Mondale had "surrendered" to the feminists; Richard Cohen of the *Washington Post* called him *henpecked*. The *New York Times* made itself look utterly foolish when it insisted for a time on calling her "Mrs. Ferraro-Zaccharo," when during all of her public life she had been referred to by her maiden name.

(The media in fact went through an orgy of resistance to the term *Ms*. What threat was implied in a woman's not using her husband's name? Editors insisted that they were interested only in correct usage, but their emotion over the issue illustrated that something larger was at play. When the *Wall Street Journal* interviewed me for a story in the early eighties, the reporter asked if I was "Mrs. Rivers." I said no, Mrs. Rivers was my mother. I use my maiden name professionally. He then said he would use "Miss Rivers." I said that would indicate I was a single woman, which might be a bit upsetting to my children. The publication went with the inaccurate *Miss.* The editors preferred inaccuracy to using Ms. or simply my last name.)

As the nominee, Ferraro herself was subject to a barrage of attacks—so unprecedented that columnist Richard Reeves referred to it as a *stoning.* Both the Myth of Female Weakness and the Myth of Female Strength were out in full force. As a woman Ferraro was seen as not able to deal with a crisis or to cope with the emotional demands of public life. She writes in her autobiography: "There it was again; crisis: Can you push the nuclear button, Congresswoman Ferraro? Emotion? Did you cry when you read the newspaper account of your father's alleged arrest? What will we have to do to prove that women are as steady, if not steadier, as men when facing a crisis, that women are not the emotional jelly our stereotypes portray?" On a *Nightline* interview Ted Koppel interrogated her with unusual fierceness on her foreign affairs positions. He later acknowledged at a Georgetown forum that because she was a woman he and other commentators had been harder on Ferraro on foreign affairs than they would have been on a man.

On the other hand, she was seen as too feisty and too irreverent; her approval ratings fell when she criticized Ronald Reagan. "Who was this pushy woman from Queens to criticize him?" was how she described the reaction. And she was attacked as a murderer and baby killer for her stands on abortion. Catholic clergy attacked her with a vigor they had never directed against Catholic male politicians such as Ted Kennedy and Mario Cuomo who were pro-choice. Also, a vicious anti-Italian campaign was launched against her, with bogus Mafia connections reported in the media.[11]

The tones of hysteria about women in politics did not abate after that campaign. In 1991, when members of NOW toyed with the idea of a third party, *Newsweek* lectured that the "shrill voices of NOW" could harm the pro-choice movement.[12] (Are Republicans ever *shrill*? How about socialists? Vegetarians? Libertarians?) Susan Faludi, in *Backlash*, noted that a torrent of scorn was unleashed on the surprised women. An anonymous source suggested "taking out a contract" on NOW head Molly Yard. The response, Faludi observed, was phobic: "No editorial writers proposed taking a contract out on John Anderson or Barry Commoner when they made their third party bids eight years earlier." Noting that polls in 1989 found American women feeling that both the Democratic and Republican parties were out of touch with women's lives, and that young women identified least with political parties and most with feminist groups and leaders, Faludi senses that women might have made great gains if they had been able to mobilize these vast numbers of women. "But in the 1980's, the backlash in the Capitol kept this historic political opportunity in check—with a steady strafing of ostracism, hostility, and ridicule," she writes.[13]

Bernice Buresh, director of the Women's Press and Policy Project, Cambridge, Massachusetts, notes several themes that emerge in media attitudes toward women and political power:

- Women's demands are always excessive—no matter what they are.
- Women's anger is terrifying.
- Once loosed, women's power cannot be contained.

Buresh also notes, "To just be seen as normal in the public world is a major achievement for women." She says that the press either portrays political women as total neophytes (read *weak*) or as harridans. She points to a *Los Angeles Times* profile of Dukakis campaign manager Susan Estrich in which Estrich is referred to as an "imperious witch" and a "snotty bitch." NOW, an organization that is no less mainstream than the American Dental Association, is often labeled "ultra feminist" or "radical feminist" in news accounts. (Women's demands are always excessive.) Is the American Medical Association ever called "radically pro-doctor?" Or the Chamber of Commerce "ultra pro-business"? Extreme words are almost never used to described men's groups that have generally mainstream positions.[14]

When women are seen as powerful, the words used by the media often have overtones of dread and menace. Anita Hill was labeled as a vengeful "scorned woman" or an equally revenge-obsessed feminist crusader, determined to bring a man down into the dust. That she seemed the epitome of a cool, self-possessed young lawyer from Yale, and that she had no visible feminist credentials—in fact was a supporter of the conservative Robert Bork—was simply disregarded. You don't have to act like a dragon lady to get tarred as one. Take, for instance, first ladies. Unless they remain locked in the attic, like Mr. Rochester's crazy wife, they can't win. A Niagara of print is devoted, each election season, to whether the president's spouse has some kind of Svengali-like power over him.

If she's Nancy Reagan, a traditional wife who devotes her career to her man, she's a meddlesome shrew who ought to stay in the kitchen and chat with the astrologist; if she's an activist like Eleanor Roosevelt, she's caricatured as a silly woman in a hat going down mine shafts. If she's got a southern accent like Rosalynn Carter's, she's the "steel magnolia." Kitty Dukakis was called a dragon lady because she had ideas of her own.

But perhaps no woman in politics has been treated with as much hysteria as Hillary Clinton. In truth, Clinton is not atypical of her baby-boom generation, a bright young woman who went to a good school, decided to get a law degree, and performed well in the competitive field of corporate law. Like many smart women her age, she wanted to marry, have a child, *and* do well in her field. The only thing that sets her apart from thousands of other women today is that she happens to be married to the president of the United States. But if the proverbial Man from Mars had to judge Hillary Clinton by the media coverage, he would have to assume that some otherworldly and utterly unexpected creature had suddenly appeared on earth.

The coverage of Hillary Clinton can be described only as overboard, hysterical, and phobic. The *New York Times* reported in September 1992 that the press had made no fewer than fifty references to Hillary Clinton as *Lady Macbeth*. Were any male advisers to the president ever presented as accessories to murder? Did anyone ever call James Baker *Iago?* When Hillary Clinton announced that she was going to move her office into the West Wing, eschewing the traditional first lady's office in the more distant East Wing, you'd have thought that Rasputin was moving his file cabinets in. She was compared to Glenn Close, who portrayed the murderer in *Fatal Attraction*, and to Eva Perón, the wife of the Argentine dictator ("ravenous for power"), and was called the "Wicked Witch of the East."[15]

Hillary Clinton just can't win. When she talked seriously of public policy during the campaign, she was chided for being too assertive. *Time* found her activism impolitic. "Instead of standing by like a potted palm, she enjoyed talking at length about problems and policies," the magazine complained. Criticized about her work at her law firm, she said, "I suppose I could have stayed home, baked cookies and had teas."[16]

That's the sound bite everybody reported. You'd have thought she proposed garroting Betty Crocker. Almost nobody reported the rest of that statement, although *Time* did: "The work I have done as a professional, a public advocate . . . has been aimed . . . to assure that women can make the choices . . . whether it's full time career, motherhood, or some combination."[17]

And while the Clinton quote was a megastory, the media ignored almost exactly the same rhetoric from a female member of the Republican team. Karlyn Kohrs Campbell, of the Joan Shorenstein Center for Press, Politics, and Public Policy at Harvard, notes that Marilyn Quayle said in a 1988 interview, "I'm not just a little housewife that's been sitting at home," and in her husband's first campaign for Congress she had told him, "You shake hands, I'll do the rest." But Hillary Clinton's similarities to Marilyn Quayle, Campbell notes, "seemed to escape press and public notice."[18]

When the media clobbered Hillary Clinton for being just what she was—a smart professional woman much involved in her husband's political career—she stepped back and let him take the spotlight. Did she get applause for making a smart political move? No, she was attacked for being muzzled and managed. As Catherine Corcoran points out in the *Washington Journalism Review*, the press attributed Hillary Clinton's problems not to the media mugging but to some overall societal dissatisfaction with feminism. The *New York Times* suggested that voters did not like the "hardheaded careerist who dominated her mate and seemed contemptuous of ordinary housewives."

But of course that was not the real Hillary Clinton but the version invented by the media. And Corcoran notes that there was little evidence for the *Times'* assertion that voters had been "put off by her assertiveness." A *Times* poll cited in the same article, Corcoran points out, "failed to document any mass revulsion among voters. It found that 29 percent of voters liked Hillary Clinton and 14 percent did not." A *Newsday* article also referred to some who rejected the "ambitious arch feminist."[19] Once again, over-the-top language. Would anyone have called George Bush an "ambitious arch preppie"? Or Jack Kemp "an ambitious arch jock"? How about Pat Buchanan as an "ambitious arch Catholic"?

Even Hillary Clinton's scholarly legal articles were cast as radical pronouncements. Daniel Wattenberg, in an *American Spectator* article, wrote that Clinton was the "Winnie Mandela of American politics who roams the far left fringes of the Democratic party and advocates that children be allowed to sue their parents to solve family arguments."[20] (Once again, extreme comparisons. Winnie Mandela was once quoted as saying that "necklaces" would help win the black struggle for power in South Africa. A necklace is a tire placed around a victim's neck and then set ablaze.)

The charge made by the *Spectator* was repeated in the mainstream press—which only belatedly took a look at her law review articles and found that she had never proposed that children sue their parents to resolve arguments and that her writings explored the thorny issue of children's rights in a way that could hardly be called radical.

The right wing, which likes its women silent and subservient, hates Hillary Clinton with the passion of junior-high schoolyard bullies. Here's a sample from P. J. O'Rourke: "She's a bossy little rich snoot of a goody two-shoes and not real bright who got into a fancy law school when girls were in season. Back in the sixties, the halls of academia were three deep with them."[21]

And that's one of the *nicer* comments. She's been called a "harridan," a "virago," and the "Lady Macbeth of Little Rock." Speaker of the House Newt Gingrich refers to her as a "bitch," his mother told TV reporter Connie Chung.

The right's loathing of a bright woman rubbed off on the mainstream media. The next phase of Hillary bashing cast her as either bad wife or bad feminist. Hillary Clinton was the "Yuppie wife from hell," said *U.S. News and World Report. Spy* magazine put Hillary Clinton on its cover in a black studs-and-leather dominatrix outfit, holding a riding crop, with the headline WHAT HILLARY PROBLEM? Barbara Amiel declared flatly in *Maclean's*, "The First Lady has emasculated America. I guess that is what radical feminists always wanted to do, but when the Bobbitt syndrome hits the only superpower left in the world, it's not only the Mr. Bobbitts who are in pain, we all are."[22]

The linkage of Hillary with Lorena Bobbitt threaded its way through the media. One cartoon showed the first lady—an evil grin on her face—sitting up in bed and thinking, "Hillary Rodham . . . Bobbitt."

Castration, S&M, witches, harridans, Lady Macbeth: it is the language of fear, dread, and loathing. Few males get this sort of terminology applied to them. How many male political candidates are called warlocks, devils, fiends, or sexual mutilators, no matter what their transgressions?

"Three centuries after Salem, what's going on?" asks Patricia J. Williams in the *Village Voice*. "Why are we still burning witches, or even just simmering them to death? Why are these images so powerful?"[23]

The Myth of Female Strength, that's why.

Susan Douglas, media critic and Hampshire College professor, notes that feminism and the left are both tossed into the boiling cauldron: "Images of the Bastille, of Salem, and of dark, swirling secret cults swirled together in punditland, creating a vision of complete societal breakdown should the ideas of feminists and leftists co-mingle and cast their evil spell over 'normal' people." Morton Kondrake worried on a TV panel that Clinton would persuade her husband to appoint "a bunch of wacko-leftists to the Supreme Court" instead of "decent people."[24] (Such wackos as

Thurgood Marshall, Earl Warren, and William O. Douglas, perhaps?) As it turned out, the first two appointees were Ruth Bader Ginsberg and Steven Breyer, both more to the center of the Court than to the left.

And where once she had been criticized for being an arch feminist, now Clinton was called not enough of a feminist. "Is Hillary Clinton a liability for feminism?" asks Michael Barone in *U.S. News and World Report*.[25] (His solicitude for feminism touches the heart.) Why? Because her "possible" involvement in questionable activities in Whitewater could undermine the ideas with which she has been identified. Would he have said that George Bush's "possible" knowledge of illegal events in Iran-Contra made him a liability to white Protestant men? Or to Republican ideas to which he was linked? And of course as of this writing, there is absolutely no evidence that Hillary Clinton did anything illegal in regard to Whitewater.

Or maybe she's not a good feminist because she is the first lady, not the president herself. "She's a false feminist," writes Mickey Kaus in the *New Republic* in 1993. "She has hitched herself firmly to her husband's career and used his success to promote herself. Nepotism is not feminism."[26] He does not mention that it was Hillary Clinton's corporate salary that allowed her husband to take the low-paying job of governor of Arkansas without totally depleting the family finances. Who was hitched to whom?

Abe Rosenthal writes in the *New York Times* that "political power must not be bestowed with the marriage vows" and says, "The First Ladyship cuts across what feminists are supposed to cherish and usually do; equal dignity, status and rights, in relation to men and to each other." He decries "power by wedding ring."[27]

How come none of these pundits decries power by college-roomate-ship, or by old-navy-buddyship, or same-law-firm-friendship? It's considered quite acceptable in Washington for men to use their personal contacts to further their careers. Ronald Reagan's old pals from California weren't elected by the people. Did William French Smith and Ed Meese—to name just two—get their jobs strictly on merit? Was Bobby Kennedy a bad attorney general because he was JFK's brother? We all know it's who you know that matters. Why should a woman play by different rules? And why should journalists demand it, when they make nary a sound about male buddyship?

Not only is Hillary not a feminist, Kaus suggests, but she's probably going to blackmail Bill because she stood by him when the philandering charges came up: "Her sudden post-election assertiveness, her name change, even her headband's return only add to the sense that she is cashing in on some sort of I-stood-by-you-now-it's-my-turn-deal."[28]

Or just maybe she's being herself—the bright activist lawyer she was trying to be when everybody told her to put a sock in it and act like a potted palm.

No matter what she does, Hillary Clinton takes a pounding. If she's quiet and wifely, she's being cynically managed. If she speaks out, she's bossy, a radical feminist, and a ball breaker. If she tries to support policy objectives, she's manipulative and unfeminine. The *New Yorker* weighed in (accompanied by the most unflattering witch-like illustrations of Clinton imaginable) with a long piece complaining that she has an agenda, making that notion seem more than faintly sinister. Jonathan Rowe, writing in the *Columbia Journalism Review*, calls Connie Bruck's *New Yorker* story

> almost a clinical case study in the way reporters project onto people in public life the very traits they indulge in themselves. We learn, for example, that Hillary Clinton has a tendency to use people for her own purposes. Reporters don't use other people? In their working lives, that's about *all* some of them do. . . . They enlist the subjects' confidence, pump or cajole them for quotes, and cast them aside or else reward them with favorable mention if they confirm the reporter's thesis. What is Bruck doing with Mrs. Clinton, if not using her to advance her own celebrity journalist persona?[29]

If the first lady isn't a harridan, a Lady Macbeth, a witch, or a psychobitch, maybe she's—a saint. That's the way the *New York Times Magazine* pictured her in a cover piece.[30] The article gave her views on the politics of meaning some serious attention, but the cover picture—which pictured her in a white dress with a haloish effect in lights—was another caricature. Saint Hillary is no more real than Dragon Lady Hillary. As media critic Ellen Hume observes, "A friend of hers said, when she saw that cover, that's the kiss of death. . . . Guess what. It's a set up."[31]

But Hillary Clinton's greatest offense is that not only is she a liberated woman, but she acts like it. No simpering, no pious incantations that she lives through her husband, no attempt to hide her brains (except during the campaign when she had to), no gazing adoringly up at Bill, no pretense that she's anything but a smart policy-wonkish lawyer and activist who is not used to behaving any differently than the guys do at work. That seems to drive some people *nuts*. As Patricia Williams writes in the *Voice*,

> It was Hillary who betrayed her husband, by not carpooling, by speaking other than when spoken to and by having the uppity audacity to write law review articles, and not just any law review articles, mind you, but those that suggest that children have rights too, that children as well as their mothers ought to be liberated from the common law of property. Hillary Clinton's great sin was that she left the nicely wallpapered domestic sphere with a slam of the door, took up public life on her own, leaving big feminist footprints all over the place, and without so much as an apology.[32]

Although all the wailing and cries of doom have occurred when first ladies stray from rearranging the china, in fact it's been all the president's men, not the first ladies, who have led him down the garden path. There were Ed Meese, Ollie North, Mike Deaver, et al. in the Reagan years; LBJ had Bobby Baker and Truman the "five-percenters"; under Ike it was Sherman Adams—all accused of a blind spot where ethics were concerned. Nixon's happy warriors, Bob Haldeman, John Mitchell, John Erlichman, Howard Hunt, G. Gordon Liddy, and company, cost their boss his job and nearly got him impeached. Why do there seem to be no questions about Svengalis where male aides are concerned?

And the ladies? Eleanor Roosevelt made things better for blacks and the poor; Rosalynn Carter helped the mentally ill; Lady Bird Johnson cleaned up the country; and Nancy Reagan tried to get her husband to work for world peace. Hillary Clinton's goals are universal health care and the welfare of children.

The idea of an all-powerful woman dominating a president seems unlikely, given the sort of men who get to that office. They are nearly always men with towering egos and iron constitutions; your average shrinking-violet guy does not suddenly wake up one morning and say, "By golly, I'd like to be president!"

But I guarantee you, come next election, once again we'll see the clichés trotted out: dragon ladies and iron fists in velvet gloves, flowers made of steel or other base metals, and all forms of reptile life attached to a word indicating the female gender. And if the candidate is female, the clichés will go through the roof.

After all, the Myth of Female Strength goes back to those snake-bedecked evil-eyed goddesses and was helped along by nothing less than religion and the rise of the nation-state. It is probably not going to go away any time soon.

5. VANISHING ACTS

How Good News About
Working Women Disappears

⑥

Journalists, like bird-watchers, are always on the lookout for creatures that hide in the brush, difficult to spot, offering the thrill of discovery when they come into view. But while birders seek the yellow-throated grackle in the reeds or the tufted titmouse high on a limb, journalists comb through the underbrush of census data, stomp about in the weeds of legislative reports, and hunt through the tangles of psychological research to spot the elusive species known as the Trend.

Editors love the little critters, especially if they come, like purebred dogs, with pedigrees attached in the form of hard numbers from the Census Bureau, the Centers for Disease Control, the Hoover Institution, or almost anyplace at Harvard.

Nothing makes an editor sit up and take notice like a trend with at least a patina of legitimacy. I have bagged more than a few of the creatures myself.

The problem is that journalists, like bird-watchers, can mistake one species for another from time to time. The birder, overeager after seeing nothing but mottled leaves, may think he's just seen a yellow-throated grackle, but perhaps it was just a piece of a yellow plastic bag from the local Kmart stuck in a tree.

Where women are concerned, mistaken spottings are all too common. Trends are bagged, examined, and proclaimed to be the real McCoy. The small voices saying, "Are the statistics right? Do any other statistics contradict the findings? Why does it say Kmart on the belly of your prize?" often don't get heard—at least not until more bits of distorted information have seeped into the general consciousness, there to remain.

Susan Faludi, author of *Backlash*, calls the trend story one of the major journalistic inventions of the twentieth century, and she notes, "Claiming to mirror public sentiment, its reflections of the human landscapes are strangely depopulated. Pretending to take the public's pulse, it monitors only its own heartbeat—and its advertisers."[1]

The trend story often gets the reporting process backward. A reporter or editor decides there is a trend—maybe by talking to another editor at a cocktail party or by reading another publication—and then tracks down experts and other folks who will validate that idea. As Faludi says, "Trend journalism attains authority not through actual reporting but through the power of repetition. Said enough times, anything can be made to seem true. A trend declared in one publication sets off a chain reaction, and the rest of the media scrambles to get the story too. The lightning speed at which these messages spread has less to do with the accuracy of the trend than with journalists' propensity to repeat one another."[2]

The Misery of the Working Woman is a trend story that has been recycled so often it should be retired to the Trend Hall of Fame.

YOU CAN'T DO EVERYTHING! announces a 1989 *USA Today* headline on a story suggesting a slower career track might be a good idea.

MOMMY CAREER TRACK SETS OFF A FUROR, declaims the *New York Times*, reporting that women cost companies more than men.

PRESSED FOR SUCCESS, WOMEN CAREERISTS ARE CHEATING THEMSELVES, sighs a 1989 headline in the *Washington Post*, going on to cite a book about the "unhappy personal lives" of women graduates of Harvard Business School.

WOMEN DISCOVERING THEY'RE AT RISK FOR HEART ATTACKS, Gannett News Service reports with alarm in 1991.[3]

If you believe what you read, working women are in big trouble—depressed, sick, risking an early death from heart attacks. *None of this is true.* It is quite simply false. In fact, research shows the exact opposite to be the case.

Scores of studies on the emotional and physical health of working women have painted a picture that psychologist Rosalind Barnett and I saw outlined in stark black and white when we examined the research: paid employment provides a substantial health benefit for women—and this benefit cuts across income and class lines. Even women who are working not because they want to but because they have to share in enhanced good health.

A curious gap exists between the studies and what you read and hear in the popular media. The more the research shows that employment is good for women, the more bleak the media reports seem to become. Ever wonder why? Ah, we're back again to the Myth of Female Weakness.

Back in 1982 *Newsday* editor Ilene Barth noted that she sensed a media crusade against the working woman that attacked "the heresy that women can be successful on several fronts." Major articles with titles like VOICES FROM THE POST-FEMINIST GENERATION cataloged the woes of working women, making them seem barely a cut above the people in Bangladesh in terms of misery. This all left Barth singularly unimpressed. "Any journalist worthy of her video display terminal can find six walking-talking examples of any trend," she said, and added that the misery of the working woman was "one of those unprovable theses that gather legitimacy as anecdotal reporting about them rolls off the nation's presses."[4]

And those stories continue to roll. Hardly a month goes by without some major publication offering a dire portent for working women: they are going to start having heart attacks, they are never going to get husbands, they'll send their kids running to shrink's couches, they'll be such bundles of nerves that they need a mommy track to keep working at all.

"The majority of working women are under stress," UPI reports. WORKING WOMEN STRESSED OUT, headlines Reuters; FEMALE MANAGERS FACE SUPER STRESS, warns the *Chicago Tribune*. *Business Week* declares a "blues epidemic among working women," *Redbook* asks working women, "Are you headed for overload?" and the *National Journal* wonders about A GENDER AT RISK.[5]

The warnings are dire, suggesting that women should either quit working or cut way back on their aspirations. But what about the *good* news about working woman? Mostly it got buried on page 105 or simply wasn't believed. Although the editors about whom Barth wrote continue to assign the problem stories, few people point out the dire predictions that *didn't* come true.

Are working women dropping dead of heart attacks, as expected? Cardiologists Meyer Freidman and Ray H. Rosenman, in their 1974 book *Type A Behavior and Your Heart*, predicted that women would lose their survival advantages over men as they entered the labor force, when they had to work "under conditions whose essence consisted of deadlines and hostility."[6]

This prediction turned out to be untrue. The federal Framingham Heart Study, a major ongoing project, shows that working women are not showing more symptoms of heart ailments. In fact, only one group of working women does have problems: women in low-paid jobs with high demand and little control, who have several children and little or no support at home. Overall, women are not having more heart attacks, nor has there been any decrease in their life span as they enter the workforce.[7]

What about that Gannett News Service headline—and many other stories—about women being at increased risk for heart attacks? None of this has anything to do with work. Women are older and frailer when they are stricken—sixty-seven is the average age for women, six years younger for men. Also, heart attacks are treated less aggressively in women—fewer coronary bypasses, for example.[8]

But aren't women at risk for all sorts of stress-related illness? In fact, there's solid evidence that work *reduces* depression and anxiety for women. Studies consistently show the mental health of working women to be significantly better than that of nonemployed women. A national longitudinal study detailed in the journal *Women and Health* in 1989 finds that women involved in both work and family roles report better physical and emotional health than homemakers.[9]

Reviewing a federally funded three-year study of 745 married women, sociologists Elaine Wethington of Cornell University and Ronald Kessler of the University of Michigan write, "The findings clearly suggest that employment benefits women emotionally." They report that women who increase their participation in the labor force report lower levels of psychological distress, whereas those who lessen their commitment to work suffer from greater psychological distress.[10] (These findings are the exact opposite of a claim made in a 1988 *Newsweek* magazine feature about women who drop out of professional jobs. "Women who give up career aspirations," the magazine said, "are much happier." But Susan Faludi notes that the magazine offered as proof the stories of only three women, two of whom were complaining about self-esteem problems because they weren't working full-time.)[11]

A study from the University of California at Berkeley followed 140 women for twenty-two years. At age forty-three, homemakers had more chronic conditions than working women did and seemed more disillusioned and frustrated. Working mothers were in good health and seemed to be juggling their roles with success.[12]

I'm not talking about a scattered study here and there. The evidence is stacking up, and in scientific research the more that findings can be "replicated," the more reliable they are considered to be. The truth is that work offers women a chance for heightened self-esteem, a buffer against depression, and enhanced mental and physical health.

But isn't this true only for women on the fast track? Not at all. Working-class women share the benefits of work. Dozens of studies of such women with jobs as waitresses, factory workers, and domestics show that these women are quite committed to their jobs, satisfied with their diverse roles, and would not leave the labor force even if they did not need the money.[13]

But don't women make less efficient workers than men because they have so much on their minds? Do you really want a *mommy* making that multimillion-dollar corporate decision or reading your X ray? Won't she be so worried by little Tommy's broken toe from soccer that she'll give your money away or tell you you've got cancer when it's just a spot on the film? That's what the media stories about all those stressed-out women seem to imply.

Surprising results come from studies of married couples by sociologists Wethington and Kessler. It was the *men* who brought the family stresses with them to work. Wethington and Kessler speculate that this may be true because women get the message early on that they'll handle the home front, whereas "men are taking on jobs they weren't trained for and didn't expect."[14]

Perhaps the most dangerous myth about women and work is that the solution to any problem is for women to drop back—or drop out. It's bad enough that these poor frail creatures with their PMS and their bad math genes and their unreliable hormones are at work at all. Poor dears, maybe if they work only part time things will be much better.

Wrong. There is evidence that these solutions will actually harm a woman's health. Mommy tracking your way to inner peace sounds great, but it can be risky. Studies show a significant connection between reducing commitment to work and psychological distress. Having a child does not increase psychological distress for working women—*unless* the birth results in their dropping out of the labor force. Wethington and Kessler found that low-hour, part-time work has a negative effect on mental health. They speculate that women who have these kinds of jobs try to do all the housework and all the child care and wind up being more stressed out than women working full time.[15]

So why do the media keep churning out stories about the wretched working woman? Probably because many adults today grew up in an era when soldiers were returning home from World War II and a way had to be found to get the women who had taken their jobs in industry back to the kitchen. The result was a barrage of propaganda that turned at-home moms into saints and the backyard barbecue and the station wagon into religious artifacts.

This mythology was at play in one of the big trend stories of recent years: Women Over Thirty-Five Who Have as Much Chance of Getting Killed by a Terrorist as They Do of Getting Married. The story is a prime example of how a major "trend" can grow from the barest of seedlings. Three Harvard-Yale researchers published a study, "Marriage Patterns in the United States." Not, on its face, a real headline grabber. But embedded in the study was what appeared to be bad news about women, a commodity that sells like fat-free cookies.

ARE THESE WOMEN OLD MAIDS? screeched *People* magazine in a headline that ran above pictures of Diane Sawyer, Sharon Gless, Donna Mills, and Linda Ronstadt. "A Harvard Yale study says that most single women over 35 can forget about marriage," warned the magazine.[16]

Before long, hardly a female on the planet hadn't heard the dire predictions about women who hold off on marriage. A *Newsweek* cover featured a graph showing how, as they age, the marriage chances of women allegedly drop faster than an Olympic downhill skier on course. The message beamed to women was that the price of ambition and independence is misery. So widespread did the story become that it entered immortality through pop culture. One of Nora Ephron's single women in *Sleepless in Seattle* cites the "fact" that it's easier to get bumped off by a terrorist than to get married once you've hit a certain age.

But is it true? No. The researchers themselves said their work was being wildly misinterpreted. As it turned out, women who choose to marry when they are past their twenties suffer no dire consequences. The massive coverage the national media gave to the story had no basis at all.

The researchers had looked at census data on baby boomers in the light of an established trend for women to marry men who are two to three years older and who are at least as well educated. The researchers noted an interesting demographic fact—that during the baby-boom years, each year brought an increasing number of babies; the baby crop in 1955 was larger than that in 1953, for example.

In the world of statistics a woman born in '55 would be looking for a husband among the smaller group of men born in 1953. Because the male baby crop of '53 was smaller, the females born in 1955 could be seen as a larger group of women fishing in waters that contain fewer men.

But the man shortage, as Katha Pollitt pointed out in *The Nation*, "is really an older man shortage, and a temporary one at that."[17] The dire scenario for single women is exactly this: the thirty-five-year-old woman who insists that she will marry *only* a man two years her senior who is as educated or more educated than she could face a shortage. Viewed in this limited statistical prism, the white, college-educated woman's likelihood of marrying is only 1 in 20. But of course that number is completely bogus. Why should we assume that this woman will scorn a man her own age? Or the thirty-four-year-old man? Or the twenty-eight-year-old man?

This is a cover story? No. It's an example of a narrow statistical study, having little relation to how men and women behave in real life, that was hyped into a phony trend.

Why so? Pollitt nails the answer when she says that "media coverage of the study, if not the study itself, is just another crack of the backlash. Women can't have it all, women must choose. A career or a husband."[18]

However, the Miserable Working Woman has a mirror image in the media—Superwoman, who does everything without mussing a hair. She was perhaps best pictured in the commercial for Enjoli perfume, in which a svelte blond woman, dressed in a power suit, croons, "I can bring home the bacon," then appears in a domestic scene in which she adds a stanza, "Fry it up in a pan," and thence to a boudoir in which Superwoman—nary a blond hair out of place—slinks about in a sexy negligé, warbling, "And never let him forget he's a man."

Of course the mass media never insist that men be good at *all* this stuff. You might see Jim Palmer posing in his Jockey shorts but never Donald Trump. Have you ever seen an ad in which a man is a tiger on

Wall Street, whips up a mean souffle, and wears a cute little string brief in the bedroom?

On the surface the Superwoman stories in the media seem to encourage women's ambitions. In fact, they do quite the reverse. These women are so magnificent, so able to transcend the limitations of ordinary women, that the average woman reading such a story is bound to conclude that the creature is of species different than hers. As Edwin Schur writes in *Labeling Women Deviant,* the process of "exceptionalizing" women who achieve—cutting them off from the herd, if you will—is "an implicit claim that 'typical,' 'normal' and even 'natural' women do not and cannot do such things."[19] The "superizing" of individuals creates for others disconnection with those of their own kind who have been trailblazers.

But almost as soon as the media invented the Superwoman Trend Story, they created another: Superwoman Gives Up. It's the ultimate media inside activity, deconstructing an icon they created in the first place. MORE SUPERMOMS ARE HANGING UP THEIR CAPES, announced the *Orlando Sentinel* in 1994, and a week or so later the *Atlanta Constitution* asked, IS SUPERWOMAN SHEDDING HER CAPE? *Ebony* said that black women are revolting against their mothers' careerism and the "Failed superwoman."[20] Superwoman is not only white and black, she's British. Also in 1994 the *Guardian* claimed that modern feminism is "concerned only with Superwoman (Good job, good man, good house, better car, good children with good child care)," and the *Independent* said, SUPERWOMAN HAS HAD ENOUGH, citing young women "who heard stories from women who've done it all and don't want to be Superwoman."[21] A *Newsday* article decreed that whereas some women are "fed up with the rat race and fast pace of modern life, others are frustrated by the feminist formula that said you could have it all."[22]

In story after story Superwomen bite the dust. Mind you, none of these stories offers any data other than a few anecdotal comments. The death of Superwoman (or her retirement) is a trend that doesn't exist, because Superwoman never existed except in the imagination of the media.

If the working woman—super or otherwise—is a favorite target of the media, the working mother virtually has a bull's-eye painted on her forehead. Next to Jack the Ripper and Attila the Hun, few people get more bad press than Mom. *Newsweek* magazine headlined one story MOMMY VS. MOMMY, saying, "Tension between mothers is building as they increasingly choose divergent paths; going to work, or staying home to care for their kids."[23]

Look at those choices. Either they go to work or they *care for their kids.* Can we assume that working mothers lock their children in the closet each morning? Or perhaps just send them out to pal around with the homeless?

Over the years I have read literally hundreds of stories blaming working mothers for every social ill except the heartbreak of psoriasis. The *Texas Monthly* charged that day care was so harmful to children that mothers ought to run right home. (The editor of *Working Mother* found the piece so slanted she called it "cheap shot" journalism.)[24] The *Washington Monthly* all but said outright that working mothers were neglecting their children. A *New York Times* feature, JOB VS. BABY, featured a series of working mothers saying they were giving up, they just couldn't do it all.[25]

Then there was the *Fortune* cover designed to warm the cockles of a working mother's heart: CAN YOUR CAREER HURT YOUR KIDS? YES, SAY MANY EXPERTS. The subtitle reads, "Mommy often gets home from work too tired to talk. Daddy's almost never around. Says one expert, 'We can only guess at the damage done to the very young.'" (The expert can only "guess" because there is no evidence that working mothers harm children. That doesn't stop the guessing.) The piece trumpets a list of woes of children of working mothers—smoking, drinking, using marijuana, feeling lonely, and even this gem: "In high achiever families, dinnertime conversation can evolve into a series of didja's—didja ace that test, win that election, score that touchdown."[26]

The media have been screaming for years that SAT scores are declining and blaming it on working parents who don't spend enough time on kids' homework. Now here's *Fortune* slapping high achievers around for pressuring their kids to do well. Parents are damned if they do and damned if they don't. The fact is that mothers can't do anything right. If they stay home, they are brain-dead parasites living off the sweat of their husband's brow and ruining their children by pampering. If they go to work, they are selfish harridans trampling on the old values, emasculating their husbands, and turning their kids into love-starved zombies.

Working mothers get hit doubly hard by these myths and by the idea that a mother must sacrifice everything for her children. Many people look at studies showing that work is good for a woman's health and say, "Hey, forget all this focus on the mothers. What about the kids? Aren't they the ones being harmed?"

But does maternal employment harm children? The answer is emphatically, unequivocally no. In 1989 University of Michigan psychologist Lois Hoffman reviewed *fifty years* of research and hundreds of studies of maternal employment. Few psychological issues were studied more. Guess what happened? What the psychologists were looking for wasn't there. There simply were no significant differences on child development measures between children of employed and nonemployed mothers.[27]

Despite the definitive research, the worries linger. Recently, my husband and I were watching a television report on new research showing that children's brains develop at a much faster rate than previously believed and that children who receive inadequate stimulation from ages one to three may fail to reach their full potential. "Maybe we didn't give the kids enough stimulation," my husband said, a stricken look on his face. (Parental guilt can strike both sexes.) The baby-sitters we hired when the kids were young were nice older ladies but hardly rocket scientists.

The chill hand of guilt clutched at my throat. Had I been a selfish mommy? Had I been a self-absorbed yuppie (before the word was even invented), focusing on my own career and leaving my children's minds to molder? Fortunately, sanity returned. "Wait a minute," I said, "are we talking about our son, who got a three point six grade-point average in grad school and was the valedictorian of his class in the police academy? Or about our daughter, the Shakespearean actress, who gets glowing reviews for reciting perfectly page after page of dialogue, in iambic pentameter? We should feel *guilty* about them?"

But it doesn't matter how well your kids are doing; guilt is like a Teflon bullet, able to rip through all your defenses. And of course anyone who has a bad word to say about working mothers immediately gets headlines. A 1994 book by British psychologist Penelope Leach entitled *Children First* got megacoverage, including a front-page review in the *New York Times* Book Review section and a profile in the *Times Magazine.*

Leach declares that institutional day care is not the answer to children's needs because she believes it interferes with the bonding process between mother and child. She declares that we should entirely remake our society, giving generous maternity leaves, restructuring business and industry so that either parent has the option of working part time—with prorated pay and benefits—until children are eight years old. All of this would be wonderful, but given the current economic realities, none of it is going to happen. Chances are that the only part of *Children First* that will be remembered is the attack on day care.[28]

Leach's firm belief that day care for young children interferes with the bonding process may be her opinion, but it is not based on scientific research. In fact, the research shows quite the opposite to be true. She relies on "attachment theory," which is a slim reed on which to hang a blanket condemnation of day care. The theory grew out of research in the forties and fifties on children in institutions—hospitals and orphanages. These children spent hours with no loving care or human contact, and they suffered from emotional problems and the impairment of many of their skills. The term for this loss became *maternal deprivation*. But these children were deprived not only of their mothers but of any true human contact. No wonder they were below average in the growth of skills and perceptions. But children aged two to four in the same era who were cared for in day nurseries while their mothers worked in factories were normal. However, the maternal deprivation studies have often been used as arguments against day care and the employment of women. It is social mythology at work. The elements of the studies that supported the idea that women's place is in the home became part of the "scientific" arguments.[29] Those that did not fell right off society's radar screen.

Which brings us to attachment. Scientists try to determine whether children are sufficiently bonded to their mothers by using this test: an infant is brought into a playroom and observed interacting with its mother and with a stranger. If the baby clings to its mother and recoils from the stranger, the child's reaction is taken to indicate a special infant-mother bond.

The attachment studies have come under fire as too simplistic. Some babies are outgoing and may not be upset by a stranger. Others who have been in extended families or in day care may be quite comfortable with relating to someone other than their mothers. And what about those cooing babes who relate to their mothers but get anxious around strangers? Harvard psychologist Jerome Kagan argues that some infants who become upset in the "strange situation" do so not because they're securely attached but because they can't deal with uncertainty. They've been trained to be dependent on a mother alone and are showing the less-than-wonderful side of this dependence. Kagan suspects that perhaps researchers are looking too hard at security, because that's what they think is important, and putting little emphasis on independence. A parent called insensitive by researchers might really be giving a child a leg up in dealing with the real world by not catering to his or her every whim.[30] But the media have a tendency to simply accept any story, any expert, that suggests everything would be better if mothers were home with their children.

Making sweeping generalizations from attachment tests seems to defy common sense. And few experts share Leach's notion that day care should be jettisoned. Alison Clarke-Stewart, a professor at the University of California at Irvine who has examined the research in detail, told the *New York Times Magazine* that Leach is "doing mothers who want to work a disservice. A good mother can counterbalance even average day care."[31]

We now have a storehouse of scientifically collected evidence on the social, emotional, and intellectual development of children in day care compared with those raised exclusively at home. "By and large no one could tell the former from the latter," notes psychologist Faye Crosby of Smith College. Crosby says controlled studies have "reassured most educators and researchers that children suffer no psychological harm and may reap some emotional benefits, from day care and other non-family care. . . . Basically, the evidence indicates that small children develop nicely under a number of circumstances and may reap some emotional benefits from child care and other non-family care."[32]

In fact, no evidence exists that day care harms children, although it is generally agreed that sub-par day care has the potential to be harmful, especially when parents are from low-income families and dealing with multiple stresses. In general, though, research has shown that at-risk children benefit from day care in terms of their overall development.

However, alarmists like Leach get massive publicity, even when they have no evidence for their opinions. But researchers who have been studying the data for years, and have come to opposite conclusions, do not get major profiles in metropolitan newspapers or invitations to television talk shows.

We hear a lot about working moms—and dads—who shove their kids off on other caretakers while they work long hours climbing the corporate ladder. I am sure such people exist, but I don't know any of them. Most of my friends who are working parents dote on the kids and spend lots of time with them. When my kids were small, they often accompanied either my husband or myself on assignment. I sometimes wonder whether my actress-daughter got bitten by the bug at age seven when she went backstage with me at the tryout of a Broadway musical. As the curtain closed on the first act, she was led out to sit on the king's throne while she could still hear the applause. She said, with royal dignity, "Bring me a bowl of chicken soup!"

I read media stories about the sixty-hour-plus career women who hardly see their kids, but are they typical? It seems not. Studies show that when both parents of preschoolers are working, they spend as much time in direct interaction with their children as do families in which only the fathers work. The difference is that working parents spend more of the time on weekends. When only the father works, couples spend more leisure time with each other.[33] So working parents are cutting down on their personal pleasure to be with their kids. At one point in our lives my husband and I never saw a movie that didn't have either a dog or a guy with a light saber in it. When at a chic Cambridge party the conversation got around to symbolism in film, people stared at me oddly when I suggested *Benji* was a Christ figure.

Rarely do researchers ask whether working mothers could be *good* for children. But when psychologists Cynthia Longfellow and Deborah Belle of the Harvard University School of Education investigated sources of stress for children, they found that the health and well-being of the mother had a direct effect on children's adjustment. They report, "Maternal employment appeared to benefit both mother and child; employed women were generally less depressed than non-employed women and their children had fewer behavioral problems."[34]

But the media can't get over their enchantment with the myth of good mommies at home and bad mommies at work. As a result, one story is largely ignored—the very real problems of the homemaker. Although the headlines sigh about the terrible problems of working women, the mental health of homemakers is rarely mentioned. A data base search for 1993–1995 turned up 353 stories about stress and working women but only 43 stories that link stress and homemakers.

By the early seventies the dismal statistics on the mental health of married nonemployed women in the industrialized West had come rolling in like the tide. Rates of depression and other symptoms of psychological distress were quite high among homemakers. Long hours of housework combined with a sense of always being "on call" led to high stress; when housework was compared to assembly-line jobs, it was found to be more monotonous, fragmented, faster paced, and involving much longer hours.[35]

But the myth of the happy homemaker was the driving force behind one 1994 trend story that was greeted with what can only be called delight by the media. "Reversing a decades-long trend, young women are opting out of the job market and staying home, with major implications for the economy," announced *Barron's* in a major feature article. The accompanying illustrations were happy pictures of moms in the fifties serving dinner to a husband or smiling contentedly over a washing machine. The pictures and the captions gave the idea that women (at long last) were going home to a better life. In fact, *Barron's* predicted, "It is not impossible that the liberated woman of recent years could meet the fate of the Gibson girl—prototype for the larger-than-life female who invaded the all-male professional world at the beginning of the century and, over the course of two generations, disappeared."[36]

Barron's announced, "Demographic trends suggest a retreat by women who will realize they're better paid—in every sense of the word—at home," under a picture of a happy mom at her Maytag. Taken as a package, the story clearly implied that (a) young women were going home, (b) they'd be better off, less stressed and "better paid" for what they did, and (c) they would be just as happy as those smiling fifties moms.

The problem is, no such trend exists, and, as noted, a major risk factor for depression in women is leaving the workforce. This is a classic example of the Ersatz Developing Trend. How did it come about?

An economist at the brokerage firm of Donaldson, Lufkin, Jenrette noticed a dip in the numbers of women aged twenty to twenty-four in the workforce in the early nineties. That would be the age range in which women would be having children, he surmised. Then he looked at the drop in mortgage rates. Ah ha, he said, women are finding it too expensive to work, they're getting too stressed out, and now they and their husbands can afford to buy a house. So they are going home and letting their husbands bring home the paycheck.

The economist, Richard Hokenson, envisioned a world described thusly by *Barron's*: "By the late nineties, Hokenson sees stores filled at midday with stay-at-home mothers, rolling serenely from aisle to aisle, comparing prices and ounces, taking risks on generics and house brands." And when she gets through with that, she can hunt through bargain basements for her new wardrobe, jeans and sweaters, sweats and t-shirts, more comfortable for her work week. "And she can now buy Nikes at its own factory outlet." In this scenario women will spend the time they used to devote to earning a paycheck to combing the stores looking for the best buys, having time to "drive to a factory outlet two towns away."[37]

What fun!

The women of America must be panting at this scenario. They can scrounge around in supermarket racks for cheapie diapers, prowl bargain basements for generic jeans, bypass the glitzy malls for the stores with bins of seconds on children's overalls. What's wrong with this picture? First of all, women aren't really rushing home. Labor force participation by young women has indeed dropped—from 72.9 percent in percent in 1989 to 71.2 percent in 1994. But what's happening with *men* aged twenty to twenty-four? If the theory were correct, they should be charging ahead, now that their wives are going home and they are the breadwinners. In 1989 men's labor force participation was 84.6 percent. In 1994 it was 81.6 percent. Men's labor force participation dropped *more than women's*.[38]

But where are the stories about men going home? Are they out there, prowling through the Nike outlets, reaching for the bargains at the back of the cut-rate racks?

Are we seeing a lemminglike rush homeward by stressed-out women? Or simply a weak labor market in the aftermath of a recession and a slowly recovering economy? Maybe women aren't entering the labor force at such a fast clip for the same reason that men aren't—the economy is losing jobs, and the competition for good jobs at good wages is much greater.

Hokenson assumes that affordable home prices are sending women scampering back to the kitchen. But he didn't bother to factor another statistic into the equation. At exactly the same time that he was making his predictions the Federal Reserve was announcing a heavy burden of debt carried by the working middle class. The *New York Times* reported that middle-class families remained stuck with unusually high debt payments, nearly a quarter of their income, a much higher percentage than in past recoveries.[39] The high debt was a result of stagnating wages combined with low rates of income. Low interest rates did prod people to buy things— including houses—but the lag in wages made it hard for them to pay for the things they'd bought. So, although low interest rates might allow twentysomething couples to buy homes, high debt might be keeping women at work. It all depends on which statistics you look at.

Barron's colors in another picture as well—of the harried working woman who is a "frenetic" consumer, the working wife who dashes into the grocery store at 6 P.M. en route from the office to the day-care center. She grabs whatever she can from the shelves, whereas the at-home mom is "rolling serenely from aisle to aisle." Note the language. The working woman is harried and frenetic, the at-home mom serene.

But how serene will she really be? *Barron's* has just said she's driven "to a factory outlet two towns away." There she is, with a couple of screaming kids in the car, driving for forty minutes to the factory outlet so she can pick up the cheap sneakers to save two bucks. She's at home with kids, she has no income, her husband's wages are declining, she's given up her chance for career advancement and retirement income, and she's at risk for being plunged into poverty if her husband is laid off or she's divorced. This is serenity?

Interestingly enough, even the women interviewed by *Barron's* as an example of the trend said that if their companies offered affordable on-site day care, they would probably go back to work.

These facts did not stop the *Christian Science Monitor* from hopping on the story, headlining, MORE WOMEN CHOOSE TO STAY HOME. The *Monitor* quoted *Barron's* on a "shocking about-face" and a "trend that seemed unthinkable just a short time ago."[40] Here's a perfect example of one media outlet's using another media story to validate a trend that doesn't exist; it's a game that could be called Media Merry-Go-Round. And others hopped on for the ride. The *Chicago Sun-Times* decreed, THE RETURN OF THE SINGLE BREADWINNER. The *Courier Journal* of Louisville, Kentucky, announced, NUMBER OF STAY-AT-HOME MOMS ON THE RISE, and Gannett News Service headlined, MOTHERS JILT JOBS FOR HOMES, FAMILIES.[41]

These stories, saying women are running home—and implying it's high time—tend to make the woman who is at home believe that she must be "serene" because this is her natural place. It can heighten the tendency for women at home to think there's something wrong with *them* if they get to feeling depressed, isolated, or unhappy, rather than understanding the risks built in to the role of housewife. If women at home have to be saints, always serene and happy—with the media telling them it's their fault if they're not—they will be seriously vulnerable to risks to their health.

6. MONKEY BUSINESS

Why the Media Love
Our Primate Cousins

⊚

Who can forget the opening of *2001: A Space Odyssey?*—the apes huddled together on the plain long before the dawn of man. As the sun breaks across the empty plain, one ape begins to play with the bones of a carcass, and as the music swells, suddenly, dramatically, he forges the world's first weapon; triumphantly, he hurls it skyward—where it hangs against the sky for a few seconds—and then turns into a spinning spaceship. The story is clear: man has invented weapons, and the path to civilization has begun. The simian with the weapon has taken the first step toward the moon.

As anthropologists Adrienne Zihlman and the late Nancy Tanner point out, the explanations for how we became human are shrouded in the mists of the primate past, and so we have to invent stories of how it all came about. Of these stories, "some can be summarized by evolutionary slogans such as 'The Killer Ape,' 'The Naked Ape,' 'Men in Groups' or 'Man the Hunter,' which emphasize competition, aggression, sex, meat-eating and hunting. Hunting in particular has been the basis for interpreting early human fossils."[1]

Man the hunter is dramatically prefigured in the gripping opening sequence of *2001* (1968). The problem with this wonderfully dramatic scenario of course is that it ignores women altogether. In the arc of time from the hurled bone to the spaceship we are seeing history as the story of men. The ape-man as ancestor is a story that fascinates the modern media; man the hunter tames the planet, invents language, fire, religion, the fast-food franchise, and dentures. Magazine articles liken CEOs to leaders of the hunt and write of the male bond of hunting as one that leads through the executive washroom to the company Lear jet. Chances are we will be seeing even more of this Paleolithic drama, as women make more strides and some men long for a mythological past of freedom and power that was never quite real. One segment of the men's movement pines for the good old warrior days, when you could do some serious bonding with another guy by sticking a sharp pointed javelin into his appendix. In *Iron John* Robert Bly sees modern men as being too weak and passive, too . . . well, civilized.[2] We are in for more of a major romance with our primate-warrior past, when men were men and life was short and bracingly brutish.

Biological determinism and the idea of a biological basis for male dominance fit neatly in an era of a changing economy within which some men feel they are losing ground. In the late 1970s and early 1980s an argument that nature, not nurture, explained human society was in vogue under the rubric of *sociobiology*. During the eighties and nineties scientists began chipping away at such notions as crediting hunting males for taking us across the divide from prehuman to human, a process from which women were largely absent. But biological determinism is making a comeback today. Newt Gingrich gave it voice when he said that combat roles for women are ill advised because men are programmed to go out and hunt giraffes.

Where did this "hunter chic" come from? According to anthropologist Robin Compton, the most recent vogue for Man the Hunter probably began with anthropologist Raymond Dart in the 1950s. Dart reasoned that because early humanoid bones were found on broad plains, or savannas, plants would have been scarce and early man would have turned to meat eating. He examined bones from caves in South Africa that were from both early man (*Australopithecus*, 2 million B.C.) and animals and decided that the jawbone of an antelope had been fashioned as a weapon by the inhabitants, who had stalked and hunted large game with this weapon—much like the one the ape wields in *2001*.[3]

From this scenario grew the picture of our early male ancestors as hunters, out stalking game in groups while women and children waited patiently by the campfires for the men to literally bring home the bacon. Piles of stones and the remains of bone were seen as the "homes" of prehistoric families. A concurrent idea was that monogamy developed early to avoid social disorder and chaos in the group. That this picture of early civilization seemed to approximate that of the 1950s family did not seem to occur to many researchers. But science historian Donna Haraway, in her book *Primate Visions,* points out that reconstructions of the past are made not in a vacuum but in a crucible in which culture, politics, and science meet. The Man the Hunter ethos arose "in the face of deep post-war anxieties about the fate of civilization . . . coupled with the equally compelling image of the mother-infant pair," she writes.[4] Moms at home, dads out providing, females monogamous—that was history. As anthropologist Adrienne Zihlman, of the University of California at Santa Cruz, told *Discover*'s Ellen Ruppel Shell, "It's a typical projection of the ideal American family back in time."[5]

Ironically, liberals used the Man the Hunter theme to deliver an antiracist message in the early fifties. "The task of human beings after Hiroshima," Haraway writes, was "to discover our humanity, i.e., the sharing way of life once lived by all of us, in the heterosexual idyll of the hunter gatherers."[6] United Nations declarations about the "Family of Man" were backed by anthropologists who hoped to prove our common roots. If all men hunted, gained language through the experience, and became human because of the hunt, why would racial prejudice exist? That this "humanist" picture of the family of man was also deeply sexist would not have occurred to most scientists in those prefeminist days.

In the 1960s and '70s a series of books, including *African Genesis* (Robert Ardery), *The Naked Ape* (Desmond Morris), *The Imperial Animal* (Lionel Tiger and Robin Fox), and *On Human Nature* (E. O. Wilson), received gallons of ink. These books claimed that the male bonding of the hunt meant that "men were making and using tools, obtaining and sharing food, developing communication, and becoming more intelligent for more effective hunting," as Zihlman puts it.[7] The media were enchanted—and continue to be. I wish I had a dollar for every story I've read over the years that likens corporate males to killer apes or Paleolithic hunting packs. One good example of the genre is an extended piece in the *Chicago Tribune* headlined, APES IN THE OFFICE: IT'S A JUNGLE IN THERE. The writer reports, "In human and chimpanzee politics, everyone participates in politics in some way, but it is the males who play the most aggressive, opportunistic game." He juxtaposes the activities of a group of chimpanzees with a group of businessmen thusly:

Chimps: He comes in with a bit of a swagger, like many chief executives. Mr. Yeroen usually is the first to arrive in the morning. . . . Yeroen is clearly admired and respected by all, and there is a distinct sexual undertone in the way the female members greet him.

Men: Atkins couldn't wait for the weekly meeting; he had to get his adoring secretary cranking this out right away so we'd all know: his division performs.[8]

In the chimpanzee scenario the females' role is to lust after the dominant male; in the human scenario the secretaries do the drudge work, happily and admiringly, for the males, who are the main players. Strange, how animal behavior and primate history echo twentieth-century corporate structure. And in an *Omni* story in 1993 on an anthropologist, man actually becomes beast, right before our eyes as he lectures at Harvard: "Four hundred students watch as a slide is projected of a large silver-haired gorilla in his natural habitat. The lecturer shifts back on his heels, throws out his chest and intones, 'and this individual rejoices in the scientific name, *gorilla, gorilla!*'"[9]

The media pick up on this theme in myriad ways that have nothing to do with the reporting of science, including a 1992 review in the *Dallas Morning News* of a comedian who does a caveman routine. The reviewer, noting the comedian's theme that men and women are universally different, observes, "We always laugh hardest at what is tough and true. We can handle the tough truths when they're sugar-coated with the comic's sure touch. But we run from them when they're given to us naked. That's why the serious sociologists and psychologists have been having so much trouble. Men are hunters and women are gatherers . . . which accounts for the variations in our shopping and driving styles."[10]

Of course, many serious scientists by this time had reservations about Man the Hunter, but it was too late. The idea had already made it to the entertainment page. The media's fascination with the naked ape and his blustery ways is understandable. It's great theater. It just may not be great science, because it leaves out half the hominid race. As Zihlman points out, "There isn't much to elaborate upon about the picture of women: it was drawn with disappearing ink. Home bases seemed to be invoked as places for women to stay home. While there, they were losing estrus, in order to be continually sexually receptive, thereby doing their part to reduce sexual chaos."[11]

In this scenario women are peripheral to evolution, except for having babies and letting out a few admiring grunts and coos now and then. This idea enchants the media, even women's magazines that ought to know better. *Cosmopolitan* puts this notion in its own cloying way: "Flash: Authorities now say nature, not nurture, makes him thump and thunder while you rescue lost kittens and primp."[12]

These kittenish lines hide an ominous message. Psychologist Naomi Weisstein, writing in *Ms.,* defines it this way: "Men are biologically suited to their life of power, pleasure and privilege, and women must accept subordination, sacrifice and submission. It's in the genes. Go fight city hall."[13]

Of course, the debate over the real story of evolution is about what happened millions of years ago, so why is it important? As anthropologist Linda Fedigan observes, "If people become what they think they are, then what they think they are is exceedingly important."[14] And the naked ape theorists argue for a world of male primacy because of hunting:

Females play only service roles of one kind or another to males. . . . The business team is most often all male. Women, usually, seen as disruptive to enterprise, are only there to serve in some way. . . . In each case, men will want to keep them from controlling the system, and women will be unlikely to make inroads into the centers of economic history. Women do not hunt.   (Lionel Tiger and Robin Fox, *The Imperial Animal,* 1971)

If the concept of the weapon had been part of our animal legacy, then our devotion to the weapon must be reckoned as a possible animal instinct, and politics and philosophy, education and psychiatry must alike grapple with the speculative consequences.   (Robert Ardery, *African Genesis,* 1961)

Even with equal education for men and women and equal access to all professions, men are likely to remain disproportionately represented in political life, business and science. . . . We know in particular that the earliest true men . . . hunted game.   (E. O. Wilson, *On Human Nature,* 1977)

And Ardery declares: "We are uniquely human even in the noblest sense because for untold millions of years, we alone killed for a living."

But by the early 1970s challenges to Man the Hunter were beginning to appear—first as underground rumblings, then as full-fledged revolt. "Is hunting the only behavior worth talking about, and what were the women doing?" some scientists began to ask. The work of Jane Goodall with her chimps, Dian Fossey with the gorillas in Rwanda, and Richard Lee with the hunter-gatherers of the Sahara—and many others—began to chip away at old ideas. First of all, the fieldwork—scientists observing primates close up and for long periods of time—gave a new focus to the studies.

The young researchers, many of them women, began to note mistakes in older research, including male bias. For one thing, scientists were looking only at the high drama of primate life—the highly visible sex and violence—and thus getting a skewed picture of our ancestor. The media of course love sex and violence, one reason that outdated views persist in their reports. For example, a 1993 Reuters story on a book about primates is headlined, RACISM, MURDER, GENOCIDE—THEY'RE IN OUR GENES. The interview with Jared Diamond, author of *The Rise and Fall of the Third Chimpanzee,* centers on murder and mayhem among male gorillas and chimpanzees.[15] Those in fact do exist, but as Jane Goodall's longitudinal studies have shown, primate societies are rich in a variety of experiences, and to focus on just the violence is like saying New York City can be explained by a mugging in the Bronx.

The young researchers in the field who were questioning the status quo focused on the dailiness of primate life—not just the high drama—and quite a different picture emerged, one in which females took a much more active part. Most social organization centers on the females and their offspring, and sibling ties remain strong throughout life. Males of high status get their status through the mother, the behavior of female primates is often assertive and central to the life of the group, and females compete for status, food, and sex.

The researchers note that scientists once had classified females only by reproductive status, whereas they classified males according to a much more complex set of behaviors, and that some data-collecting methods just didn't support the conclusions they reached about the centrality of males.

Meanwhile, new analysis from African fossils casts doubt on the notion that early man hunted large game. Teeth have provided compelling evidence. Studies of molars reveal they were large and well worn. Electron microscope scans, which examine tiny scratch marks to determine the diets of our early ancestors, show that some of our ancestors and "even early *Homo* seem to have eaten a diet dominated by tough, fibrous fruit. The meat content of the diet appears inconspicuously small," Compton reports.[16]

In fact, early man was more likely *on* the menu than out for the kill. The bones that Raymond Dart identified as remains of the meals eaten by early man and as weapons turned out to be something quite different, according to paleontologist C. E. Brain, now director of the Transvaal Museum in South Africa. His study of bones in the sorts of caves Dart had examined concludes that it was the carnivores—especially leopards—who were doing the eating, and the human remains were those of humans who had been eaten, Compton reports. The fossil record does not show weapons, as Dart believed, but tools for chopping, shredding, and flaking.

A human skull in a cave that Dart examined showed several dents that Dart said were made by a weapon—and he theorized that it was a record of early men killing one another. These fossils became the basis of the argument, made by Ardery and others, that warfare began early—a good example of how huge theories can blossom from scant evidence. But Brain's analysis of the bones creates a much different probability, Compton points out: "The canine teeth of a leopard fit the dents better than any hypothetical bone club. *Australopithecus* was prey, not predator or murderer. [E. O.] Wilson's model of the development of male dominance as a genetic adaptation to hunting life represents an unacceptable distortion of the available data—or at best, pure speculation."[17] And noted paleontologist Richard Leakey says, "There is absolutely no evidence that we became human through hunting. Up until very recent times, there's no record at all of human aggression. If you can't find it in the prehistoric record, why claim it's there?"[18]

Such leaps as Dart's show both the tentative nature of developing science and the need of the media for a roaring good tale. Murderous cavemen and great hunters make a much better story for the media than weak frightened prehumans who wound up on the dining table of carnivores. But when later analysis of data proves the latter to be the more likely scenario, the news appears in the fine print someplace. What readers remember is the purple prose, even years after the scientific thinking has changed. Robin Compton's 1984 article warns,

The appealing and insidious nature of myths like "The Killer Ape" are dangerous. They become part of the human consciousness, the common set of preconceptions and biases that color thinking, and linger on against any number of devastating scientific criticisms. Responsible scientists, armed with these preconceptions, and a natural desire to make their work more interesting and popular, feed the flames of misconception by making illegitimate and unwarranted speculations when publicly announcing their data. The media pick up on these myths as the result of "science."[19]

And, he points out, our behavior is constantly being modified by our environment. That some behavior has a biological component does not mean it can't be changed. Even if a hunting lifestyle had put genetic pressure on *Homo sapiens,* it would "tell us nothing of how such genetic characteristics might respond to a change in environment; how they might be changed or even eradicated as behaviors. Careful scientific study of human origins, not speculation, may tell us much about where we have come from and how we got here. It has little to tell us of where we may go from here," says Compton.[20]

The idea that men were bringing home to passive waiting women the prey they had hunted was challenged not just by the examinations of bones but by such work as Richard Lee's studies on the !Kung hunter-gatherers of southern Africa. The Man the Hunter theory has the male bringing home food to one female and to their offspring, and this pair bond was key. But as Adrienne Zihlman explained to science writer Ellen Ruppel Shell, the data anthropologists were getting on the !Kung showed the women were pretty independent. They controlled the resources they collected, and the !Kung women wandered far afield to gather the tubers and roots that formed much of the tribe's diet. Zihlman speculates that it makes sense to assume that our early female ancestors, like the !Kung, were not helplessly tied to a campfire waiting for males to provide but walked far afield to gather food and used tools to hack through the tough vegetation or pry open shells and nuts.[21]

Zihlman and Nancy Tanner looked at chimpanzees and theorized that early hominid behavior may well have been much like theirs. Studies on blood proteins showed that genetic similarities between humans and chimps go well beyond what was imagined—genes of chimps and humans are 99 percent identical. And chimps make and use tools; they catch, kill, and eat small animals; they share food and sometimes stand and walk upright.

Tanner and Zihlman speculate that gathering—rather than hunting—was the activity that took humans across the divide between animal and human: "Sticks for digging and containers for carrying may have been among the first regularly used tools. . . . Because mothers had more reason to collect and carry food, they would be most likely to select and modify appropriate objects regularly for use as digging tools and containers in order to make the job easier and quicker."

The tools they used were not for hunting large, dangerous, and swiftly moving animals but for gathering and digging and cracking and cutting. Tools began to replace teeth. Mothers were the primary socializers of the young, teaching them the skills of surviving in the Savannah.[22]

The idea in *2001*—that the first weapon led directly to the spaceship, an unbroken chain of male invention—was challenged by a number of scientists, including anthropologist Sally Linton.[23] Donna Haraway says, "Linton understood the ideological and mythological core of the debate about the first tools: so she shifted the linguistic terrain from those originary tool-weapons that are so potent in masculinist Western technologically preoccupied cultures. She changed the focus instead, to 'cultural inventions' and suggested that two of the earliest would have been containers to hold the products of gathering and some kind of sling for babies to be carried in."[24]

Primatologist Linda Fedigan, noting the evidence that early man was not the warlike fearless hunter but a small vulnerable species that hovered on the edge of extinction, says that the sexual division of labor happened rather late, that in the beginning both men and women did similar work, prompted by the key human invention: food-getting tools. The weapons for big-game hunting came much later, and, as Haraway explains, "In the narrative code of evolution, late means less fundamental to human nature"[25]—and thus easier to change.

Fedigan also looked at the work of Richard Potts, who examined the assemblages of stone and fossil remains that earlier scientists had identified as the "homes" where women waited patiently for the men to return. He said they were more likely tool caches and places where food was processed from time to time, not places where early people lived for long periods of time. The remains in the area showed that both early man and large carnivores had been active at the sites, and if the carnivores were there, the humans weren't. Early life wasn't *The Flintstones,* with Fred and Wilma snug in their well-upholstered cave-house. The hominids—males and females—were most likely constantly on the move, and "home" was no more the domain of women than it was of men.

"If there is not evidence for home bases . . . then we can perhaps free our minds of the image of dawn-age women and children waiting at camp-sites for the return of the provisioners," Fedigan argues.[26] Mom and kiddies waiting happily and patiently at home is a staple of sitcoms projected back into history—not a real story of what our ancestors were like.

Other scientists have speculated that early man walked upright because of the male need to roam far and wide in the hunt. Isn't it just as likely that the upright posture could have come from *women's* need to walk? It makes no biological sense to picture prehuman or early human females as sedentary—unless you are looking through the lens of *Leave It to Beaver.*[27]

The media's bias in this area shows clearly in an anecdote Haraway relates in *Primate Visions*. For an article on human locomotion for *Natural History* Adrienne Zihlman wanted to use a photograph of a modern gathering woman—pregnant, with a young child, carrying a heavily loaded bag, and walking swiftly a long distance from her home camp: "The magazine editors, without consultation, substituted two photographs of a modern white American football player, one . . . with the whole body musculature poised for receiving a pass."[28] Illustrations of what early humans did are nearly always illustrated by male figures. A 1993 *Omni* article on the history of walking was illustrated by serial photographs of a nude muscular male striding briskly along.[29]

In biological research, as well as in history, you see what you look for. In both areas the story of human development has been told as one of male achievement. Some scientists have theorized that language evolved as the need to communicate between male hunters. But isn't it more likely that the close communication between mother and infant—which is a universal, whereas hunting is not—may have played more of a role? Nancy Tanner argued that mothers and their young, learning and gathering in a social environment, their cognitive skills increasing with each new discovery, working their ways toward language, were in fact the main players in the drama of evolution. But it has been only recently that this seemingly obvious hypothesis has been put forth.[30]

Marilyn French writes in *Beyond Power*,

> At whatever point in the human past language began, it had to emerge from
> mothers communicating with their infants and children. The old notion
> that males on the hunt developed language to communicate is absurd: one

doesn't learn to speak after one is physically developed. We know that language develops young, or it doesn't develop at all. It is reasonable to assume that mothers cooing to, warning and teaching their youngsters, developed a symbolic system that was then built on and transmitted by children.[31]

It does seem odd that the hunt—rather than the mother-infant relationship—should be thought of as the reason for language. But then female behavior is simply not regarded as "species making." The story of Imo, the Japanese macaque, is a case in point, as psychologist Naomi Weisstein points out.

Imo was a member of a troop of Japanese macaques studied intensely by scientists. The monkeys were fed sweet potatoes, which were hard to eat because grains of sand and gravel clung to the food. Imo figured out that washing the potatoes in water got the sand off. Her innovation spread among the other children in the troop, who taught their mothers, who in turn taught their infants. The adult males never got the knack. The scientists then flung grains of wheat into the sand to see what the troop would do. The ingenious Imo didn't bother to laboriously pick each grain from the sand. She took globs of wheat and sand to the water, where the sand sank and the wheat floated. Once again, the knowledge spread from mothers to kids—not adult males.

"The fact that these Japanese macaques had a rudimentary culture has been widely heralded, but what are we to make of the 'way' culture spread in this troop?" Weisstein asks.

> If Imo had been male, we would never have heard the end of the inventive capacities of primate males, and since generalization spreads like prairie fire when the right sex is involved, no doubt their role in the evolution of tool use—and why not—language as well. But the urge to grand theory withers when females are primary actors, and when the task relates to food—at least food without killing. Imo has been described as 'precocious' and left at that. Precocious indeed!—How would *you* get the sand out of the wheat?[32]

But what if the scenario so popular in the media was *not* that of the naked ape? What if it were one in which women were active, social, independent, and free ranging, not passive beings huddled by the fire. In that case, there is no biological imperative—such as the one Tiger and Fox describe in *The Imperial Animal* (1971)—for men to keep women out of the public arenas in which human dramas occur. Under the Man the Hunter scenario it would be "natural" for men to control everything. But if prehistory wasn't that way, there is no biological inevitability about men being in charge of politics, religion, and technology—just as there is no evidence of the inevitability that whites will rule the earth, another corollary of biological determinism.

But Zihlman finds strong resistance to the idea of woman the gatherer as the main engine of evolution. Some critics charge that it is a "feminist" construction and thus to be discounted. But what of "masculinist" scenarios of chest-thumping apes and macho monkeys? Are they any less biased? As John Pfeiffer, author of *The Emergence of Man* (1981), says, "Human evolution has long been regarded as a male achievement. . . . The putdown of women is generally implicit. They were bit players in the human drama." He calls this a result of male bias and says, "Big game hunting, for all its glamour—had nothing—and gathering had a great deal—to do with the crossing of the line between ape and human."[33]

But Zihlman says the pace of change—in science and the media—is slow. Recent articles "are totally male or hunting oriented" despite the growing body of evidence to offer an alternate theory. "Why," she asks, is there "reluctance to bring ideas about women's roles in evolution and give them the same thoughtful consideration" as male-centered scenarios? She sees sexism operating, as do others who observe the struggles women have in science. Men are perceived as neutral, value-free observers when they put men at the center of the universe. But when a woman sees a female at the center of the drama, she is attacked as feminist and biased. Zihlman says, "One aspect of the gathering hypothesis that is so threatening is that it brings women in as central participants throughout the history of the species, not only in contemporary life, but in a vision that reclaims the past."[34] The naked ape, however, is a story that fits perfectly with the notion of capitalism and male dominance. We can almost picture our simian ancestors reading *Wall Street Journal* and watching *Rambo III*.

It's probably no surprise that the portrait of prehistoric man the killer fits the picture of the modern nation-state with its many territorial wars. But prehistory was not like that—and neither is much of human life today. When Harvard anthropologists Mary Maxwell West and Melvin Konner studied male and parental behavior across eighty cultures, they found a wide variance in behavior but much evidence for paternal involvement in nurture and child rearing. This was most evident in societies in which warfare was sporadic or nonexistent. They say that most human evolution was probably characterized by a fairly high amount of paternal behavior and low aggression and violence. Our ancestors relied on cooperation between men and women in gathering food. And gathering societies probably had a fair amount of equality between men and women—as there is in such cultures that exist today.[35]

But somehow the image of Sam or Sally the Salad Maker just doesn't have the panache of the Great Hunter. Can you see a picture of a guy with a salad bowl and a little stone chopper painted on the wing of a B-52?

Many scientists now argue that the subjugation of women didn't begin until humans settled down and claimed territory. Anthropologist Eleanor Leacock has argued that equality persisted well into the agricultural stage; some researchers speculate that it was the rise of the state, with its notions of property and hierarchy, that reduced the status of women.[36]

What this all means is that as a species we are remarkably "plastic." We can be murderous and nurturing, assertive and passive, monogamous or promiscuous, involved with our young or totally indifferent. Different situations call forth widely differing behavior. As Naomi Weisstein says, "We belong to an order stunningly flexible in its social arrangements, and capable of great change within species. Biology tells us that there is nothing genetic stopping us [women] from having full sexual and social expression."[37]

And the noted primatologist Sarah Hrdy notes the irony in the frequent use of primate studies to justify second-class status for women: "The real irony is that women in so many human societies occupy a position that is far worse than that of females in all but a few species of nonhuman primates."[38] Robert Wright, in the 1994 book *The Moral Animal,* suggests that women would be better off with polygamy, in which a male shares a number of women, than with monogamy. He says that women in polygamous cultures are perhaps "less than eager" to share a man, but "typically, they would rather do that than live in poverty with the undivided attention of a ne'er do well." He thinks that what we have now, "serial divorce," is bad for women, because men abandon their old families, whereas in polygamous cultures men must support old as well as new wives.[39]

Missing entirely from this scenario is another possibility—that women can take care of themselves and their children. As women are no longer denied entry to decent jobs, such independence becomes a fact. Tell a modern woman that her choices are inclusion in a harem or living with a ne'er-do-well, and she'd probably say, "No thanks, I'm off to law school."

In fact, women initiate the majority of divorces in the United States; they do not come about because men abandon their wives.[40] It is arguable that in the postindustrial world women have just as good a shot at economic independence as men do. The idea of the cringing little woman and the big bold hunter bolsters the notion of female helplessness as inevitable. It is not a picture that squares with the historical record.

So, next time you see one of those ape-man CEOs in his hunting skins marching across the printed page in four-color glossy glory, remember Imo, the "precocious" macaque. While the guys were out hunting, she would have been busy gathering food, taking care of the kids, inventing language and calculus and a maybe a new microchip to boot.

Who would *you* want running the R&D department?

7. BORN TO BE BAD

The Fault, Dear Brutus, Is in Our Genes

Jimmy Carter's malaise speech was one of the great miscalculations of the modern political age. Carter said that things weren't all champagne and roses in America, and we were living in a world in which resources were starting to get scarce. Maybe all of us would have to tighten our belts, learn to live with a little less.

We embraced that idea as if it were a huge dose of castor oil and invited Carter right back to the peanut farm in Plains, Georgia. We liked it a lot better when Ronald Reagan said, "Sure, we're still number one" and "Deficit? What deficit?"

But beneath the beer commercial optimism, even during the Reagan era anxiety was boiling, roiled by the suspicion that maybe it wasn't really true. Maybe resources *were* dwindling, and maybe we'd better hang on to our share. Today there isn't much doubt about that proposition. In times likes these, those who have want to hold on to what they got. Change becomes risky, generosity downright foolhardy. It is a time tailor-made for shoring up the status quo.

In the past it was the Calvinist God who rewarded the wealthy and socked it to the poor; the Calvinists called on Jehovah himself to vindicate the haves. But God—if not actually dead—hasn't got quite the box office clout he once had. Now we call on science. God didn't give the rich their lucre; biology did. It's all written in the genes.

This is a comforting thought; *The fault, dear Brutus, is not in our stars, but in ourselves,* especially if we hold the view that we are somewhere near the end point of evolution, that nature has spent all that time laboring to create glorious glittering US. We can write off obvious past inequities as having been resolved. Just like the song about Kansas City in *Oklahoma!*—"They've gone about as far as they can go."

The media and many politicians have eagerly taken up the notion that social problems such as poverty and crime are the result of faulty genes, so all we can do about them is build more jails.

And indeed this supposition was voiced by the late Harvard psychologist Richard Herrnstein, who mused, "The privileged classes of the past were probably not much superior biologically to the downtrodden, which is why revolution had a fair chance of success. By removing artificial barriers between classes, society has encouraged the breaking of biological barriers. When people can take their natural level in society, the upper classes will, by definition, have greater capacity than the lower."[1]

In place of "upper classes," read "we." After Marie Antoinette sniffed, "Let them eat cake," the wretched of France certainly had a right to storm the Bastille. Now that *we're* in the high-rent district, things are surely different.

This is the very shaky leg on which rests one of the media literary sensations of recent years, *The Bell Curve* by Herrnstein and conservative guru Charles Murray. A NEXIS search reveals no fewer than fifteen hundred mentions of the book in the news media in less than a year.

The Bell Curve is an elephant of a book, some eight hundred pages of mind-numbing review of scientific studies interlaced with political advocacy and sloppy science. As the noted scientist and critic Stephen Jay Gould notes, "*The Bell Curve* fails because most of its premises are false."[2]

First, there's that notion that society today is a meritocracy and intelligence determines who succeeds or fails. Do we really believe that the son or daughter of two Harvard professors has no advantage over the equally bright child of an unwed mother in Harlem? The second major problem with the book is its assumption that racial differences in IQ are not only hereditary but unchanging. However, as Gould points out, height is far more heritable than IQ—but good nutrition can change average height substantially in a few generations. Although a 15-point average difference between whites and blacks in IQ is well documented, there's no reason to assume that this won't change. In fact, in some countries average IQ scores have risen by 15 points and more since World War II.

Few geneticists have anything good to say about *The Bell Curve*—they think the authors grossly oversimplify a complex issue. Dozens of better-researched and more thoughtful books about the issues *The Bell Curve* covers have been written over the past few years. Why didn't they get such massive media attention? *The Bell Curve*, after all, broke no new ground, revealed no new research, suggested no new theory that hadn't been argued often before.

Gould concludes—and I agree—that the magazine covers and the editorials and the newscasts dedicated to the book "must reflect the depressing temper of our time—a historical moment of unprecedented ungenerosity" when the urge to take a machete to social programs can be justified by the idea that the poor (especially the black poor) are stupid and likely to remain so.[3] Harvard geneticist Richard Lewontin points out that "such a view does not threaten the status quo, but on the contrary, supports it by telling those who are without power that their position is the inevitable outcome of their own innate deficiencies and therefore nothing can be done about it."[4]

Think what would have happened if Martin Luther King Jr. had believed that. *Sorry brothers, but you're just meant to be sharecroppers; being allowed to vote and send your kids to the U of Alabama just won't help.*

However, the notion of genetic inferiority has special appeal to the media for two reasons. It validates the privilege of middle- and upper-class white folks—which most media managers are. And it offers simple solutions for complex problems. Complexity cannot be squeezed into a 72-point head or limned on a four-color bar graph or compressed into a thirty-second sound bite. We in the media today want things short and snappy, no more demanding of attention than your average music video. So it's no wonder that *The Bell Curve* has garnered such attention; after all, "criminal genes" and "violence genes" have been a media staple for the past decade or so.

Once again tentative and unproved scientific findings are making wonderful copy. The Case of the Criminal Chromosome, which garnered massive publicity in the 1970s should have been an object lesson in the dangers of this sort of rush to judgment. In 1966 a drifter named Richard Speck brutally murdered eight nurses in Chicago. He later was found to have had an "extra" Y chromosome, an abnormality that some researchers suggested might be related to antisocial acts. Suddenly, the Criminal Gene was born. (Most males have one X and one Y chromosome.) Not only was there a media feeding frenzy, but a group of researchers associated with Harvard set up a project in Boston to test children for the extra Y. It was said that national testing procedures might have to be set up, to determine early on which children had the "criminal gene" and could be helped with early intervention. The Harvard researchers called people who objected to testing—because it might stigmatize children—radicals who were simply antiscience. And because of the news reports some women who found they were carrying a fetus with an extra Y chromosome chose abortions, and some prisoners with the extra Y were sterilized.[5]

What happened in the Case of the Criminal Chromosome? Where are the national testing programs? The massive intervention? They don't exist, because further research simply showed no evidence that the extra Y predisposed anyone to criminal behavior. The main problem for men with the extra Y, it turned out, was a tendency to have learning difficulties. The criminal gene—the extra Y—faded from the headlines and from the scientific literature. It did make a brief reappearance in the 1986 book *Crime and Human Nature*, by Herrnstein and his Harvard colleague James Q. Wilson. The book got major media coverage in such places as *Time*, *Newsweek*, *U.S. News and World Report*, *Vogue*, National Public Radio, and many others. The authors cited research that purportedly validated the idea of the criminal chromosome. What was it? A study that found five of twelve XYY males had arrest records. That sounds like a high percentage indeed. But critics pointed out that three of the five "criminals" had been arrested for relatively minor crimes—such as calling in a false fire alarm while drunk.[6] Hardly the sort of behavior that makes suburban householders cower in the beds. *Ethel, he's out there, drunk again, and he's gong to get at that fire alarm, I just know he is!*

The lesson of the criminal gene did not impress itself on the news media, however, which remain as enchanted as ever with the notion of a dramatic, headline-making, simple cause for crime and violence. A sampling of recent stories makes it clear the criminal gene—or hormone—is alive and well; if the extra Y wasn't it, well, it's lurking around someplace.

The media search for a genetic basis for crime continues unabated: Some examples: THE GENETICS OF BAD BEHAVIOR (*Newsweek*, November 1, 1993); EVIDENCE FOUND FOR A POSSIBLE AGGRESSION GENE (*Science*, June 18, 1993); HOW BRAIN'S CHEMISTRY UNLEASHES VIOLENCE (*Chicago Tribune*, December 13, 1993); GENE TIE TO MALE VIOLENCE IS STUDIED (*New York Times*, October 22, 1993).

Time magazine in 1993 headlined, SEEKING THE ROOTS OF VIOLENCE, and the lead reads:

> It's tempting to make excuses for violence. The mugger came from a broken home and was trying to lift himself out of poverty. The wife beater was himself abused as a child. The juvenile murderer was exposed to Motley Crue records and Terminator movies. But do environmental factors wholly account for the seven-year old child who knifes a teacher? The employee who slaughters work mates with an AK-47? Can society's ills really be responsible for the savagery that is sweeping America? Or could some people be disposed to violence by their genes?[7]

Guess what the answer is to all those questions. When a reporter uses this technique—piling up a series of questions and incredulously asking if they could be true, the reader of course knows the right answer. (This list, by the way, tosses trivial arguments—like the Motley Crüe defense—into the same pot with the demonstrated fact that abused children themselves often become abusers.)

And indeed *Time* argues that "advances in genetics and biochemistry have given researchers new tools to search for biological clues to criminality." Answers may be "a long way off," but science is galloping to the rescue, sure to "offer new solutions for society."

Beyond the gee-whiz language readers should wonder at the naïveté of one question asked in that lead. How could social conditions (gasp!) be responsible for the "savagery" sweeping America? Read your history, *Time*. Savagery has swept across America with some regularity. The urban ghettos of the 1890s were every bit as cruel, vicious, and as full of sociopathic behavior as some city neighborhoods today.

BORN BAD? NEW RESEARCH POINTS TO A BIOLOGICAL ROLE IN CRIMINALITY, said the consumer magazine *American Health* in 1993. The lead on the story reads:

The tattoo on the ex-con's beefy biceps reads: BORN TO RAISE HELL. Much as it may defy the science of the past, which blamed crime on social influences such as poverty and bad parenting, and Americans' bias against biological and genetic explanations for behavior, the outlaw may be onto something. Though no one would deny that upbringing and environment play important parts in the making of a criminal, scientists who study all types—from muggers, murderers and school yard bullies to Armani-clad embezzlers, increasingly suspect that biology also plays a significant role.[8]

The story gives the readers the idea that a scientific consensus has been reached—when indeed no such thing has happened. In fact, most scientists reject the simplistic notion of BORN TO RAISE HELL out of hand. The *American Health* story is an example of the ahistorical nature of too much of what appears in the media. Throughout our history Americans have often happily embraced biological explanations for crime and social problems, and our science has been just choc-a-bloc with them.

In the first three decades of this century seventy thousand Americans were sterilized as the result of a "eugenics movement" backed by professors at such prestigious schools as Harvard, Columbia, and Stanford and with money from the Rockefeller and Carnegie foundations. This "science" was also the rationale for restrictive immigration quotas passed by Congress to keep out Asians, Slavs, Jews, and other "undesirables." (The Nazi death camps also owe their existence to the twisted science of racial superiority.) Brain size of course has been used to argue that blacks have low intelligence and are prone to crime and that women are dumber than men. Scientists once argued that certain body types and facial features (most often non-Aryan ones) make the criminal easy to spot. After the riots of the 1960s two Boston neurosurgeons suggested it might have been "brain dysfunction" that made people riot. (Surely, someone in Chevy Chase or Bel Air or Scarsdale had the same sort of brain abnormalities as people in the ghetto. Why were they not out throwing rocks?)

Through much of our history white scientists have not been loathe to make sweeping statements about the "inferiority" of African Americans. Twenty years before *The Bell Curve* Herrnstein argued in a much-debated article in *Atlantic* that blacks had lower IQs than whites and society simply had to accept that fact and that such programs as affirmative action were ill advised.[9] The old canard that blacks are closer to animals than whites was echoed in a recent comment by Dr. Frederick Goodwin, when he was head of the federal Alcohol, Drug Abuse, and Mental Health Administration. He suggested in 1993 that the behavior of monkeys in jungles could help us understand behavior in the inner cities: "Maybe it isn't just the careless use of the word when people call certain areas of certain cities 'jungles.'"[10]

To what areas was he referring? Rodeo Drive? Park Avenue? Certainly, African Americans got the message.

The dreary history of trying to find biological bases for crime—and the long line of theories that have been advanced and disproved—does not seem to dim our enthusiasm for that one neat tidy answer. No matter how many times it gets batted down, the criminal gene pops up again, like a child's punching clown. The news media often recycle—uncritically—studies that "prove" criminality is inherited. The *Los Angeles Times* reported in 1993, "Studies have shown that adopted children whose biological parents broke the law are more likely than other children to be lawbreakers themselves."[11] The story offers no critique of the research, and the reader assumes that the research is sound and that it solidly establishes a link between crime and heredity.

The studies are based on detailed records on adoption kept in Denmark, where all criminals are included in a national register and scrupulous records of adoptions are kept. But psychologist Leon Kamin, who has studied those records, points out that adoption policy there tends to have a strong overlay of issues of social class. The child of an unwed mother who is a college graduate is likely to be placed with parents who are also college educated. Kamin notes,

> It is also true that if you are an adopted child in Denmark and you grow up to be criminal, the odds that your adoptive father will be in the criminal register are also extremely high. . . . In short, children who come from biological families where there is criminality are likely to be selectively placed into adoptive families where the adoptive parents are not paragons of civil virtue. . . . There simply is, in the real world, no effective separation of genetic and environmental variables.[12]

Still, the media keep looking. Lately, an "aggression gene" has made the bold type: in that *Science* headline mentioned earlier (EVIDENCE FOUND FOR A POSSIBLE AGGRESSION GENE) and in the *Los Angeles Times*: RESEARCHERS LINK GENE TO AGGRESSION.[13] The aggression gene found its

way into the headlines of a number of American newspapers and magazine. Just what was the aggression gene, and who had it?

One family in the Netherlands, that's who.

Some thirty years ago a Dutch schoolteacher who was concerned about
violence among male members of his family traced his genealogy and
wrote about it under the title "A Curious Case." In 1993 researchers studying the family found that the men in the family possessed a mutant gene
that might predispose them to aggressive behavior.

Why the headlines on one family and its problems? Because every time
somebody purports to have found a gene for crime, the media work into
a lather. Besides, scientists in the field of human behavioral genetics desperately need a "win"—rather like prosecutors who have lost too many
high-profile cases. It is a field, writes Natalie Angier of the *New York Times*,
that "has lately been in disarray as previous announcements of genes for
manic depression, schizophrenia and alcoholism have either been disproved or come under withering criticism."[14]

Critics pointed out that the evidence of the violent behavior in the family was meager and mainly anecdotal. One man who had repeated out-
bursts of aggressive behavior had the abnormality, but his brother—who
also has it—did not have such problems.

Researchers who concentrate on the genetic roots of crime seem to
focus almost exclusively on violent street crime, not the kind of crime
upper-class folks commit. Is there, one wonders, a gene for insider trading,
linked perhaps to an innate tendency to buy Mercedes automobiles?
Or for s&l fraud, linked genetically to contributions to a member
of Congress?

One of the latest ideas grabbing headlines is that the neurotransmitter
serotonin is linked to violent behavior. A lab experiment linked low levels
of serotonin to aggressive behavior in college students in Montreal.
Previous studies of criminal populations had shown that people who had
long histories of criminal violence also had low serotonin. So did 1,043
arsonists and prisoners convicted of manslaughter. The *Chicago Tribune*
story reporting this development in December 1993 went on to say that
"another piece of the violence puzzle fell into place in October."[15] The
article then recounted the story of the Dutch family, the significance of
which had already been questioned.

Journalists are always talking as if violence is just another puzzle to be
put together in the lab like a child's toy, giving readers the idea that this is

(a) a problem that will be solved by science and (b) much less complex than the whole issue really is.

The problem with the serotonin study is the classic question of correlation versus causality. Lots of things can be found in prison populations—left-handedness, high incidence of learning disorders, substance abuse—but to say that one of these *causes* crime is just too simplistic. Lots of young male criminals are dyslexic—but so too is Tom Cruise.

But there's big money in violence research these days. Biologist Steven Rose of the Open University in Great Britain wrote in 1994 that he was contacted by a colleague in California to be part of a Justice Department study of violent criminals that would analyze their spinal fluids. "It sounds off the wall—but it turns out that it is only one of dozens of such projects planned within the 'Violence Initiative,' a program designed to explain and combat the frightening levels of violence in the US," he wrote. With $400 million in potential funding at stake the rush to file grant applications is not surprising, Rose says, noting the current bio chic of serotonin. He sees a "headlong rush" to what he calls *neurogenetic determinism* and says one of its most eager advocates is Daniel Koshland, "the [former] editor of one of the world's premier scientific journals, *Science*, offering us genes for homelessness and also, of course, for violence and homosexuality and the rest of the usual suspects."[16]

Of course, no one talked about genes for homelessness in the 1960s, when the economy was booming and housing at reasonable rates was plentiful. Have Americans suddenly sprouted a homelessness gene? Is that what creates the irresistible impulse to sleep under bridges? The fallacies in such arguments, Rose says are "scientific, philosophical and social. First, despite the convenient genetic shorthand, there are no such things as 'genes' for behavior." What genes do, he says, is code for the manufacture of certain proteins (there are as many as 100,000 of them in the human body). Even in the formation of a relatively simple trait such as eye color, a gene "for" blue eyes means a difference in these hundreds of substances. "If the Dutch 'violence gene' story held up, it would mean that there was a gene which made a certain protein whose function in the brain contributed to the developmentally expressed difference between the violent and non-violent members of that family," Rose notes.

But such a gene difference still wouldn't "explain" violence—there are many roads to violent behavior. "Nor would finding an abnormal level of a particular chemical in the brain, spinal fluid or blood of a violent criminal mean that the chemical was the cause of the violence—any more than the snot in your nose is the cause of your cold," Rose writes.

Another problem with finding biological causes of violence or aggression is "to assume that these words label one 'thing,' a unitary biological mechanism active when a man abuses his sexual partner, police confront strikers on a picket line, skinhead neo-nazis bomb Bangladeshi houses, there is a gangland drive-by shooting—or a technician in a bunker fires a Scud missile. . . . Neurogenetic determinism would seek to account for each as engaging the same biological mechanisms as come into play when cats kill rats—one of the standard ways of measuring 'aggression' in laboratory animals," Rose continues.

Unlike eye or hair color, violence is a social construct, and it varies widely from one society another. "Murder is common in the US, relatively rare in Europe or Japan. Should we assume there is something unique about the American genotype? In both Britain and the US, violent crime has risen dramatically over the last 15 years in parallel with the increase in poverty, unemployment and homelessness," Rose points out. "Has a mutant gene suddenly arrived in our populations, accounting for all three?"[17]

Rising levels of crime—and the availability of research money—may cause a feeding frenzy among scientists looking for simple causes of crime and a media eager to report them. It isn't very sexy to say that crime is a complicated issue, that while biological mechanisms may certainly play a part in behavior, they are almost always acting in concert with more critical environmental factors where crime in concerned.

For example, harsh and erratic discipline is three or four times more common in young boys who become delinquents than in those who do not, says Dr. Felton Earls, psychiatric epidemiologist at the Harvard School of Public Health. He says that growing up in a poor inner city neighborhood can expose children to multiple hazards such as addicted parents, exposure to high levels of lead, diminished verbal skills, a dearth of role models for a steady work life, and gang warfare. Often, by the time such children arrive in first grade, "they are more aggressive than other kids, have conduct problems and low reading achievement, a pattern that solidifies by third grade, at which point these kids get marked as problems and put in special education classes," Earls told the *New York Times* in 1992. "As early as third grade they are stigmatized and at a social disadvantage."[18] The kids who drop out of school, join gangs, and start on a life of crime are often doomed forever to the criminal justice system. Those who finish their education, get jobs, or get married often do not become criminals. Clearly, finding a way to intervene in this vicious cycle early on makes more sense than measuring serotonin levels of thirty-year-old burglars. Learning to speak well and to develop social skills early in life seems a better medicine for controlling aggression than taking a drug to reduce neurotransmitter levels after you've committed your fourth felony.

Dr. Gregory Carey, a behavioral geneticist at the University of Colorado who reviewed studies that tried to link heredity to crime, told the *Times*, "There's a multitude of social, personality, cognitive and other variables that intercede between the level of DNA and a complex behavior like crime. My view is that the idea there could be a genetic marker for crime is wild-eyed speculation or science fiction."[19]

But the gee-whiz approach too often used by journalists mitigates against understanding the complexity of the issues of crime and violence. Reading through many stories about the issue, I find several patterns. First, of course is the catchy simplistic headline, which means that too often what the reader retains even from well-crafted, accurate stories is the simple idea. Then comes the propensity—on the part of both scientists and journalists—to use the dramatic quote that makes the problem seem much simpler than it is.

"The biology of violence is becoming clearer," a scientist at Yale told the *Chicago Tribune* in 1993.[20] Actually, it's very, very murky. A researcher looking at the Danish adoption records told the *Boston Globe* in 1982 that a "biological marker" could identify criminals and that this could have "disproportionate effects on the crime rate."[21] But of course people have been looking for biological markers for years. Because crime is such a complex problem, the search is likely to be fruitless. But it makes great copy and gets the scientists some dandy clippings.

It's also true that the job of the journalist is to focus on what's new—so the bulk of the stories about new research on the biological roots of crime concentrate on the scientist and his or her work, enthusiasms, and ideas. One story describes in heroic, active terms a scientist at the National Institutes of Health (NIH) who is looking for a "vulnerability gene": "His work challenges long-held assumptions that social and environmental factors—poverty, joblessness discrimination and lack of education—are the sole causes of crime and violence."[22] Even the wording presents the scientist as hero.

And in the "nut graphs" in which journalists sum up the story, or in other explanatory paragraphs, reporters too often give readers the impression that many researchers have reached a consensus where in fact there is none. Phrases such as "scientists now believe" or "research is telling us" proliferate in such articles. *Newsweek* says that the Dutch family with the "aggression gene" "helped validate the notion that heredity can foster aggression."[23] *Science* says these same researchers are "hot on the track" of the aggression gene. The *Economist* says that liberal academics are just now beginning to catch up to what the publication believes is fact: the roots of crime are found in biology.[24]

Everyone, of course, throws a crumb to the other side, by quoting a scientist or two who says this is nonsense—but they get little space. Killjoys, they play second fiddle to the scientists doing the new and exciting work.

I've also noted, after covering a number of science stories over the years, that scientists are often naïve about the social impact of their work and how it can be used to promote somebody's legislative agenda. Scientists (and, I might add, journalists) are most often upper middle class, and their kids are in no danger of being stigmatized or treated with drugs because of some other scientist's bright new idea. Their privileged lives seem to disconnect them from the reality that less-entitled people can and do become guinea pigs. Dr. Markku Linnoila of NIH told the *Los Angeles Times* that "our critics paint these nightmare scenarios based on their own imagination . . . that somewhere there is a bogeyman who wants to immediately start drugging people, and I don't see that. I think we have a very significant problem with interpersonal violent behavior."[25]

Indeed, some critics harm their own case by presenting scientists as Dr. Strangeloves trying to do crazed experiments on people. The fact is, most misguided experiments are done by well-intentioned people who believe they are doing good for humanity. And we're not talking about Victorian science here, or some benighted era past, but the recent past, when the modern scientific method was in full sway. The radiation experiments done in schools for the retarded in the 1950s were performed with good motives. Who knew it might give them cancer? The New Jersey prison experiments of the seventies—where prisoners were given a drug that paralyzed the throat muscles and gave them the sensation of strangling to death—were done in the name of preventing violence. The government employee—a husband and father—who threw himself out a window and plunged to his death because he thought he was going insane had no idea that he had been given a dose of LSD in a government research project. Prostitutes and prisoners were given psychotropic drugs in the same program. It's not the bad guys we have to be afraid of—it's the good guys with the bad science—and the overdeveloped sense of arrogance.

Few would argue today that all behavior—including violence and aggression—has biological components. But in today's world, with declining economic resources, how much less expensive would it be to test for a "genetic marker" for crime than to fund massive preschool education programs? Scientists often don't understand—or don't want to understand—how their work can be used in a political way. For example, after the *Atlantic* article on race and IQ by Harvard's Herrnstein appeared in the 1970s, his arguments went from the printed page to the White House in a flash. Pat Buchanan, then a White House staffer under Richard Nixon, wrote a memo saying that federal efforts to integrate blacks and the poor into U.S. society would result in "perpetual friction." Citing the Herrnstein article, he argued against civil rights efforts and affirmative action because of the friction that would be created as "the incapable are placed . . . side by side with the capable."[26]

Buchanan, of course, became a key aide to Ronald Reagan, whose administration gutted federal efforts to enforce most civil rights legislation.

Just as the conservative push to make welfare a moral issue has succeeded, the time may be ripe for a similar offensive on the causes of crime. A financially strapped public might well be inclined to believe that if poor inner city people are born to be bad, why not junk Head Start and just build more jails? (That the former is much less expensive than the latter doesn't seem to figure into the calculation when the American public wants a quick fix.) But we might remind ourselves that many of the descendants of the Italians, Irish, Jews, and Slavs who were the heartless vicious criminals of yesterday are today's bank managers, actors, chemists, salespeople, and cops. Did their genes simply change in the space of a few generations? Or as those ethnic groups climbed the ladder into the middle class, as they escaped grinding poverty and misery, did they start to behave as most middle-class people behave—like those who have a stake in society and something to lose?

8. FLASH—FEMINISM IS STILL DEAD

But It's Bad for You, Anyhow

⊚

The coverage of feminism, which I've observed for nearly three decades now, has gone through several distinct stages.

The first stage was one I call *The Birds*, after the Hitchcock movie.

If you remember that film, peaceful creatures much admired for their beauty suddenly turned savage, much to the astonishment of those who felt the force of flying beaks. The victims' incredulity was on the same level as that of members of the media in the early 1970s when suddenly confronted with women making demands.

Amused condescension was actually the first order of the day, before people realized that women were really serious about this stuff. On the fiftieth anniversary of women's suffrage in 1970 the massive marches across the country seemed to amuse ABC anchorman Howard K. Smith no end. He began his lead-in to the story thusly: "Quote: Three things have been difficult to tame: the ocean, fools and women. We may soon be able to tame the ocean, but fools and women will take a little longer." (The source of the quote was a man who, it turned out, had considerable acquaintance with the second category: Spiro T. Agnew.) The broadcast ended with a pronouncement from West Virginia senator Jennings Randolph, characterizing the movement as "a small band of braless bubbleheads."

On CBS commentator Eric Sevareid dismissed the movement as being led by a group of "aroused minorities . . . who are already well off by any comparative measure." He shrugged off feminism as a passing fancy and said that women now had "the unavoidable opportunity to prove that the masculine notion that women can't get along with other women is another item from the ancient shelf of male mythology." His demeanor made it clear that he believed quite strongly in that bit of myth. Then Walter Cronkite signed off with his stentorian "And that's the way it is," leaving viewers with the idea that the women's movement was silly and futile.[1]

The initial amusement of the media rather quickly turned to terror, mixed with equal portions of loathing and disgust. Susan Douglas, in her book *Where the Girls Are*, says rightly that "there is no doubt that the news media of the early seventies played an absolutely central role in turning feminism into a dirty word, and stereotyping the feminist as a hairy-legged, karate chopping commando with a chip on her shoulder the size of China, really bad clothes and a complete inability to smile."

The Myth of Female Strength was in full flower during those years. As a journalist and television commentator I was often amazed to find people regarding me—a mild-mannered reporter—as something akin to Joan of Arc. When WGBH, a public television station in Boston, thought about creating a show devoted to women's issues, the producers at first asked me to host the show. Because I appeared regularly on the station doing news and comment, I expected no opposition. But the program director vetoed me, saying I was not "warm and loving" enough. I was okay to do news, but he said that I might "threaten" suburban housewives.

Because women made up a fair share of the station's audience, I suggested that those women I would terrify were already cowering under their beds in fear, so what did we have to lose? I noted that my husband and my children thought of me as warm and loving. And because the show was supposed to be an "issues" show, why would we want a Dinah Shore wannabee anyway?

The show went on with another host who had no television experience, which didn't work out. Finally, reluctantly, the station decided it would let me go on as host, because I knew how to deal with the camera. As I prepared to go on the air, the president of the station approached me. I had never even *seen* the president of the station before. He was not accustomed to mingling with the help. He said to me rather nervously, "Now, you won't be too—aggressive—will you?" If I'd had my wits about me, I'd have said, "Gee, Stan, I guess you won't really love the castration segment." But I simply assured him that I would not be too aggressive.

Douglas notes that coverage of the movement was hopelessly schizophrenic, reluctantly conceding that perhaps women did have some tiny grievances, then flattening a rich and complex movement into cardboard cutouts of harridans and man haters. "Rage would not be too strong a word to describe the emotion felt by large numbers of feminists about media's coverage of the women's movement," journalists Judith Hole and Ellen Levine write in *Rebirth of Feminism*.

A *Time* cover piece in 1970 called the movement "borrowed" from the civil rights and student movements. "The implication, often repeated elsewhere, was that this was a copycat movement, a frivolous imitation, with no genuine basis in true oppression," Douglas says.

This was the attitude that greeted me as a journalist back then. Editors would ask me, "Have you ever *really* been discriminated against?" The interesting thing was that until I was asked, I thought I hadn't been. Then, when I started to think about it, I realized how much I had repressed in the name of staying sane.

The *National Observer*, a now-defunct Dow Jones national newspaper, had used freelance pieces of mine on page one and had given me bylines. When I applied for a reporter's job, the managing editor said he would hire no women as reporters; however, he offered me a job as his secretary. The city editor of the *Baltimore Sun* said he wouldn't hire women, period. *Newsweek* and *Time* said they would hire me only as a researcher, despite my graduate degree from Columbia and a national award for reporting. Nobody at that time (the 1960s) even suggested that I wasn't a good reporter and writer. In fact, they admired my work. They still wouldn't hire me. A university wouldn't let me teach reporting after I'd covered the White House, the civil rights movement, and the Supreme Court, because "you'd just have babies."

Still, a hallmark of the early coverage of feminism was simple denial that women like me had anything of which to complain. And feminists were regarded as evil witches seducing innocent young women. A major *Time* story in 1970 suggested that "radical feminists" were brainwashing young women who were "fertile grounds for the seeds of discontent," and it referred to feminists as "the angries." Few editors took the women's movement seriously. When Elizabeth Rhodes, then reporting for the *Charlotte Observer*, suggested a story about the motives of those backing the opposition to the Equal Rights Amendment, one of her editors said he might consider it "if you take off all your clothes and then give me the story idea."

In March 1970 *Newsweek* assigned a cover piece on the movement to assistant editor Lynn Young; she says that her male colleagues continually told her that the piece wasn't objective enough; one male editor said that only a man could write the piece that would portray the "ludicrous soul of this story." A man did rewrite it, and then the piece was rewritten every week for two months before it was given to freelancer Helen Dudar. Her piece was largely sympathetic to the movement, but *Newsweek* also featured a sidebar on how social scientists saw feminism. As Douglas puts it, "This piece was filled with typically pompous comments of primarily male experts . . . who cited a range of studies to show that, in a host of areas, feminists were simply ignorant, wrong-headed, and misguided women prone to hyperbole. Feminists were called self-hating, vituperative, militant, unpleasant and unfeminine."

The news media continually tried to vilify the movement. Reporter Marilyn Goldstein of *Newsday* revealed to another journalist that whenever reporters on her paper were assigned to cover the movement, one of her editors told them to "get out there and find an authority who'll say this is all a crock of shit." The most often quoted statements by feminists were those made by the most radical women, such as Ti Grace Atkinson's "marriage means rape."

Susan Douglas says, "Time and time again the media emphasized that members of the women's liberation movement were completely out of touch with, hostile to and rejected by most American women, when in fact, women's attitudes were much more complicated and moving towards acceptance." But the portrayal of feminists as freaks, man haters, and angry unattractive women went on.

The next phase of media coverage of feminism was the "front page" phase, in which the press simply could not ignore the massive changes in American society, including successful suits by women against major news organizations such as the *New York Times* and *Newsweek* and against other major American corporations. This phase featured the many "first" stories: first astronaut, first firefighter, first heart surgeon, and so on—and because editors and publishers had begun to understand that because they had millions of women readers, they had to pay attention. But although many media outlets featured glowing stories of women's accomplishments, they continued to trash feminism. Reading some stories of that era, you'd think that the women attorneys, journalists, doctors, and the like had magically wafted through the doors of those professions, when in fact women had to file class-action lawsuits to open them. Without the women's movement it would simply not have happened.

The front page period was brief, followed quickly by declarations of the Death of Feminism and the arrival of the Postfeminist Era. When Bernice Buresh (former head of the Boston bureau of *Newsweek*) and I proposed a book on women in politics in 1985, we were told by editors that feminism was dead, that nobody cared about women in politics. The trends the media discovered in the eighties, Susan Faludi observes in *Backlash*, were women's failure to find husbands, get pregnant, or properly bond with their children. She notes that stories in women's magazines and Style sections talked about the New Femininity, the return to domesticity, and the return of the good girl: "In each case, women were reminded to re-embrace 'traditional' sex roles—or suffer the consequences. For women the trend story was no news report. It was a moral reproach."[2]

For every story about a successful woman lawyer, doctor, professor, or astronaut the media portrayed a dark underbelly of feminine failure; it remains a constant lurking presence today. As Faludi puts it, the message was that "women are unhappy precisely because they are free. Women are enslaved by their own independence. They have gained control of their own fertility, only to destroy it. They have pursued their own professional dreams—and lost out on the greatest female adventure. The women's movement, we are told time and time again, has proved women's own worst enemy." She adds,

> In the last decade [the 1980s], publications from the *New York Times* to *Vanity Fair* to *The Nation* have issued a steady stream of indictments against the women's movement, with such headlines as WHEN FEMINISM FAILED to THE AWFUL TRUTH ABOUT WOMEN'S LIB. They hold the campaign for women's equality responsible for nearly every worry besetting women, from mental depression to meager savings accounts, from teenage suicides to eating disorders to bad complexions.[3]

And feminists dress terribly too, sniffed the media. Small wonder that a group of Ivy League women students told a writer for the *New York Times*

Magazine that they weren't feminists because those were just women who "let themselves go" and had "no sense of style."[4]

Feminism may have been dead, but it was making women miserable from its coffin, according to the media. When Anita Hill brought her charges against Clarence Thomas and was savaged by the Senate, Hill was cast, as I've noted, as a feminist virago. Even though she did not claim the label, she became one "despite her ethnicity, her color and her sociological background," writes Karlyn Kohrs Campbell. She became "functionally white." Briefly, Campbell notes, "sex trumped race. Not only was Hill 'bleached' and cast as a feminist, but she was forced into the stereotypes against which non-traditional women have struggled . . . a bitter old maid, a manhater, even perhaps, a lesbian, an erotomaniac (a category unknown to psychology), a pawn of extremists, a woman out of touch with reality and given to sexual fantasy and a cold, selfish, arrogant, ambitious person—an unwomanly woman."[5] The women of America didn't buy this notion, however, and the Death of Feminism was seen to be slightly premature. The corpus delecti revived for a time. The media recognized a brief resurgent feminism, and then we entered the current phase: Feminism is still dead. Women are still miserable.

A series of themes runs through recent coverage of feminism. One I have noticed is the message that women shouldn't be selfish by just looking out only for women. No one says this about Teamsters or dentists, or newspaper reporters—who have their own guild. It's okay for everybody to look out for number one but not for women. They always must put others first. Imagine that *every* story newspapers ran about the American Medical Association complained that doctors don't do enough for the poor, and you get an idea of the coverage of feminism.

Syndicated columnist Murray Kempton, in a 1994 column about a Women's Leaders Roundtable, lamented that participants paid too much attention to the "glass ceiling" for women and not enough attention to the poor. He longed for the good old days when the Women's Trade Union League and the International Ladies Garment Workers fought for workers' rights.

"Woman then rose up against the rich man's inhumanity to the poor one and she found exhilarations grander than are available in women's minor share in the fruits of men's greed," he proclaimed. He said women's cause must be "every deprived American's cause."[6] In other words, it's okay for women to fight for "humanity" but not for women. He neglects to mention that the class-action suits brought by feminists on behalf of telephone operators and flight attendants brought major gains for non-elite women. And no one tells the Teamsters *they* ought to quit representing their members and go picket for poor kids.

This same notion underlies the media reaction to the campaign against domestic abuse. In editorials and columns feminists are chided for not being against "violence" in general, not just violence against women. Once again it's the idea that women must always minister to others and that focusing on their own gender is somehow selfish and inappropriate.

If *selfish* isn't the media's favorite word about feminism, there's always *strident*. It's the tag the media use for even the mildest of feminist pronouncements. For example, when Governor Ann Richards of Texas spoke at a conference of high school girls, she warned the girls not to rely on Prince Charming to come along and give them a life but to develop their own skills and talents. But even that commonsense piece of advice was labeled man bashing by a writer for the *Dallas Morning News*. She called Richards's comments part of "the knee-jerk and angry militancy of one portion of the feminist movement that continues to operate. . . . The governor's sound bite is the kind of politics that seeps into the small fissures between men and women and begins to erode into chasms across which it becomes more and more difficult to breach with trust."[7]

How did the governor's witty, sensible advice transmute into man bashing? The same way that any mildly feminist idea can be seen as somehow threatening to males.

Another media practice is to see every feminist as a "radical feminist." The two words seem glued together. Reading through hundreds of stories I realized the degree to which the label gets thrown around. Some feminists are indeed radical—those who espouse a separatist agenda, who believe that all heterosexual intercourse is coercion, that women are morally superior to men, and that marriage is to be avoided because it is inherently degrading to women. Most mainstream feminists do not espouse such positions, and yet they get tagged as extremists. Gloria Steinem, a mainstream feminist if ever there was one, is constantly called radical—most recently by Christina Hoff Sommers in her book *Who Stole Feminism*, which got massive publicity. (Anyone who attacks feminists gets booked immediately on almost every national talk show.) She said over and over that Steinem and Faludi were radicals. She repeated the right-wing mantra that the "good" feminists were those who talked only about pay equity, whereas the "bad" feminists talked about date rape, wife beating, and pornography. (It's intriguing that the right now talks so glowingly about those old feminists, whom it was once busy vilifying as hairy-legged, ugly bra burners.)

Sommers was accepted uncritically by many journalists as a feminist, which is how she labeled herself. Few seemed to note that her book credited the right-wing Olin, Bradley, and Carthage foundations for financial support.[8] Foundation records say these three groups gave her $164,000 to support her work.[9] These folks are about as likely to fund a true feminist writer as the *Marxist Weekly* is to give money to Donald Trump. Olin, for example, funded the scurrilous attack on Anita Hill, David Brock's book *The Real Anita Hill.* (This is the book that peddled such trash as the idea that Hill's students found pubic hairs in papers she handed back to them.)

Why then did the *Wall Street Journal's* reviewer praise Sommers's "lack of a political agenda"?[10] If a writer had thanked the Ms. Foundation for its support, many journalists would have instantly labeled her work a feminist tract. But many reviews praised Sommers's work as objective and bias free, the work of a "skeptical feminist," when it was obviously the work of a right-wing antifeminist who has made public statements such as this one: "There are a lot of homely women in women's studies. Preaching these anti-male, anti-sex sermons is a way for them to compensate for various heartaches—they're just mad at all the beautiful girls."[11]

As Laura Flanders of the media watchdog group Fairness & Accuracy in Reporting (FAIR) writes: "By that standard Rush Limbaugh ('Feminism was established so as to allow unattractive women easier access to the mainstream of society') is a feminist."[12]

But it's not only in the books of right wingers that feminists are seen as being out of the mainstream. Radicals are omnipresent in the media. Kirkus Reviews—syndicated to many newspapers—describes a woman historian who did a study of the lives of three female medical workers during the Civil War, drawn from their letters and journals, as having a "radical feminist" view.[13] Why? Who knows? There is no indication in the review that the book espouses any notions that today would be regarded as radical.

The *St. Petersburg Times* called Hillary Clinton's story of her attempt to join the marines—when she was told she was too old, she wore glasses, and besides she was a woman—"radical feminist rhetoric, designed to polarize woman against men." Hillary Clinton had told this story in a light anecdotal way and with a grin, as I recall. How did it get turned into man bashing? The *Buffalo News*, in a review of a book about football and violence, calls Naomi Wolfe, author of *The Beauty Myth* and a moderate feminist— guess what—a radical feminist.[14] Over and over again this sort of labeling appears. Former surgeon general Joycelyn Elders is referred to as "rabidly

pro-choice." What does that mean, exactly? Does Dr. Elders strap screaming women to the operating table? Does she gnaw at their ankles, foaming
at the mouth?

Journalists by and large have little understanding of feminist positions
or theory—and women journalists join the men on that score. When
journalism professor Evelyn Trapp Goodrick of the University of Illinois
interviewed women newspaper editors, the managing editor of a large
metro paper said, "I never was a feminist" and added that she pays no
attention to feminist positions on issues. An editorial page editor at
another large paper distanced herself from feminism because "I dislike
militancy and protests." Others did not identify with feminist leaders.[15]
Can you imagine a black editor saying he never approved of the civil rights
movement and that he wanted to distance himself from black leaders
because he doesn't like protest?

As a result of this, another common media tic is to insert distortions of
feminist positions in stories to which they have little relevance. Again and
again journalists state as fact that feminists "believe" this or that, and the
stated position is either dead wrong or hopelessly out of date. It's like taking a position from the platform of the Black Panther party of the 1970s
and insisting that it applies to today's black leaders.

Georgie Anne Geyer, a veteran foreign correspondent, drags feminists
into a story on the potential danger of poor, angry, dispossessed males all
over the Third World. An interesting piece, but why put feminists into it?
She says, "Despite what radical feminists insist, men are not like
women."[16] In fact, radical feminists these days don't think men are like
women—they think women are *better* than men. And even feminists who
argue (from good data) that men and women are more alike than different do not claim that there is *no* difference in aggression.

And John Leo, writing in 1994 in *U.S. News and World Report*, reports
on a "topless" women's advocate in New York, a forty-nine-year-old
Colombian who strolls around New York City with her breasts exposed.
Leo quotes another topless advocate as saying that breasts are not really all
that erotic—they're "oversized, specialized sweat glands"—and that
women should not be barred from displaying their chests in public, just
like men do. It's quite a leap from topless fanciers to mainstream feminism,
but Leo makes it. "This movement is interesting because it shares some
assumptions with the broader feminist movement. One is that differences
are troublesome and should be minimized or explained away, no matter
what mental or legal tricks are necessary. Just as pregnancy was disguised

as 'a disability' so it could be crammed into unisex health plans, we are now supposed to believe that male and female breasts are exactly the same."[17]

No feminist I know ever really thought of pregnancy as a disability. Because the U.S. Congress has not exactly been rushing to grant women maternity leave, the "disability" ploy was simply a way to try to shoehorn such benefits into an existing system designed for men and that ignored millions of female workers. But hey, why miss an opportunity to whack feminism upside the head?

Women in the media spotlight, I notice, are always being quoted as saying they're not feminists. Typical is a story in the *Cleveland Plain Dealer* quoting the new chief of the county bar: "Mercedes Spotts is one of those Can Do people . . . and she has a credo about women and success (although she denies she's a feminist): 'When you have the position and the power, you have an obligation to look out for those who come after.'"[18]

Because feminists get only slighter better press than the gun-toting militia groups, it's no wonder women say they don't want to be one. Feminism is the only major human rights movement that is consistently not endorsed by many it has benefited. A 1989 poll by *Time* and CNN reported that 77 percent of women thought the women's movement had made life better, 94 percent said it had helped women become independent, and 82 percent said it was still improving the lives of women. But only 33 percent identified themselves as feminists.[19] Polls show that college women repeatedly refuse to call themselves feminists (while buying most of the feminist ideas about equality) and that even women who agree that feminism has helped their lives still think it has "led women astray."

The media have had a major role in creating Fear of Feminism. If you are constantly told that the word equates with hairy, ugly man haters that it dooms you to never getting married, never having children, being unloved and neurotic, getting depressed and anxious, and being a selfish hysteric to boot, you are probably not going to run headlong to the office of the National Organization for Women with your membership fee in hand.

The unremitting media trashing of feminism will probably go on. I notice with dismay that even the favorable pieces about feminism come with a caveat. The *Washington Post*'s Richard Cohen, in a column lauding Governor Richards for her Prince Charming speech, agreed that indeed the women's movement was "grounded in common sense and equality." But while chiding the right wing for its strident antiwoman stance, he felt constrained to add that "certain feminists have it coming.

Their wild exaggerations and their vision of men as rapacious beasts" have hurt the movement.[20]

Wait a minute. During the civil rights movement did sympathetic reporters say that demonstrators "had it coming" because some of their number indulged in overblown black power rhetoric? Few journalists seem to write a good word about feminism without dredging up some bad words to say at the same time. I've noticed that feminism is almost never cast in a totally favorable light. Compare that with the civil rights movement. What if, every time the name Martin Luther King was mentioned, the writer also noted that, yes, it probably was good that blacks got to vote, sit at lunch counters, and go to motels, but the movement was radical and it didn't make all black folks happy people. Feminism isn't even allowed its historical successes without taking a slam.

Will all this change? I doubt it. An unrelenting antifeminist drumbeat from the radical right is gaining in power and momentum. It is well financed from right-wing foundations and think tanks, and the message is beamed by radio talk show hosts around the country. Rush Limbaugh has made *feminazi* a household word. Right-wing politicians like Ollie North say they are running against "an army of feminists" who are destroying family values, and those messages get widespread coverage. Meanwhile, how many feminists have talk shows? How many well-funded think tanks fund feminist policy papers?

The antiwoman campaign from the right has become so intense that *Newsweek*'s Eleanor Clift called 1994 the "Year of the Smear." A popular staple of radio talk shows is to ask callers whether they'd like to go to bed with women politicians. A Denver radio jock asked that about Rep. Patricia Schroeder. Smear artist Howie Carr asked the same thing about Hillary Clinton on his Boston show. Rush Limbaugh—hardly a poster boy himself—makes jokes about the looks of Clinton's women cabinet appointees.

Clift reports that first-term politicians are getting hit hard by the talk show smears. Arizona Rep. Karan English was called a feminazi by a caller—and she ran with the blessing of Barry Goldwater. Other women in Congress are being smeared with falsehoods about their marital status and with whisper campaigns that they are lesbians.[21]

However, the ideas of feminism will not be beaten back. Women have slammed the door to the doll's house for good. Some women's leaders sigh with resignation and say, "Forget the word—if women buy the package, not the wrapping, that's progress." But the word is important, because without it women have no history, and the accomplishments of women can be presented as simply those of isolated individuals and the opposition to their progress downplayed. As George Santayana noted, those who forget their history are condemned to repeat it.

For now, however, we will probably have to settle for half a loaf. Susan Douglas says we need to "reclaim the word feminist from the trash heap it's been relegated to by the media and remind them and ourselves that a woman who says, 'I'm not a feminist, but . . . ' is, in fact, a feminist."

So the hate-fascination relationship between the media and feminism will go on, entering who knows what phase in its next incarnation. It may even give the movement some (underhanded) encouragement. Douglas says, "Despite their best efforts to keep feminism a dirty word and women under control, the media will continue, often inadvertently, to play a critical role in providing that encouragement. They are still our worst enemy and our best ally in our ongoing struggle for equality, respect, power and love."[22]

9. THOUGHT POLICE, TRIBES, AND VICTIMS

The Media and Multiculturalism

Journalism and paintings by the Old Masters have a number of notable differences; among them is the frame. Put a Rembrandt in just about anything and it's still a Rembrandt. But a news story looks totally different depending on how it is presented.

I have noted lately that the frames of many stories hacked out by the media have been changing shape, now that white males seem to feel that they are an endangered species.

Mind you, many white men have been at the forefront of promoting justice in America for people of genders, colors, and sexual persuasions other than their own. It is also true that men have been confronted with a bewildering array of changes, which many have accepted with grace. And I am quite fond of white men, being the wife of one and the mother of another. But I notice that a great many men who were passionate champions of justice and equality as young journalists or aspiring academics back in the days when the economy was blazing and nothing was at stake for them personally have become neoconservatives now that their promotions, their jobs, or their tenure are on the line. They rant against affirmative action and political correctness and immigration. Can this be because—for the first time in American history—the hegemony of white men, who have always run the culture, is not only loudly criticized but threatened as well? Describing "white male paranoia," David Gates writes in *Newsweek*:

> This is a weird moment to be a white man. True, one of them just became president—but then one of them always becomes president. . . . A black female poet read at his inauguration, welcoming everybody to the party— the Asian, the Hispanic, the Jew, the African, the Native American, the Sioux, the Ashanti, the Yoruba, the Kru . . . and dropping in the occasional Swede and Scot almost as if they were . . . tokens. WASPs didn't even rate a mention. Some party. Suddenly, white males are surrounded by feminists, multiculturalists, PC policepersons, affirmative action employers, rap artists, Native Americans, Japanese tycoons, Islamic fundamentalists and third-world dictators, all of them saying the same thing—you've been a bad boy.[1]

In fact, for the first time many affluent white males seem to be feeling like women, blacks, Jews, and others have often felt—like outsiders who have to keep explaining themselves. As a woman I have often marveled at the way some men so often seemed to sail along, sure of the waters, sure of their course, while I saw a world much more convoluted and complex then they. Sometimes it seemed we were gazing at utterly different vistas. Things they absolutely took for granted, I questioned or simply did not believe. It's no wonder the neoconservative movement has gained such popularity. Scrambling back to familiar turf is a basic human instinct, and to many men the days when white males and their culture went unchallenged must seem like Paradise lost.

Often this is a subconscious reaction, but it has its effect on the news business. As journalism scholar Austin Scott Long says,

> The news business today is governed to a large extent by the values, instincts and sense of fairness of people whose supporting cultures were shaped one, two, three decades ago. A lot of these people are hostile to the

notion that there has been a multicultural revolution since the framework through which they view events was shaped. And it's that old framework, that old culture, that they fall back on . . . these are not people who deliberately distort and misinterpret the news. These are people who think—wrongly—that most other people who matter see things sort of the way they do.[2]

The sense of threat experienced by white men, combined with that cultural time lag, creates certain frameworks around many current stories. Three in particular reflect a subconscious hostility to a new culture that does not accept the old white male verities: I call them the tribalism, political correctness, and victim culture frames.

For many years American politics was the exclusive province of upper-class white men (as were banking, law, academia, manufacturing, marketing, and so on), and media hardly whispered a complaint about this state of affairs. It was assumed to be quite normal. Growing up in the fifties, I did not hear one charge that the United States was an oligarchy, a tyranny, or any of the other nasty words we hear about societies that are controlled by one caste. Although not a single person on the Supreme Court, on television anchor desks, in any of the cabinet posts that mattered, at the controls of jet airplanes, or at the helm of Fortune 500 companies looked remotely like me, the American media seemed gloriously unperturbed by this fact.

Why then the shriek of alarm now that people other than white males are gaining power in politics, the arts, and elsewhere in the culture? Why, if white male monopoly stirred no outcry, is there suddenly the conviction that everything is going to hell, that the country is falling apart because of "tribalism" and "Balkanization"? Perhaps is it not the *country* that is falling apart but white male privilege, and for some it is not easy to tell the difference.

This is not to minimize the difficulties of absorbing new waves of immigrants and maintaining a sense of who we are in the midst of great change. But guess what, folks? We've done this before. Indeed, it may be hard to absorb people whose skins are a different shade, whose language falls strangely on our ears—but think of how a New Yorker of Scottish-English descent must have felt when confronted with a bearded Jew from Romania clad in a long black coat and speaking in a strange tongue. Some critics today speak of the ease with which we absorbed all these European immigrants, because they were "more like us." That's not the way the people who were around at the time saw it. The *Boston Republic* spoke for many native-born Americans in 1880 when it wrote of "hordes of illiterate laborers who have no notion of permanent settlement and who never intend to become part of our population. It is from these elements that the Republic has reason to fear danger."[3] Pat Buchanan, in a 1991 column that the *Boston Herald* headlined, AMERICAN VALUES ARE DROWNED IN RISING TIDE OF IMMIGRANTS, writes of "a mortal threat to American civilization."[4] Familiar?

The fact is that modern Americans will probably have an *easier* time confronting strangers than did our great-grandparents; thanks to television and other modern media we are at least vicariously acquainted with strange lands and strange peoples. And because formal religious affiliation plays less of a part in our sense of identity than it once did, we are less threatened by people whose religious beliefs are different from our own. In the days when great numbers of European immigrants came to our shores, religion was a major source of friction between groups, and superstitious people readily accepted such ideas as the notion that Jews have horns or that nuns steal babies. A convent in Charlestown, Massachusetts, was burned to the ground in 1831 on the basis of such rumors. The idea that assimilating the immigrants was easy and went smoothly just doesn't jibe with history.

Tribalism and *Balkanization* have become buzzwords in the media. I found more than a thousand references to them in NEXIS since 1990. They are also scare words, casting the new state of affairs in a frightening and negative light. But they are used quite promiscuously. Irving Kristol writes in the *Wall Street Journal* of the "Balkanization of America" brought on by such horrors as affirmative action; Thomas Sowell writes that *multiculturalism* is a euphemism for the Balkanization of the country, a "jobs program for race racketeers"; William Bennett talks about the Balkanization of campuses on *This Week with David Brinkley*; Charles Krauthammer says the left promotes Balkanization and attacks the idea of common American citizenship. Historian Arthur Schlesinger says that individual rights are the backbone of the nation and that an emphasis on group rights will unravel the nation's binding cords.[5]

On and on it goes, with the neoconservatives leading the charge, and the media picking up the terminology, with *Balkanization* used routinely in stories on such issues as voting rights; affirmative action; diversity of college campuses; school funding, hiring, and promotion; women's studies; and black studies. At play in all this is one fallacy that seems to affect journalists as much as the rest of us, the dream of the Vanished Eden, when things were so good in America. The late Max Lerner—a liberal icon— wrote a 1990 column in the *New York Post* that "the difference between past eras in America and the present is that we have moved from the Emersonian and Whitmanesque confidence and self-reliance of the individual ego, which held the center together, to the grandiosities of the ethnic, gender-group ego which tear the center apart."[6]

In which era did these Emersonian virtues hold the center together? During the Civil War? The draft riots? The lynchings in the South? The Vietnam War? America has always been a contentious place, with various groups jousting for power and place. And Jews, as Lerner certainly must remember, always had a strong group identity and sense of ethnic roots that stood them in good stead in surviving the often virulent anti-Semitism in America. Are they to be chided for not "holding the center together"?

Joe Klein writes in *Newsweek* that in America "group identities are irrelevant; individual rights are paramount. The times we have made exceptions to that premise have proved disastrous. The first and most odious was slavery. The most recent was kindly, but misguided, that blacks, and later other protected groups should be given special preferences because of their historic grievances."[7]

Only a white guy could compare affirmative action to slavery. Maybe there could be a miniseries in which the heroine recounts the horrors of being dragged in chains to the 32d floor, where, because of a class-action suit, she is forced to be a CEO. Besides, white males have been a group with "special preferences" for a long time, because no one else was even allowed to compete for most good jobs. Giving special benefits to people who are not white guys, Klein says, hasn't worked: "The acceptance of racial distinctions gave leverage to those who, like Louis Farrakhan, made hay off the differences. It made possible poisonous reactionaries like Meier Kahane."[8]

Gee, it must have been affirmative action that gave rise to Father Coughlin, the Ku Klux Klan, Gerald L.K. Smith, and maybe Hitler.

Or maybe letting folks other than white guys have any power will wreck creative endeavors. Robert Brustein, director of the American Repertory Theater, complained to the *New York Times*, "You have to cast a black woman in a law school as a law professor. . . . You have to cast Asians, homosexuals, everyone, in order to get sufficiently diverse representation."[9]

Funny how no one complained when Lena Horne wasn't allowed to play a mixed-race woman in *Showboat*, but Ava Gardner was. No one complained when Caucasian actors grabbed off all the good Asian parts in films and plays, when Marlon Brando in makeup got the choice Asian role in *Teahouse of the August Moon*. How come no one complained about authenticity when only whites were cast?

Chester Finn, the director of the Education Excellence Network in Washington, D.C., is quoted in the *New York Times* as saying, "A Beirutization of American higher education is taking place. More and more we are identifying ourselves in terms of race, ethnicity and sexual preference."[10]

This makes me consider the fact that I went through most of high school, college, and graduate school barely reading the works of any women or people of color. Dead white guys, that was it. Some of the dead white guys were great, mind you, and I am not knocking Western culture, but in terms of role models for intellectual achievement I often felt like the young black man in Richard Wright's *Native Son* who looked up at an airplane in the sky and thought, "Fly that plane, white boy." What word—what would be the antonym for *Beirutization?*—might be used for the education I got, in which only one sort of person was allowed to speak? The *Moscowization* of education? No such word was ever coined.

There are charlatans and plenty of silliness among the devotees of multiculturalism, just as there are among white guys. There are people who say that the darker "sun people" are morally superior to the "ice people," that Jews ran the slave trade, that women are morally superior to men, that only blacks can teach about blacks or women about women, or that white men are all racists by nature and created all the ills of the world.

But when white guys tell me that studying women's history is bad for me, or when Arthur Schlesinger says that "I regard blacks as part of American culture, not African culture,"[11] my tendency is to say, "Who asked *you* to decide, kemo sabe?"

When John Leo writes in *U.S. News and World Report* that newsrooms are seeing a "new tribalism" because women and people of color are demanding more diversity,[12] I wonder if he wants to go back to the good old days—when the *Los Angeles Times* had to send a black messenger to cover the Watts riots because it had no black reporters. When my friend Carolyn Toll Oppenheim, then a reporter for a Chicago paper, was told she couldn't write about the problems of children after she became a mother because she would be too biased. When the *Baltimore Sun* would not print pictures of engaged couples who were black. When the word *homosexual* couldn't appear in a family newspaper. When editors thought the women's movement was just a bunch of nutty bra burners.

As a white woman I am delighted by the new mix of cultures and genders that is gaining a foothold in the halls of power in America. I think that in the long run we will benefit from the mix, as we did when the last wave of immigration swept across our shores, despite the upheaval it created. When I see Asian-American kids picking up their diplomas from my college, when I see white teenagers dressing like black rappers, when I see two women from California getting elected to the Senate—sorry, guys, I just can't feel threatened. Unlike the white male neoconservatives, I was never really accepted at the table. When it came to Western culture, I was in the back of the bus. Maybe that's the difference.

If tribalism is one echo of the threat to men heard in the media, the huge media hype given to political correctness is another. As I noted earlier, I discovered 9,724 stories about the subject in NEXIS (most of them since 1991).

Does PC exist? Yes. Is it a problem? Certainly. But are there *really* armies of Thought Police (as a *Newsweek* cover piece put it) marching across the land, threatening the rights of Americans?[13] No. Are people being blacklisted, en mass, as they were in the McCarthy era? No. Are they being jailed, stripped of their livelihoods? No. Are Hollywood screenwriters blacklisted, forced to write under other names? Are playwrights being hauled before Senate committees? No.

On some college campuses people whose views deserve to be heard have been intimidated into silence; some groups try to shout down or otherwise harass those with whom they don't agree. Sometimes college administrators get chicken and let bullies get away with it. Some spurious suits have been brought. This is wrong, and it should be opposed. But what I see happening in the media is that any progressive opinion is being labeled PC, and any attempts to increase diversity are being tarred by that label.

The media view American college campuses with alarm. As critic Todd Gitlin writes, "Just note the degree of alarm, of alacrity, with which the media have jumped on this issue. *Newsweek*, the *Atlantic*, the *New Republic* and *New York* jumped up with cover stories on race, multiculturalism and the politically correct movement on college campuses. The *New York Times* has given extensive coverage to the PC trend."[14]

If you believe the headlines, you'd think that our colleges are nothing but warring camps. Indeed, bringing young people of many ethnic groups, races, and cultures together at an age when the hormones are flowing and the energy level is high is going to cause some frictions. But the media panic hardly seems warranted. A (New Orleans) *Times Picayune* story refers to colleges as being "flash points of separatism." ASIAN INFLUX AT CAL STIRS QUESTIONS, headlines the *San Francisco Chronicle*. An educator is quoted in the *New York Times* as saying, "Separatism and even tribalism in the old-fashioned sense are increasing" and that this is frightening.[15]

But is it really all that frightening? Not to Troy Duster, director of the Institute for Social Change at Berkeley, who did a two-year study of diversity on campus. He concluded that campus fragmentation, if its components are as many and varied as they are at Berkeley, might lead to a social revolution, a minisociety without a dominant group, able to work in the multicultural global economy that is now taking shape: "Now we have to start talking not in the old tradition of 'How can you be like me' but 'How can I understand you?'" Berkeley is no longer a Caucasian island in an ethnically diverse sea, as it was when Duster was an undergraduate there in 1969. "Students are brighter and standards are higher," he says.[16]

Such a positive view of diversity on campus is rare in the media, however, which prefer the alarm headlines: SEPARATE ETHNIC WORLDS GROW ON CAMPUS. The thrust of many stories is that blacks and gays and Asian-Americans are segregating themselves. Richard Bernstein writes in the *New York Times* that there is a "determined assault" on college campuses against required courses in Western culture and that a "radical minority assertiveness, that cult of otherness, permeates the mainstream."[17] This theme is echoed again and again.

But who is really into "otherness?" Little notice was taken of a 1994 study of six thousand students of all races across the country showing that minority students—far more than white students—had contacts with other groups, studied with them, and dined and socialized across racial and group lines. Sylvia Hurtado, a professor at Michigan University and one of the researchers, told the *Boston Globe*, "Students of color are crossing ethnic and racial lines the most, while white students seem to be segregating themselves." She said the study suggests that "current concern about whether minority students are promoting and practicing self-segregation is misplaced."[18]

Because whites often cluster together—and have often set up barriers against those of other races—white self-segregation on campuses may seem normal. But when blacks or Asian-Americans cluster, they get noticed. Professor Arthur Levine of the Harvard Graduate School of

Education says that both students and outsiders have perceived racial separation on campus to be deeper and less complex than it actually is.[19]

The media seem alarmed at what's happening on campus, but when groups do hang out together, it is nothing new. My husband remembers the Jewish corner of the student lounge where he hung out at the University of Massachusetts. My friends and I often clustered with other Catholic students when we got together in large groups. (In fact, the nuns told us not to go to non-Catholic schools lest we lose our faith.) We still managed to find ways to meet and deal with students of other religions and ethnic groups. Students today do the same. The Michigan study reported that membership in black or other ethnic organizations did not limit students' broader interactions.

However, the media's ever-present framework of conflict/tension, which decides what is and what is not a story, leads to the "trouble-on-campus" articles. If a reporter goes out and interviews a lot of students, and they say, *Yeah, a few problems, but no big deal,* that's not much of a story. Let somebody hurl a racial epithet, though, and it makes the headlines.

And although the media decry the "PC" aspect of diversity, a study by Alexander Astin of the Higher Education Research Institute at the University of California at Los Angeles (UCLA) shows that students who take ethnic and women's studies courses tend to be more tolerant of others' views. In a study of 25,000 students at 2,217 U.S. campuses, such courses were linked to "a whole range" of positive outcomes, Astin says, including being satisfied with student life, being able to work well with faculty members, having good listening and writing skills, and developing critical thinking. Such courses, he said, do not appear to be fostering "Balkanization" or the heightening of racial tension. Quite the opposite seems to be the case.[20] However, this study, with its positive findings, got little media attention.

Whereas the focus of many stories is on the comfort level of white professors and students, less attention is paid to studies showing that the level of harassment and violence toward minorities in increasing. A huge media outcry went up over "speech codes" that were drafted to end such harassment.

Some codes indeed went too far and could have choked off the free-wheeling speech that is the life of a college community. But many actions barred by the rules deserved censure. For example, Brown University was charged with being "PC" for expelling a white student who leaned out of his windows and screamed *nigger* and *kike* at other students. For my money he deserved to be out of there. This was a second offense, and we should not allow students to behave like hooligans. Once, maybe you get a warning, but twice and you're history, pal.

If speech codes raise hackles, the notion that some dead white guys' books might get the boot leads the media to positively shiver with the fear that all of Western scholarship just might vanish in a puff of smoke. Replace one pretty good white guy writer with a superb black or Latino writer, and you'd think the entire edifice of Western thought had just collapsed. Critic Todd Gitlin says, "Hysteria rules the response to multiculturalism. Academic conservatives who defend a canon, tight or loose, sometimes sound as if American universities were fully and finally canonized until the barbarians showed up to smash up the pantheon and install Alice Walker and Toni Morrison in place of old white men. . . . Moreover, the hysterics gave the misleading impression that Plato and St. Augustine have been banned."[21]

The truth is that academia is much like the ground under Los Angeles—always moving around. The work of the greatest of the dead white guys will always remain enshrined; it is at the edges that some of them will lose out to newer voices, but that happens in academe all the time. Some newer works now in favor will in time fade too, to be replaced by new books, ideas, theories.

Often the hysteria the press exhibits about the whole PC issue—which seems to intensify as the shade of the skin color of Americans darkens—elevates minor squabbles to the levels of "thought police." For example, a claim in Dinesh D'Souza's *Illiberal Education* about the "harassment" of Harvard historian Stephan Thernstrom led to reports in the *New Republic* that the professor had been "savaged," and *New York* magazine called Thernstrom the victim of "demagogic black students."

What really happened? Three black students complained about Thernstrom's depiction of the black family in a course he taught. One student said that the professor noted that black men beat their wives, and then their wives kicked them out.

Then the story was picked up by the *Harvard Crimson*, which prompted a vigorous debate on campus. The denouement was that the Harvard dean of faculty felt the students had a point and said that their course of action—not going public but coming to the administration—was judicious and fair. According to Jon Weiner, who teaches history at the University of California at Irvine, and who interviewed a great many of the principals, the Harvard administration commented only on the manner in which the students took action, not on their complaints. It did not, as D'Souza alleges, characterize the substance of their complaints as fair. In fact, a Harvard dean declared that "in disputes over classroom material, instructors exercise full discretion over the content of classroom discussion" and noted that "in the classroom, our students are entitled to question views with which they disagree."[22]

This may not have been the ringing endorsement Thernstrom would have liked, but neither was it any sort of censorship.

D'Souza never interviewed the students involved, according to Weiner, who did. One student said she told Thernstrom that she felt his blanket statements about black men and women were inaccurate. He reportedly replied, "If you don't believe me, read Toni Morrison." Another student felt his perspective on black life "came across as simplistic and not reflective of our own experience."

Harvard sociologist Orlando Patterson talked to one student who complained. "She was genuinely upset about one of his lectures. This was not an ideological reaction. It was a personal and emotional one," Patterson told Weiner. "She said she did not want to make it into a political issue, and she had deliberately rejected attempts by more political students to make it into a cause. She was trembling with rage at the *Crimson* for making this public."

It was the type of issue that universities confront all the time, when students differ with professors over incendiary issues. But the media presented it as a storm of harassment and PC terror. *New York* magazine began its story this way: "Racist! Racist! The man is a racist! Such denunciations, hissed in tones of self-righteousness and contempt, vicious and vengeful, furious, smoking with hatred—such denunciations haunted Stephan Thernstrom for weeks."

But when Weiner asked Thernstrom if the passage was accurate, he replied, "I was appalled when I first saw that. Nothing like that ever happened."

Professor Jon Womack, former chair of the Harvard history department, said,

There had been a case years ago involving Richard Herrnstein, who had his classroom disrupted and was harassed in the Yard [by students who objected to his writings on race and IQ]. But nobody did anything to Steve [Thernstrom] but say he was insensitive. You'd think, Jesus, he ought to be able to get over that. Instead, Steve just weirded out. He was being very combative. He acted as if his very reputation as a liberal was being wiped out. It's easy to see why the *New Republic* picked it up, but why [scholars] Gene Genovese or Vann Woodward would get on the bandwagon is more puzzling. To my amazement, this has now become an issue which stands in the annals of free speech.

And Harvard government professor Martin Kilson concluded, "There is no Thernstrom case. There were 680 black students at Harvard at the time. A couple of them complained about his interpretations of black experience. That got translated into an attack on freedom of speech by black students. Nothing like that ever happened at Harvard. It's a marvelous example of the skill of the neocons at taking small events and translating them into weapons against the pluralistic thrust on American campuses."

In another case, at the State University of New York at Binghamton, press reports surfaced about a group of students who had disrupted a meeting of conservative scholars with sticks and canes. The *Wall Street Journal* repeated this "fact" in an editorial that condemned the PC students' "storm trooper tactics," their "bullying," and "censorship." Other newspapers also carried the story of a PC mob.

But David Beers, a writer for *Mother Jones,* found what a reporter for *Newsday* also found. The story was simply not true—no mob, no canes, no clubs. Where did the story come from?

The National Association of Scholars had announced a "kickoff" lecture for the conservative group to feature talks by several professors. Rumors circulated that the KKK might attend—"gossip of unknown origin, fueled by the fact that one of the professors had invited a Klan member to speak to a class several years before," writes Beers.[23] Some two hundred students, including some leftist activists and black students, entered a lecture hall with too few seats.

During a presentation one professor offered a framed photograph of his granddaughter at the Berlin wall for the crowd to pass around. One African American student scornfully tossed the photo to the back of the room. The student and the professor exchanged insults, and the student tossed a wad of gum at another professor. Other black students near the angry young man tried to restrain him. The dispute lasted four minutes, and then the meeting went on peacefully, with audience members asking questions. Beers notes that one professor told a reporter for the school newspaper that, "other than one person who misbehaved," the meeting had gone well. A reporter for a local TV station noted in her story that the racial flare-up to which she had been tipped had not happened.

Two weeks later a columnist for the *Binghamton Press and Sun Bulletin* wrote his version of the events he did not witness. He said a cane-and-club-wielding "mob" reminiscent of "the Nazis' heyday, Stalin's Reign of Terror and Mao's cultural revolution" had terrorized the campus. He spoke of the university's "decline into savagery." Beers notes that "similar wording appeared ten days later in the *Wall Street Journal* editorial, followed by slight variations in the *New York Post* under the headings OUTRAGE AT SUNY-BINGHAMTON and THE BROWNSHIRTS AND THE COWARDS."

Versions of the story that appeared in the Binghamton paper, the *WSJ*, and the *New York Post* picked up language that also appeared in a memo written by a conservative professor at SUNY. When the president of the university did not endorse the professor's inflated version of events, the professor "blitzed" the media with copies of his memo.

Beers interviewed a number of players in the drama, including professors and students who had been present, and found that the whole incident consisted of one student's acting up and being restrained by other members of the audience. He was later put on probation. "The clubs supposedly brandished consisted of one walking stick used as such, and a handful of pledge canes carried as symbols of fraternity membership. No NAS [National Association of Scholars] member we interviewed claims that the stick or canes were ever raised or used in a threatening way," Beers says. His findings agree with those of a *Newsday* reporter, who concluded that a lone disrupter was being used to brand the audience a mob. But the careful *Newsday* story, coming a month after the incident, was too late to counter the impression left by major media outlets that a raging mob of PC storm troopers had been unleashed at SUNY.

At the University of Texas at Austin, when a committee of faculty members and graduate students decided to create a course for first- and second-year students called Writing About Difference, conservative opponents forced the cancellation of the class. They claimed that students would be forced to write "PC essays." After six months of fending off criticism, the committee resigned en bloc.

The *Houston Chronicle* editorialized "good riddance," calling the professors "Later-day versions of the Hitler Youth and the Red Guards" and used words like *fascism* and *McCarthyism*.[24]

Now, as an academic I know that such courses are often taught in universities. We teach writing about sports, about business, about politics, about personal experience. If I proposed a course called Writing About Difference, I would get little flack if my syllabus seemed sound. But the media seemed to think this course was some new, dangerous chimera.

Two members of the committee at Texas who planned the course, Linda Brodsky and Shelli Fowler, later wrote,

> Not one of the many journalists who have trotted out "Writing About Difference" as an example of the dangers of political correctness interviewed anyone who actually worked on the syllabus. Freedom from information (beyond the spin put on the course by its opponents) may explain why syndicated columnist George Will felt free to tack Race and Gender onto the course; why Richard Bernstein reported in the *New York Times* that "literary classics" had to be dropped to make room for PC materials, why *Newsweek* did not know in December that the leftist *Rothenberg Reader* had been dropped by June, why Fred Siegel, writing for the *New Republic*, mistakenly claims that English 3306 is a "remedial writing course" whose theme is "white male racism."

None of this is true, the Texas professors say. No literary classics were to be replaced—the university requires a class in expository writing. The committee had selected federal court decisions about discrimination for the students to focus on, including arguments by the plaintiffs, the defendants, and the courts, to teach students about debate and critical inquiry. Students would be allowed to take any position they chose and argue for it. That this approach would produce writing only about "white male racism" seems farfetched.

The hubbub led the university president to refuse permission to field test the course. Here in fact was a good example of how charges of PC, seemingly unwarranted, actually censored an academic course. Brodsky and Fowler write, "If the *Houston Chronicle* is really concerned about academic freedom, it should be worried rather than relieved by our resignation" from the committee.

Indeed, the right has repeatedly overblown such incidents on campuses, and a credulous media has too often fallen into lockstep. This is not to say that there haven't been real threats to free speech and times when professors have been intimidated, but the notion that a "climate of fear" is spreading across American campuses is an idea manufactured by a wealthy and aggressive cadre of the right. Dinesh D'Souza, for example, was the editor of the *Dartmouth Review* when it ran perhaps the most notorious piece of racist trash ever published in an Ivy League newspaper in the modern era. It was a desperately unfunny parody of a stupid black student at Dartmouth that caused an uproar on the campus: "Now we be comin' to Dartmut' and be up over our 'frods in studies but we still be not graduatin' Phi Beta Kappa." The piece reminds me of the trash I've seen over the years in publications by white racist organizations—crude, unfunny, and offensive. D'Souza later worked in the Reagan White House and at the Heritage Foundation. As David Beers notes, "He then decided to write a book in which he would seem to be handwringing over all the racial fuss on campus—which, of course, he had done his best to create."[25]

If PC is one way to discredit critics of the status quo, the idea of a victim culture is another. If the frame on a story is that of real people who have been discriminated against, who have felt real pain and must be listened to, that story takes on a particular seriousness. But if those who are complaining can be pictured simply as whiners, wimps, and pseudovictims, their complaints can be dismissed out of hand.

Richard Bernstein writes in the *New York Times* of the Myth of the Permanent Victim, and he manages some interesting mental gymnastics in writing of a feminist performance artist:

> The artist, the creative personality, has in modern times often been a rebel against prevailing morals and conventions. When a performing artist like Karen Finley rails against what she characterizes as the degradation of women in society, presenting herself as one lonely rebel, she seems to be in that tradition, one with the courage to be different. Her theatrical pose is that of the victim of the violence of male-dominated society.
>
> But Ms. Finley's message, with its evocations of injustice, is what has become the "politically correct attitude," encouraging audiences and critics and artists alike in reverent support of the cause of the "oppressed."[26]

Wait a minute. We should blame the *artist* because she persuades people to be against oppression? Should we blame Arthur Miller for being politically correct in being against witch-hunts in *The Crucible*? Why not knock Athol Fugard for being against apartheid and getting people to agree with him? The artist's moral voice has always been a driving force in drama. When people are convinced, that's bad? Maybe only when feminists do it. And why is drama that centers on society's effect on women said to portray "perpetual victimhood"? Dramas about fascism, communist repression, and anti-Semitism never seem to be cast in that mold.

Casting people as part of a victim culture trivializes their complaints. Arthur Austin writes in the *Cleveland Plain Dealer* that "according to the patrons of victimization, society is splintered into groups of oppressed people. Women and an ever-expanding pool of minorities are deemed oppressed. White males are per se oppressors."[27]

Ah, there's the rub. Poor white guys and their problems.

Sometimes the tables can be turned so that the victim seems the victimizer. This was the case in a *Time* feature article about childhood sexual abuse and recovered memories, titled LIES OF THE MIND.[28] The story suggests that people who remember incidents of abuse and incest as adults are merely the tools of therapists who goad them into a frenzy of doctrinaire belief that everyone's a victim. Indeed, there have been cases in which recovered memories are questionable, and safeguards have to be maintained to protect the innocent. But the frame on the story—and the slanted headline—casts doubt on all recovered memories as fraudulent.

What is at work here is a second cousin of the Myth of Female Weakness—the Myth of Female Unreliability. Women are not to be trusted, and because most victims of sexual abuse are women (or male children, also unreliable), it's easy to believe their stories are suspect, as *Time* implies.

My experience tells me this is not so. Not long ago I did a lengthy interview with Frank Fitzpatrick, the insurance investigator and private detective whose refusal to give up on a crime that happened thirty years ago led to the arrest and conviction of Father James Porter for child sexual abuse.

Fitzpatrick was nearly forty when memories of abuse when he was thirteen began to return. A lifetime of depression and feelings of unworthiness had haunted him. When the memories returned, he began to track down Porter, the parish priest in his small Massachusetts parish. Ultimately, more than sixty other victims in Massachusetts and two other states came forward—many who had not repressed their memories but had never told.

The notion of a victim culture spread by the media could put back in place the old taboos against talking about sexual abuse. My brother, who was molested by a Catholic Christian brother when he was a teenager—and committed suicide in his thirties—never told until many years later. His therapist later said he had never seen such destruction of self-esteem as had been visited upon my brother in that Catholic school. I wonder if the illness that dogged him for years and his tragic death could have been prevented if the taboos had not been so strong.

Also, there is solid evidence that sexual abuse is real and rampant. In 1991, for example, there were 129,697 *confirmed* cases of child sexual abuse, according to the National Center on Child Abuse and Neglect.[29] As Mike Males writes in *Extra*, the magazine of the media-watch group FAIR, debating the false memory issue became a media fad: "While only one major news magazine ran a comprehensive article on the prevalence and effects of confirmed child abuse (*Newsweek* 4/25/94) during the year, there were five articles—including three multi-page features—on the recovered memory issue." He notes, correctly, I think, that "the problem is not that recovered memory is being debated. Rather it is that today's media devote far more coverage to side issues like recovered memory than to the indisputable reality that millions of American children grow up in nightmarish conditions."[30]

Another victim story that can be played in several ways is that of date rape. Although the original stories about date rape brought a little-understood phenomenon into the light, a backlash quickly developed, in which date rape was portrayed as just another case of whining pseudovictims. This frame on the story was the one chosen by Kate Roiphe—and the reason her book, *The Morning After*, got such incredible hype by the media.

Roiphe, a twenty-five-year-old graduate student with no literary track record, no in-depth research, few facts, and no interviews with victims, became a publishing sensation. Why? Because she argued that the whole issue of date rape was just hype. She'd talked to a few of her Ivy League friends, and they felt the same way. Such a slight book on any other serious topic would have been laughed out of the arena. Because of its message it got the cover of the *New York Times Magazine* and massive exposure in print and television.

Of course, a debate about the gray areas—of when seduction becomes rape—is legitimate. Is a woman raped if she's dead drunk in a frat house? If she's in bed with a guy with all her clothes off and changes her mind? If she's sweet-talked into it, not thrown on the floor? Some people define almost anything as rape, and that to me is not sensible. But date rape is real. Roiphe's book wasn't credible and didn't deserve the attention it got. But her message fell sweetly on a great many ears. *(Those women are just whiners and what's more, they're asking for it.)*

Roiphe's lack of interest in studies of date rape is a glaring omission in her book. Naomi Wolfe, feminist and author of *The Beauty Myth*, noted that Roiphe had ignored several studies reporting that 16 to 25 percent of the women surveyed at four major colleges had experienced forced sex and that date rape had a serious long-term effect on their lives. Marquette professor Mary Ann Sideritz told *Newsday*, "The idea that rape crisis hype is painting a generation of women as helpless victims might make attractive reading, the thing that sells books. But it seems to be an over-simplification of what's happening. I'd like to see some data, please."[31]

Despite what the news media say, we do not have a victim culture. We do have smart defense lawyers who would try a "Twinkie defense" or an "abused child" defense for Jack the Ripper. That doesn't mean abuse is not real. We have a much deeper understanding today than in the past of how childhood traumas, addiction, abuse, and poverty can shape behavior. Some people take no responsibility for their actions and blame some external force for everything that happens. But most victims of rape (date rape or any other kind), child abuse, spousal battering, and other kinds of trauma really are victims, and to think otherwise is simply wrong.

I grew up in what might be called a Culture of Silence. Things happened, and no one ever told. What would the neighbors think? My best friend in high school remembers how she and her brother used to stand at the bottom of the stairs to catch their mother when their father threw her down them. Another friend was beaten for years by her naval officer husband; another finally threw her husband out after years of beatings. One of my students remembers that her father used to come into her room and penetrate her with a favorite shampoo bottle that had a little ballerina on the top that she loved, which made the rape even worse. A male student of mine used to listen to his father beating his mother. It took years of therapy before he could be convinced he wouldn't turn into a batterer too.

No, there is no Culture of Victimization, but there are victims, real ones. And even if there were such an artifact, if I had to choose between the victim culture and the culture of silence, I know which I would choose.

10. QUOTA QUEENS MEET AFFIRMATIVE DISCRIMINATION

When Fairness Comes Under Fire

American attitudes toward affirmative action have undergone a vast sea change since I started out as a journalist. Although some people always have grumbled about "quotas," the civil rights movement brought fairly broad recognition that blacks—and later women—had indeed faced severe discrimination in the job market and that some remedial action was only fair. That of course was in the days of full employment and a booming economy.

The Civil Rights Act of 1964 led to a series of executive orders requiring nondiscriminatory practices in hiring and promotion, setting goals for minority hiring—and later the hiring of women. They were accepted—if grudgingly—by businesses, because businesses knew that employees and job applicants could bring suit under federal guidelines. (In fact, class-action suits by women against *Newsweek*, the *New York Times*, and other media outlets led to breakthroughs for female employees in the news business.)

But in the late 1970s the tide began to turn. Perhaps the critical event was the application of a white man named Alan Bakke to the medical school at the University of California at Davis. He challenged the "set-asides"—slots for minority students that were designed to encourage African Americans and Hispanics to train for careers in medicine. The case finally wound its way to the Supreme Court, where a sharply divided Court ruled in favor of Bakke.

Since the *Bakke* decision (1978) the American media have exhibited what can only be called a tidal wave of disapproval of affirmative action. For example, a NEXIS search reveals no fewer than 5,732 stories on "reverse discrimination" and nearly three hundred on "affirmative discrimination" from 1985 to 1995; in the past two years alone (1993–1995), the data base shows more than two hundred stories on quotas. (In a 1988 study of how *Time* and *Newsweek* covered racial issues researchers Jack L. Daniel and Anita L. Allen found that the publications gave more attention to "reverse discrimination" than to issues black readers thought important, such as poverty, civil rights gains, and improving education.)[1] Conservatives have made affirmative action a prime target. And in reading through the flood of stories on the data base, the ever-useful Man from Mars would assume that women, African Americans, Latinos, Asian-Americans, and Native Americans had special privileges and that white men were a disadvantaged class.

A sampler of such stories would include a men's group complaining in the *Chicago Sun-Times* about Take Your Daughter to Work Day on the ground that it "discriminates against boys who haven't had any history of discriminating against anyone." The *Sacramento Bee* editorialized that a new policy encouraging women and minorities to compete for city contracts was "affirmative discrimination." The *Atlanta Constitution* complained in an editorial in 1994 that "Diversity and social leveling have become the sacred cows of our time." On CNN firefighters working for the U.S. Forest Service claimed women get all the jobs, and male gymnasts at UCLA claimed their sport has been shoved out because of affirmative action and requirements that women's sports get equal funding.[2] The late William Henry, a *Time* critic, argued in 1994 that affirmative action is as unfair to its beneficiaries as it is to white men, because it causes members of minority groups to wonder whether they were hired to fill a quota. Syndicated columnist James Kilpatrick sees good news in the fact that white males are now bringing discrimination suits. A writer for the *Houston Chronicle* claims in a book review that affirmative action has made white males second-class citizens.[3]

On and on and on it goes. The news makes a reader sense a growing feeling in the culture that white males are steadily losing ground, even though the statistics show that men are still firmly atop the pyramid of power in America. White men are 39.2 percent of the population, yet they comprise 82.5 percent of the Forbes 500 listings of individuals who are worth at least $265 million apiece; white men hold 77 percent of the seats in Congress, 92 percent of state governorships, 70 percent of tenured college faculty slots, nearly 90 percent of daily newspaper editorships, and 77 percent of TV news director jobs.[4]

Minority groups are in fact advancing slowly. When the executive search firm Korn Ferry prepared its ten-year survey of senior executives in 1989, it found that blacks had gone from 0.2 percent to a mere 0.6 percent of top corporate jobs, Hispanics from 0.1 percent to 0.4 percent, and women executives from 0.5 to 3 percent. Yet white men's perception of being under siege is intense. In a *Newsweek*-Gallup poll in 1993, 48 percent of white men thought their kind was losing influence in American today, 56 percent believed they were losing an advantage in terms of jobs and income, and 52 percent thought they were losing influence over American culture—style, entertainment, and the arts.[5]

Many white men have the feeling that they are surrounded by aliens, and in fact the United States is in the throes of a major transition, from a predominately white Protestant nation to one that is multicultural and diverse. White power is holding, as the statistics show; still, whites seem to see the "others" everywhere, and media coverage that presents affirmative action as an unfair attack on the jobs and privileges of white men only heightens that paranoia. A 1990 Gallup poll, for example, found that the average American estimated that 32 percent of the population was black and 21 percent Hispanic. The accurate figures were far lower: 12 percent and 9 percent.[6]

"Why would white men feel they are pushed to the wall when they hold most of the jobs?" asks Ellis Cose, *Newsweek* essayist.

> One clue was offered by a black female executive on a large newspaper who said that her employer routinely told unqualified white male reporters that they could not be hired because the next slot had been promised to a black, a Latino or a woman. It was a way, she surmised, of allowing the applicant to salvage his pride in his competence—which raises the possibility that despite all the bellyaching affirmative action may turn out to be the best tonic for the white male ego since Edgar Rice Burroughs invented Tarzan.[7]

The myth that white men are falling behind whereas hordes of women, blacks, Hispanics, and Asian-Americans are making spectacular gains fuels male resentment. "White male paranoia," notes *Newsweek*, "isn't old-fashioned liberal guilt. It's atavistic racial and sexual dread, and it achieves critical mass when a rapidly contracting economy becomes overcrowded."[8] Incendiary too is the notion that the poor are lazy and undeserving and that minorities get jobs only because they are held to lower standards.

Neither perspective is real, but both are flourishing.

Given the historical facts of slavery, followed by blatant discrimination in education and economic opportunity, blacks didn't even get to start playing the American Game until very recently. Women only began to move into the workforce in massive numbers in the 1970s. The race and gender discrimination that were the targets of the civil rights and women's movements of the sixties and seventies were blatant and widespread. Liberals viewed affirmative action as a nonviolent way to address the obvious unfairness of the distribution of jobs and resources. It was intended to be a temporary measure to give those who had faced centuries of discrimination a fairer shot, a way of getting into the game. Author and scholar Cornell West sees affirmative action not as a cure-all but "playing a negative role—namely to ensure that discriminatory practices against women and people of color are abated. Given the history of this country, it is a virtual certainty that without affirmative action, racial and sexual discrimination would return with a vengeance."[9]

The Myth of the Incompetent Minority Worker only fuels the anger of many Americans. It is almost sacred writ to many whites that an army of incompetent African Americans, women, and Hispanics has invaded the American workplace, taking *their* jobs. And of course the stereotype contains just enough truth to make it powerful. Do white men sometimes lose out to less talented "others"? Of course. It happens. Just as talented women lose out to less gifted men, and blacks and Hispanics of superior ability lose out to white men—or women. The American workplace is just chock full of mediocre people, of all colors, shapes, and sizes. Just as talented performers come in all races and both sexes. (My lawyer mother once gave me one of the best pieces of job wisdom I ever received. She said yes, it was true that a woman had to be twice as good as a man to get ahead, but that was not hard, because there were so many dumb guys out there.)

But when the Myth of the Incompetent Minority Worker meets up with the American Myth of the Meritocracy, resentments are bound to flare up. We like to believe we are a classless society in which a person's talents can carry individuals as far as they want to go. But in fact we all know that a class structure exists and that it shapes the destinies of many of us. White Americans accept with hardly a protest the special treatment given to those fortunate enough to have had a family member, somewhere in the past, smart enough or lucky enough or rapacious enough to have amassed wealth or property. We all know company heads, store owners, publishers, police officers, or union stewards who are not all that bright but who had a parent who owned the store or an uncle who was on the force. A national outcry erupts over the question of college admissions for members of minority groups, but hardly a stir is created by the substantial numbers of less-than-brilliant sons and daughters of alumni who get admitted to elite colleges, pushing out more talented students.

A twenty-one-year-old Harvard graduate, John Larew, the son of a midwestern farmer, probed the admissions systems of elite universities after seeing the "caste" of children of "old Harvard," with their airs of wealth and privilege. "What did it for me was seeing classmates I knew were on their way to immense wealth and power who were just not very impressive people," he told the *Boston Globe*.[10]

A federal study showed that the kids of alumni admitted to Harvard were significantly less qualified than the average student, the *Boston Globe* reported. Comments scrawled by admissions officers said such things as "Without lineage, there would be little case. With it, we will keep looking." One official wrote, "Classical case that would be hard to explain to dad [if he were not admitted]." These less-than-brilliant students *were* admitted to Harvard.[11]

White upper-class privilege continues unabated with scant notice, but let one not-so-talented black guy or one unbrilliant woman move ahead, and the story spreads like wildfire. On the other hand, do you ever hear anyone say, "My daughter didn't get the job in sales, because there was this really great black man who deserved it more"? Or "I lost out on the editorship to a woman, but she was really much better than I was"? If you believe the new American folk tales, hordes of unqualified minority applicants are gobbling up American jobs like black holes eating stars.

If the stories were true, black folks would be running America. But where are they? I have a friend who swears that white males can't get any jobs in the newspaper business and warms gloomily that white women will be the next to go. But I look around and see that 94 percent of executives in the business are white and 85 percent are men.[12] The newspaper business serves as a microcosm of the larger society; it is a business that is confronting both the demands of a diverse workforce and difficult times. Tensions exist on both sides, as those in power seek to retain their position against advances by those seeking entry to what has long been a white man's club.

Suspicion about why minority applicants are hired and resentment over the "costs" of diversity run deep, says Ted Pease, former editor of Gannett's *Media Studies Journal.* He cites some comments by whites in his study, "Race and Resentment in the Newsroom":

- "Managers seem to believe that minorities and women automatically are qualified for jobs, while white males must prove themselves."—Male reporter
- "When will people look at me for what I have to give instead of weather [*sic*] or not I'm a minority ? Reverse discrimination is hurting more than helping."—White male photographer, late 30s
- "I think there is a serious problem with minorities and women receiving preferential treatment in the newsroom. White males are being passed over or pushed out"—White male sports reporter, late 30s
- "We reward jobs and promotions in the newsroom to people of inferior talent in order to meet . . . company goals of minority representation. . . . We deny jobs to qualified white men because they're white."—White male newsroom manager, 50s

Another white reporter says, "I think we have a problem when newspapers look at the color of a person above who can do the job best." And the general sentiment is perhaps best summed up by this comment: "Who cares about white males? No one."[13]

With so many news professionals worried and angry about affirmative action in their own backyard, is it any wonder that their copy reflects that resentment? Indeed, newspapers are a shrinking industry—as are most businesses these days, and times are tough not only for white males but for all job applicants. I do not minimize the problem that white males are having these days—as are all Americans looking for jobs in a downsizing economy. There is a huge gap, however, between the ways whites and blacks see the state of the business. "Whites and nonwhites are coming from different planets, not just different perspectives," Pease writes. Minority journalists say they are expected to "look black and think white" and to be seen and not heard. Whites either don't see race as much of a problem, or, when minority journalists don't do well, blame their failure on affirmative action politics that pushed them too fast.[14]

Minority journalists, on the other hand, think their race works against them when managers make assignments and promotion decisions and that managers have serious doubts about their professional abilities. Journalists of color also think they have less opportunity to succeed than whites and are more likely than whites to be overlooked for training. Sixty-three percent of minority journalists say race is a distinct factor in managers' decisions on story and beat assignments.[15]

A black reporter from Pennsylvania complained, "Black journalists are presumed inferior even by editors who hired them based on a great interview and a butt-kicking resume. . . . Black journalists also feel that if they make one slip, they're dead meat."[16]

The constant criticism about the evils of affirmative action in the white-dominated media can perpetuate the myths of minority incompetence and widespread white suffering. By exaggerating minority progress, by seeing every white male under siege and facing discrimination, the media can heighten tensions that already exist in a tough economy, which can also lead to the cry for the repeal of the fairness measures that do exist.

The saga of Lani Guinier is a classic example of how incendiary those tensions can be.

"Strange name, strange hair, strange writing; she's history," is the oft-repeated line in the media about Guinier.

How did a soft-spoken, respected academic with a reputation for working cooperatively with her peers and avoiding confrontation turn into a weird extremist radical known as the Quota Queen? The story of Lani Guinier is a tale of how a character assassination plot hatched on the right raced through the mainstream media and destroyed a presidential nomination before it could even get off the launch pad. It also is an example of how the media tend to shoehorn a story into a familiar frame. "A lot of my colleagues had the reaction, 'We know what this is about, we know this is about quotas,'" writes *Los Angeles Times* media critic David Savage.[17]

Few could have predicted that the nomination of Professor Guinier to head the Civil Rights Division of the Justice Department would have produced such a media feeding frenzy. She was a respected attorney and litigator, and her qualifications in those arenas were never on question. New York University law professor Derrick Bell notes that although the complaint is often heard that enough "qualified blacks" can't be found to fill top positions, in this case "you can't imagine anyone being more qualified than Lani Guinier . . . and suddenly, qualifications mean nothing."[18]

She was being nominated for an important job, but she would be under the direction of the president and the attorney general, and she would be well aware that she would have to persuade a largely conservative judiciary in order to win her cases. Robert Bork, who was savagely attacked as a Supreme Court nominee, was not even asked about his law review writings when he was appointed to the lesser position of solicitor general in the Nixon administration.

But Lani Guinier moved into the sights of activist Clint Bolick at the conservative Institute for Justice, who—taking a cue from the successful anti-Bork campaign—went fishing in Guinier's law review articles. Just as conservatives trolled through Hillary Clinton's writings and tried to portray her as a feminist radical, the right lifted passages from Guinier's dense and lengthy articles on voting rights and her complex writings about securing minority representation through formulas of proportional representation. The Institute for Justice campaign to get Guinier began with a series of press releases, all calculated to portray her as a left-wing radical who wanted to scrap American democracy and replace it with weird schemes of reverse discrimination.

But the "killer metaphor," as Guinier calls it, was supplied by a *Wall Street Journal* headline, CLINTON'S QUOTA QUEENS. (The other queen was Norma Cantu, nominee for assistant secretary for civil rights in the Department of Education.)

Quota Queen. It was a perfect sound bite, a snappy headline. Who could resist it? Apparently no one. The *New Republic* reported that 337 articles used the term in stories on the nomination. The words *quota queen* might as well have been blazoned on her chest like the scarlet letter. That Guinier had specifically *rejected* the use of electoral quotas or affirmative action remedies in voting rights cases in articles for the Harvard and University of Michigan law reviews did not seem to give the columnists, headline writers, or the authors of newsmagazine cover pieces any reason not to use the label. In her detailed critique of the Guinier coverage for the *Columbia Journalism Review*, Laurel Leff points out that *Newsweek*'s first story on the controversy was titled, CROWNING A QUOTA QUEEN? Leff writes, "The article's author, Bob Cohn, says the use of the term was justified as long as it wasn't in '*Newsweek*'s voice' because the 'term was around town. It was the way most people identified her.' Of course, the term was 'around' because it appeared in the *Los Angeles Times*, *USA Today*, the *Chicago Tribune*, and the *Washington Post*, not to mention *Newsweek*."[19] Pat Buchanan opened an edition of the CNN news show *Crossfire* with the words, "They call her the quota queen,"[20] and news stories used the words *radical, weird, outlandish, far out,* and *unacceptable.*[21]

Was Lani Guinier really a flaming radical out to abolish American democracy? No. But the media simply accepted at face value the characterization her by the Institute for Justice and the *Wall Street Journal* and made only a half-hearted attempt to investigate what her ideas really were. For example, Bolick repeatedly picked up minor points made in footnotes about complex voting issues and distorted their meaning. In a complicated argument Guinier described an "authentic" black elected leader as one elected by blacks and culturally similar to his or her constituent base. By this yardstick former Virginia governor Douglas Wilder would not be considered authentic, because he had to appeal to a majority of white voters to win election. *Authentic* in this context is a word used in voting rights legal jargon and understood by scholars. But the press took it to mean she was calling Wilder an Uncle Tom.

And Guinier later told *Editor & Publisher*, "As I was to learn the hard way, only one message, and not even the one I thought I was sending, was received by the press. It turned out I was not skilled at the task of facing down journalists, projecting symbols and reducing complex ideas to sound bites."[22]

Leff points out that few journalists seem to have waded through the difficult articles. Stuart Taylor Jr., a columnist for *American Lawyer* newspapers, received frantic calls from reporters asking what the hell Guinier had actually said. That gave Taylor, a columnist not known for supporting civil rights, a disproportionate influence over the debate.

Leff writes that by the middle of May *Newsweek* had done its report, other columnists had joined in, and "the view of Lani Guinier as a radical leftist had hardened beyond repair."[23] Here, *Newsweek* was reporting on a process of which it had been a part—the media chasing its own tail, as often happens.

And few publications took the time to point out that a nominee should not be judged—as Bork surely was also—by scholarly articles, the purpose of which is to suggest ideas, even profligately, and expand the horizons of the debate. No one expects them to be the sole basis of policy. As Leff points out, the *Chicago Tribune* was an exception; it endorsed Guinier despite some criticism of her legal writings, saying, "The error here—as in the case of Bork—is to assume what a scholar suggests in an academic article shows what she will suggest in public office. . . . Guinier, even if she were so inclined, will not be allowed to push any radical agenda in litigation."

Once labeled, Guinier tried to fight back but got little support. Leff notes that the story then changed quickly: "The initial and decisive stories swung quickly from 'controversy' stories to 'doomed nominee' stories." Both story lines dictated that the most objectionable parts of her work would be the focus. The Clinton White House backed off the nomination, saying that some of her ideas seemed undemocratic.

Newsweek reported the crash with the flip headline SO LONG, LANI. The story suggested that "maybe she didn't understand the code" by not dropping out earlier. In this piece Guinier became the naïve pol who didn't understand the Beltway game (as Washington reporters undoubtedly *do*), and the story, all insider stuff, said the White House was "caught napping." The *Newsweek* piece repeated two of the "footnote fantasies" about Guinier—that she had questioned the legitimacy of Doug Wilder and that she stood for "equal outcomes," not simply a fair process. Said *Newsweek*, "To many in Congress, these are euphemisms for quotas."[24]

In retrospect, Lani Guinier told *Editor & Publisher* magazine, she saw four potential explanations for the failure of journalists to report her story accurately. First, she said, there isn't enough diversity among media decision makers, and second, those media that do pursue hiring diversity often employ a few "tokens," who must continuously prove their qualifications. As isolated achievers, their very visibility and token status can be paralyzing. Others are silenced by their own self-censorship. And she added, even when there is diversity, there is still "viewpoint monopoly." (Most columnists and top editors are white men.) Finally, she said, "We are in a state of denial about issues of race and racism. The media's treatment of my nomination suggested that officially there should be no serious public debate or discussion about racial fairness."[25]

Guinier may have taken some consolation from the fact that in 1994 a federal judge in Maryland ordered an Eastern Shore county to adopt cumulative voting to make it possible for black candidates to get elected. The court was using a voting scheme that was exactly like the ones Guinier had been suggesting, a form of which had also been practiced in Illinois for nearly a century.[26] In a different political climate Lani Guinier's ideas might have been welcomed as novel approaches to the problem of legislatures that still deny blacks voting power, especially in the South.

The problem was, Lani Guinier, with her "strange hair" (probably a covert way of referring to the fact that she was part black, part Jewish), walked into a story that already had a frame. Journalists were familiar with one big story where hiring and voting were concerned, and quotas was it. Period. On top of that she was swimming against the tide of American individualism. Some of her ideas about proportional voting, she said, came from reading an article on turn taking in the *Sesame Street* magazine. Six children had to decide whether they would play tag or hide-and-seek. Guinier's son Nicholas decided that the children should play both games; tag first, hide-and-seek second. "In a nutshell," she said, "that is the theme of many of the ideas that got me into trouble last spring. It is about taking turns. It is about figuring out ways that we can all get along, in which no one group gets everything and no one group loses everything."[27]

Would John Wayne have said that? No way. American individualism, unfortunately, seems to be about who gets all the toys.

So Lani Guinier confronted the American Myth of the Lone Hero, as well as the backlash against affirmative action, the reluctance of the press to abandon a familiar frame around a difficult story, and the machinery of the right wing going full tilt. It is no wonder she didn't get confirmed. It's a minor miracle she survived.

11. STRANGERS AMONG US

Zoo Stories and Ice Queens

Who are Americans, anyhow? As we as a nation become darker in shade and more diverse in custom, religion, and country of origin, the sense of threat felt by white Americans grows more intense. This is nothing new, as I've noted. When waves of immigrants from Eastern Europe, Ireland, and the Mediterranean arrived on our shores, Americans already here were often close to hysteria about it—how close, we often forget, now that all those folks have been happily assimilated. But in the American media images of people who are nonwhite, non-Christian, or non-Anglo sometimes take on strange and wondrous contours.

When David Shaw of the *Los Angeles Times* interviewed 175 minority editors, reporters, and publishers in 1990, they came up with a laundry list of complaints about the mainstream media's depiction of minorities:

- Harmful stereotyping
- Ignorance of cultural differences

- Use of racially based or insensitive language
- Unfair comparisons between different ethnic groups
- A double standard in the coverage of minority politicians
- Failure to photograph or quote minority news makers
- Anointing unrepresentative and sometimes irresponsible minority "spokesmen"
- Automatically lumping together all Latinos or, in particular, all Asian-Americans as a single community, without recognizing the substantial differences in cultures and language among the various elements of those communities[1]

Next to stories about criminality, minority journalists complained most that the media convey a much broader cross-section of white life than of minority life.

"As far as the press is concerned, we don't exist," Craig Matsuda, assistant editor of the features section at the *Los Angeles Times*, told Shaw. Even in papers that have high-ranking minority editors, the coverage is not as inclusive as it should be. In Detroit, Shaw notes, the paper's features section is called The Way We Live—which African Americans sardonically refer to as "The Way *They* Live."

Ben Johnson, then-assistant managing editor of the *St. Petersburg Times*, says that coverage of white America gives white readers a sense of normality. But minorities see little "normality" in coverage of their communities. "The coverage gives reader the impression that 'people of color' don't buy houses, die, get married," Johnson told Shaw. When the stories are about lawyers, doctors, fathers, mothers, people starting business, writing screenplays, or doing the myriad other things people do in the course of their lives, minorities are simply not included. Felix Gutierrez, vice president of the Gannett Foundation, says minority coverage still falls into predictable categories: "We're either beset by problems . . . or we're causing problems for the white society."[2]

In a report titled *Kerner Plus 20* a group of journalists revisited the recommendations of the Kerner Commission, which was set up after the urban riots of the 1960s. The group noted that in twenty years not much had changed in many aspects of the media's portrayal of African Americans:

> Blacks are not yet part of the normal flow of the news, even in the areas where they have over-achieved, such as sports, music and entertainment. . . .

It is a strange place this black world the media project by commission and omission. Within the feature pages of many newspapers, snowstorms and floods rarely disturb black residents. Gypsy moths don't attack their lawns or eat the leaves of their trees. Their children don't run away from home or go on vacation, or get married, or shop at suburban malls. Or take in a play.[3]

When the Unity '94 News Watch study, sponsored by black, Asian-American, and Hispanic journalists, compared *Newsweek* and *Ebony* magazines, it found striking differences in perspective. A *Newsweek* story on the black family featured the headline THE WORLD WITHOUT FATHERS: THE STRUGGLE TO SAVE THE BLACK FAMILY. On the cover a lone boy looks somberly off the page. On the cover of *Ebony* sits a family of four, well dressed and neatly groomed. The cover says, THE NEW BLACK FAMILY: DETERMINED, DYNAMIC, AND DIVERSE. "The chasm between the perspectives illustrated the criticisms most often voiced about the way mainstream American journalism covers African Americans," the report says. "It focuses on the downside rather than on the more everyday—and representative—side of black life, thought and culture."[4]

It is this notion—that white life is *real* life and that the white perspective is the only one that matters—that so irritates those whose skins are not the shade of bleached flour. It is what I have often found most baffling in the reactions of some otherwise sane and sensible white male journalists. They are simply so used to having the world presented from their point of view that they cannot imagine a world that is quite different. I suppose it's rather like a fish trying to imagine walking on land and breathing air. (Some white women journalists are just as obtuse, but for the most part women have the experience of being outsiders, so they have at least a sense of what I am talking about. Some women of course deny it completely and try to be more like the guys than the guys are. There's a recipe for disaster! I would much rather deal with a real guy than an ersatz one.)

When the media cover only the violent or unusual side of minority life, bad news seems to be the norm. As a result, minority journalists often get criticized for not emphasizing the negative. White reporters rarely get such criticism. The *Washington Post*'s Dorothy Gilliam points to a column in *U.S. News and World Report* that criticized a gay reporter who covered a march on Washington and focused not on drag queens but on the issues. Now, drag queens may be quite exotic to middle-class heterosexual reporters, but who says they are the story? Gilliam, president of the National Association of Black Journalists, says, "It's calling into question a gay reporter's ability to be objective in covering a gay rights march because he didn't write as much about people in drag as he did about substantial issues. Similar judgments are made about people of color. A white reporter makes decisions about what he or she is going to cover and its called news judgment. You send a black reporter and judgment is suspect. It becomes a convoluted attack on diversity."[5]

Another category of coverage "where we're defined as a people," the Gannett Foundation's Felix Gutierrez told Shaw, is what he calls the "zoo stories": "Chinese New Year, Cinco de Mayo, Black History Month—basically they come and see us in our cultural garb—out of the context of our normal daily living."[6]

An example of this mindset comes from the *Washington Post*'s much ballyhooed launch of its redesigned Sunday magazine. In the nation's biggest black metropolis the product that emerged seemed nothing so much as a showcase of white fears about African Americans. The cover piece was a long profile, written by a white writer, of a black rap singer from New York who had been charged with killing a District drug dealer. Prominently featured was a column by Richard Cohen in which he defended white shopkeepers in the District who shut their doors when young black males approach.

If either article had been presented as simply a part of the *Post*'s ongoing coverage, there probably would have been little complaint. But with the two articles juxtaposed in the much touted new launch, the reaction in the city was immediate and explosive. Demonstrators appeared at the door of the *Post* from some forty organizations in the city. The Association of Black Psychologists published a paper saying that the premiere issue was unfair, unhealthy, and dangerous. The leader of the protest, Cathy Hughes, told the *Boston Globe*, "This magazine reinforced all the negative stereotypes about blacks. To make that kind of statement in a magazine's premier issue is to glorify deviant behavior and to say to the young black men of our community, 'You don't have any hope. You want to make it, take drugs and steal and get your picture in the *Post*.'"[7]

The *Post* editor at the time, Benjamin Bradlee, wrote an apology on the op-ed page, but the whole incident left some black readers unhappy with the paper. A *Post* editor who appeared on a journalism panel with me wrote the whole brouhaha off to "political correctness" and defended the stories.

It seems that no image of blacks these days is believed unless it has something do with crime and drugs. When black film director Kevin

Hooks shot a park scene in Harlem, his studio's white executives wanted more trash, filth, and litter dumped onto the set—Harlem was simply "too clean" for white folks to accept. And although films about young black gang members in the 'hood are boffo box office, hardly any feature films deal with the reality of black middle-class life. "As long as it's in the ghetto and people are carrying guns and even the dogs speak in four-letter words, they'll give it four thumbs up and nine stars," says director Robert Townsend. Townsend, who also is a comedian, does a hilarious send-up of this attitude in a skit called "Black Acting School," in which he plays a Shakespearean actor who has to go to school to learn how to talk like a pimp and a thug to get a job.[8]

The media's presentation of the United States as a place constantly terrorized by gun-toting thugs—most of them people of color—has seriously skewed our image around the world. I once had a student from mainland China who rode the subway in utter fear, clutching her purse to her chest as she came to classes, until it slowly dawned on her that the peaceful morning commute was the usual reality in America. She told me she really expected to see black men with AK-47s rushing though the cars, firing at will at any second. The news media join with the entertainment media to create this deranged picture of American life.

If blacks find themselves distorted by the media, Asian-Americans also complain that coverage is dictated by a white perspective. *Project Zinger*, a 1992 study sponsored by the Asian American Journalists Association (AAJA), found '92 a year of some notable Asian-American triumphs. Kristi Yamaguchi won the Olympic gold medal in figure skating, Amy Tan hit the best-seller list with *The Joy Luck Club*, her novel of Chinese-American life, and George Takei finally got his own Starship command in a *Star Trek* movie.

On the other hand, Japan bashing reached an all-time high. Michael Crichton released the book *Rising Sun*, a "paranoid thriller" presenting clever, evil Japanese executives out to dismantle American industry. Hate crimes against Asian-Americans escalated. Many Korean merchants were the targets of looters in the Los Angeles riots.

Scanning the American media, the report said that simple-minded stereotypes still litter the landscape. It cited a story in the *Philadelphia Inquirer* on a tennis match between Boris Becker and Michael Stich. The reporter commented on Becker's shirt changes, saying, "The shirts were piling up behind Boris Becker faster than they do at a Chinese laundry."[9]

Chinese as laundry owners is a stereotype so hoary that it had begun to lose any basis in fact by World War II. In a review of the film *Shadow of China* in the *San Francisco Bay Guardian*, the reviewer said, "The plot is resolutely and inscrutably Asian." He later acknowledged, "I gave the maker the benefit of the doubt by saying he was intentionally inscrutable, when it was probably just plain bad writing."

An opinion column by James O. Goldsborough published in the *San Diego Union* was headlined, JAPAN NIPS CREATIVITY IN THE BUD. The story resurrected another old chestnut, that Asians are merely imitators. *Project Zinger* noted, "The author compares Japanese workers to bees, merely manufacturing the products resulting from American technology, implying the Japanese lack creativity. The word 'Nip' in the headline recreates a slur used frequently during World War II."

Echoes of the "yellow peril" seep through media coverage, *Project Zinger* says.

THE JAPANNING OF SCARSDALE was the headline of a *New York* magazine article. The AAJA criticized the article for its "sensational headline and its written-to-scare" content. Although the article overall was deemed to be generally evenhanded, the headline raised the old "yellow peril" echoes.

"The phrase *Asian invasion* has been used through United States history to whip up antagonism against Asian immigrants. . . . In modern times, *Asian invasion* has become a metaphor used in stories about international trade, immigration and demographic changes in neighborhoods," the AAJA noted. "It has become an offensive cliché for many Asian Pacific neighborhoods."[10]

Unfortunately, *Asian* rhymes with *invasion*, making it irresistible to editors who are prone to the June-moon style of verse. Asians "invade" all over the mass media, notes *Oakland Tribune* columnist William Wong in the Gannett Foundation's *Media Studies Journal*:

SHOW BUSINESS: HONG KONG'S WOO LEADS AN ASIAN INVASION—*Time*,
   September 13, 1993
THE ASIAN INVASION—*New Yorker* photo caption, March 31, 1993
MOVIE TRENDS: ASIAN INVASION—*Indianapolis Star*, January 1, 1994
A TWO-MAN ASIAN INVASION HAS HIT BASEBALL—*Sports Illustrated*,
   March 28, 1994

The mysterious Orient, another cliché, pops up again and again, Wong observes. When ABC's *Good Morning America* spent a week in Hong Kong in 1991, "the white American hosts occasionally laced their chatter with references to 'strange' and 'mysterious' things. Strange and mysterious to whom?" Wong writes.

Sometimes reporting is simply inaccurate, as in a story in the *Santa Clarita* (California) *Signal* in 1993 that said a Japanese husband would slap his wife's face if she didn't have dinner ready when he came home—and would slap her again if she hadn't done the dishes. "These outrageous generalizations should have been checked with Japanese cultural experts," says Wong.[11]

Project Zinger homes in on a *Newsweek* cover story on Olympic ice-skating champion Kristi Yamaguchi, written by Frank Deford. Although it found much to praise in the writer's condemnation of prejudice against the Japanese, and condemnation of the internment during World War II, it objected to the sexist portrayals of skaters Yamaguchi and her rival, Japan's Midori Ito.

Other critics agreed with the Zinger report. Elena Tajima Creef, of the University of California at Santa Cruz, writes, "As Kristi is rewritten from Japanese-American into all-American, racial difference becomes displaced onto the figure of Midori Ito, who bears the traditional burden of the *real* other at Albertville. Given the strong Americanization of the former, it is hardly surprising that when paired with Midori, Kristi seems to transcend Asian representation and even comes to embody the Western ideal against which Midori cannot possibly compete."[12]

She quotes *Newsweek*'s portrayal of the two women:

> [While] Yamaguchi is almost five inches taller than the 4 ft. 7 in. Ito and totally of Japanese descent, she perfectly represents the stylish Western ideal that the stout little Midori is so envious of. Although absolutely petite, a size 1, 93 pounds, Yamaguchi is cut high with a Betty Boop mouth and two beauty marks wonderfully positioned under the left eye and the lips. Ito, though, is simply short, her powerful legs bowed in an old fashioned way, what the Japanese once called unkindly, of their women, *daikon* legs, after the archipelago's big, squat radishes. In matters of appearances, it doesn't seem that Yamaguchi and Ito grew up in different lands so much as if they came from different centuries.[13]

Can you recall such a derogatory passage about a male athlete in any sport? Males with powerful muscular legs get admiring adjectives from male writers; rarely if ever are they cast as radishes. Nor are they sexualized in comparisons between them. The physiques of Chinese and Japanese male divers and Caucasian ones often show marked differences—and, as in figure skating, grace, precision, and skimpy clothing are all part of the sport. However, their bodies go unremarked upon.

Creef writes,

> Kristi represents a new type of Japanese—one where Americanization and assimilation have transformed her into a type of beautiful model minority of modernity where racial difference is muted in favor of Western style. As one who "perfectly represents the stylish Western ideal," she becomes an honorary Caucasian, complete with beauty marks and cartoon lips, who is cut *high* even though she is only five feet high.
>
> Compared to her modernized and Americanized counterpart, (Ito) remains behind the times, "a squat peasant-bred Mongoloid on skates."[14]

Coverage of Midori Ito in American publications, Creef notes, bears an uncanny resemblance to the stereotyped notion of Japan:

> Midori is presented less as a gendered Japanese subject than as a kind of relentless and nearly perfect jumping machine who is able to outperform most men. There is no question that the representation of Midori Ito in the winter Olympic games at Albertville invokes the contemporary narrative of Japan as a rising economic superpower now threatening to compete in global affairs. She is the "industrious Japanese athlete (with the superior body technology) who threatens to take over the women's figure skating competition—until now one that has always been dominated by the West."[15]

If the press makes a cartoon of Midori Ito, the actual cartoons that represent Asians are especially hurtful. *Project Zinger* reports, "Cartoons depict Asians with buck teeth, slanted eyes and big round sunglasses." One example cited was a cartoon by the *Boston Globe*'s Paul Szep, showing horrified but grinning Japanese car dealers rushing to President Bush's side when he fell ill. The features of the Japanese are outlandishly stereotypical, reminding me of the old Tojo and Hirohito caricatures. Szep defended the cartoon, saying he treats everyone the same way: "I've got complaints from everyone—blacks, Asians, Hispanics." But the *Globe* ombudsman disagreed, saying, "Portraying every man in Japan as a buck-toothed ninny is a mischievous oversimplification, the equivalent of caricaturing every American as a long-nosed oafish boor with dollar signs on his vest. Fifty years after Pearl Harbor, it's time to dump the too-easy image of Japanese men as toothy World War II soldiers in business suits."[16]

In American newspaper cartoons buck-toothed Japanese seem to be everywhere, selling cars, taking away American jobs, doing business in an underhanded way. One cartoon in the *Detroit Free Press* showed two Japanese businessmen buying silicone breast "imprants." A sign reads "crearance sale."[17]

But cartoons even impute stereotypical Asian features to inanimate objects. *Project Zinger* noted a cartoon that appeared in the *San Jose Mercury News* with a story about Japanese cars; it gave an automobile an Asian face. "The car's headlights portray slanted eyes and the grill portrays a toothy smile. The car is painted yellow." A graphic illustration in the *Orange County Register* portrayed Asian investors as a two-headed extraterrestrial bug in a package of business stories entitled WHERE'S THE MONEY?

But perhaps even more pervasive is the Model Minority stereotype. By now many Americans seem to believe that Asians are born with genes that program them to be math whizzes and valedictorians at Berkeley. But this myth has a down side: envy. David Shaw writes, "Asian Americans are successful—even wealthy. They are polite, even passive, Hmm. Sounds as if they might make good targets for a mugging.

"Bingo."[18]

As the *New York Times* pointed out in October 1990, there is a "growing and disturbing trend of subway attacks against people of Japanese, Korean, Filipino and Vietnamese descent."[19]

The Model Minority Myth creates resentment among other Americans and gives a caricatured idea of Asian-Americans. In fact, poverty rates among Chinese, Korean, and Vietnamese families in the United States are much higher than for whites, but, Shaw writes, "Asian Americans are generally perceived as being successful. They often find it difficult to obtain necessary social services and may be denied access to affirmative action programs."

The portrayal of Asian-American success is often double edged. Just as Jewish success was caricatured as the unfair success of pushy money-grubbing people, Asians are thought to have an unnatural cunning, clannishness, and deviousness that give them an advantage over whites.

Already, prejudice has taken the form of "quota" systems at prestigious colleges and beatings and shootings in several cities. A poll taken before the Soviet collapse showed that more than twice as many Americans thought the security of the United States was threatened more by the economic power of Japan than by the military power of the Soviet bloc. Headlines about Japanese economic power only underline this perception: JAPANESE EXPECTED TO TAKE OVER ANOTHER MAJOR HOLLYWOOD STUDIO. Although Europeans have more investments in the United States than do the Japanese, rarely are there scare headlines when a British or a Dutch firm buys an American company.

The growing numbers of Asian immigrants—increasing by 80 percent between 1985 and 1995—have made many Americans suspicious, certain that these "alien" people are taking jobs and college slots from deserving Americans. In 1982 a former Detroit auto worker clubbed to death Vincent Chin, a Chinese-American, mistaking him for a Japanese. During the beating Chin's assailant yelled racist remarks at him and blamed people like him for the problems in the American auto industry.[20]

The unrelenting press coverage of the success of Asian-Americans often fails to mention their backgrounds. Seventy-five percent of the Korean greengrocers in New York had college degrees before coming to the United States, and running a small store is not the pinnacle of their economic dreams, says Ronald Takei, professor of ethnic studies at the University of California at Berkeley. It in fact represents "dashed dreams, a step downward in status."[21] The media's failure to note this fact helps exacerbate tensions between Asians and blacks and leads to unfair comparisons of the two groups by whites. The *Asians made it, why can't blacks?* argument can be used against social programs for unskilled blacks, who are seen as not as "enterprising" as the more educated Asians.

If Asian-Americans suffer from model minority coverage, Hispanics complain that they are barely seen or heard from at all. Although Asian-Americans comprise only 3 percent of the population, they get as much press coverage as Hispanics, who now make up 10 percent. The National Council of La Raza says that Hispanics are too often portrayed as illegal aliens, drug dealers, or violent macho men.[22] The Unity '94 News Watch study noted that "major papers frequently fail to represent Hispanic perspectives in their coverage of the news."[23] When journalist Jorge Quiroga analyzed five hundred articles about New York mayoral campaigns in 1989 and 1993 for the Joan Shorenstein Center at Harvard, he found a "transparent if not invisible quality in the way Hispanics were covered." In 60 percent of the articles containing references to Hispanics, such references were "so limited the term was used only as a noun or adjective such as 'Hispanic community' or 'Hispanic neighborhoods.'" No actual Hispanic sources were quoted.[24]

The News Watch study noted that coverage of Hispanics as "problem" people or victims dominates the news, rarely counterbalanced by portrayals of Hispanics in more positive settings.[25]

One Hispanic journalist noted sadly that the highest-profile Hispanics in the American media recently were parent killers Lyle and Eric Menendez. Another Hispanic journalist observed that a paper she once worked for ran a story saying that Hispanics were one-half of all drug felons in the United States. Would the paper have run a story, she wondered, noting that 99 percent of white-collar crime was committed by white men?[26]

As for Native Americans, this country has a long history of treating the first Americans either as savages or as quaint and colorful lesser beings. The media are especially insensitive when it comes to language of concern to Native Americans. A *New York Daily News* headline about Donald Trump's opposition to Indians' owning and operating casinos prompted this headline: TRUMP STARTS INDIAN WAR: DONALD SAYS UGH TO INDIAN GAMBLING. When Native Americans complained about the headline, a *Daily News* editor said he didn't think it was insensitive; the *News* would use *oy vey* if the story were about Jews, because Jews say oy vey (never mind that Native Americans don't say ugh).[27] When I told my husband about the editor's comment, he said, "Yeah, we'd say oy vey when we saw that headline."

It is not always the race or ethnicity of Americans that can make them them strangers in a land that is their own. Class may sometimes be the issue. Because the media have moved upscale, because so few journalists today are from working-class neighborhoods, blue-collar folks can be covered as if they were as exotic as the new immigrants. The megacoverage of Tonya Harding is a case in point. Long before it was known whether Harding had been involved in any way in the attack on figure-skating rival Nancy Kerrigan, the news media had indicted and convicted her—for her lifestyle.

Early on Kerrigan was set up as the "good girl"—the "feminine one" with the nice family—whereas Harding, who won the national championship after Kerrigan was attacked, was the "bad girl"—tough, unfeminine, wild. None of this had anything to do with guilt or innocence. Harding later admitted to knowledge of the plot to maim Kerrigan and was barred from the sport. But the coverage centered on her blue-collar roots and convicted her long before she admitted anything.

Writers gushed about Kerrigan's beauty, her "ice princess" style, her pristine looks, her long legs, her elegance. Harding, meanwhile, was called—

in disparaging tones—a jock, an in-your-face competitor, and much was made—both by print reporters and TV commentators—of her muscular arms and legs. The same terms used admiringly about male jocks became epithets when applied to Harding. Physically, Kerrigan fit our ideal of the feminine athlete, lithe and graceful. Harding was too tough, muscular (like Midori Ito), and by inference—masculine. Had the roles has been reversed—had a member of Kerrigan's entourage been the attacker and Harding the victim—might the coverage have been quite different?

And although Kerrigan comes from a less-than-upscale background herself, that fact was glossed over. Kerrigan was repeatedly compared to Katharine Hepburn, the very symbol of upper-class elegance, whereas Harding looked like a lot of the blue-collar kids you'd see on a street corner in East Boston, Queens—or Portland. Several stories quoted experts who advised Harding to make her blond hair less brassy and to get rid of those tacky clothes. Much was made of Harding's hardscrabble roots, that she felt comfortable in a pool hall, that her husband once roughed her up. One columnist referred to Harding as "a pathetic tart."[28] But there is no evidence that Harding was promiscuous. Kerrigan later became romantically involved with her manager, who was separated from his wife and had a child, but no one called her a tart. *People* magazine, however, included Harding in its list of "white trash" celebrities.

The news media—and advertisers—like female superstars to be stereotypically feminine. In the 1970s tennis star Chris Evert, lithe, graceful, and cool, got most of the endorsements, whereas scrappy Billie Jean King—who really made women's tennis the money-making sport that is it today—was too much of a battler, too much of a blue-collar jock, for comfort. A narrow idea of feminine beauty linked to class surfaces in coverage of female athletes. Writers gushed about beautiful Katerina Witt, the East German skater who took an Olympic medal a few years back, whereas the absence of such comments about American skater Debi Thomas—who was also beautiful, tall, and lithe but black—was marked.

The athletes don't think about themselves in the way the media portrays them. Nancy Kerrigan said about herself, "I'm tough! I'm a fighter." Beneath the sequins and the elegance were the muscle and the grit of an athlete. And if Chris Evert was a "princess," she was one who'd drill you with a lethal forehand without a second thought.

It's time to retire words and phrases like *princess* and *ice queen* and get rid of the references to movie star looks in the coverage of female athletes. After all, a number of male quarterbacks, tennis stars, National Basketball

Association forwards, and major league baseball stars have classic profiles and well-conditioned bodies that could make them candidates for the movies, but rarely are those attributes mentioned in the sports pages.

The saga of the Olympic skaters was a compelling story without being distorted by stereotypes based on class or gender. It's hard for many media professionals, however, to stop seeing reality through those frames inside their heads—the ones that package all of life into neat, easily understood categories.

12. THE COLOR OF EVIL IS BLACK

The Media Demonize the Black Male

When I looked at the *Time* cover of O. J. Simpson, my first thought was, *Omigod! It's Willie Horton!* The same sense of Black Menace conveyed by the close-up picture of Horton, the murderer and rapist the Bush campaign managed to link inextricably with Democratic presidential nominee Michael Dukakis, shone forth from that cover.[1]

The "Hortonizing" of Simpson was an amazing feat of transmutation—especially noticeable when you put *Time* and *Newsweek* side by side. Both chose to put on their covers the mug shot of Simpson, accused of killing his ex-wife and a male friend in a vicious knife attack.

Newsweek's O. J. Simpson is the familiar celebrity. Not as we have usually seen him, handsome, affable, and smiling; no, this O.J. seems weary, almost dazed, but instantly recognizable as who he is.

The *Time* cover, enhanced by an artist, is quite different. It's not only that the color of his skin has been greatly darkened but that all the light in the picture is now concentrated around the eyes, nearly washing out the other features. In the unretouched pictures the man looks weary. But in the *Time* picture the pupils have almost disappeared; they are only tiny pinpoints in nearly black circles. The eyes look not weary but hooded, menacing. The *Newsweek* cover is of a familiar individual; we know him. The *Time* cover—by darkening the hue, spotlighting the eyes, and erasing the pupils—creates a mythic portrait: Sinister Black Man. Amazing how a little creative enhancement can erase an individual and create a myth.

Time's editors seemed amazed at the outcry across the country. In an unprecedented move *Time*'s editor apologized and said no racial slur was intended. I believe him. That's the problem. It's easy to deal with an overt racist who uses an airbrush or a jar of paint; it's when well-intentioned people do the deed that we realize how thorny the problem is.

It was not "racists" in the media who believed Charles Stuart when the Boston man claimed that an unknown black man had climbed into his car, forced him to drive to a lonely spot, then shot both him and his wife. A nationwide tidal wave of revulsion against the killer—another "Willie Horton"—swept the nation.

Charles Stuart, a handsome young salesman at a chic fur salon in downtown Boston, had taken his pregnant wife to their natural childbirth class at a Boston hospital. Charles and Carol DiMati Stuart seemed to be the perfect couple; she was an attractive young lawyer, and they were happily expecting their first child.

But then tragedy struck. A 911 operator in Boston received a distress call from a man on a car phone who said that he and his wife had been shot by a black assailant, and he desperately needed help. He didn't know where he was, because he had gotten lost on the way out of the hospital, which is near one of Boston's black neighborhoods. Police cruisers and paramedics roared off in a frantic search.

By coincidence a film crew seeking material for the television show *911* was in town that night and responded along with the paramedics. Local stations and later the networks used some of the dramatic footage, as the wounded Charles Stuart and his even more seriously wounded pregnant wife were put into ambulances that went screaming off into the night. Before she died, Carol Stuart was delivered of a baby boy by cesarean section. The *Boston Herald*, a tabloid, ran a picture of the bloody scene of Carol Stuart's murder that took up its entire front page.

At Carol Stuart's funeral a moving tribute of love and loss written by Charles Stuart was read aloud; he was still in the hospital recovering from his wounds, and many an eye in the television audience did not remain dry. I know I choked up as I heard his words about how he would always love and cherish his slain wife. His baby boy did not survive, making the father's grief even more poignant.

Grief and affection for Charles Stuart flowed through the city of Boston and across the nation. It was the nightmare of the white middle class: the black man with a gun stepping out of the shadows to wreck the happy productive lives of a hard-working couple. Hordes of police descended on Boston's largely black Mission Hill neighborhood. They hassled people, conducted a frantic door-to-door search, and stopped citizens on the street and questioned them. The press wrote stories about how the neighborhood was a symbol of black crime and violence in America.

As the search for the devious depraved black man went on, glowing stories about the Stuarts filled not only the Boston media but national publications as well. *People* magazine wrote of the happy young couple, and "Chuck" was pictured as the loving husband and father-to-be much in love with his wife and enjoying the childbirth instruction: "During the classes he would look at his wife a lot and just beam."[2] We learned of Chuck's hard work as a salesman, of the couple's new house, their dream of raising a family. They were enshrined in the media as a pair straight out of Camelot—a reference to the glamorous Kennedys.

When Charles Stuart had recovered from his wounds, he identified a black man, Willie Bennett, in a police lineup. Now the demon had a face. Rumors leaked out of the district attorney's office about Bennett's criminal record and the certainty that the guilty fiend was in custody. The media lapped them up. Calls for the revival of the death penalty in Massachusetts were heard.

But even as the general public was reading about the tragedy of the Stuarts, rumors were starting to circulate in the journalistic community: that Chuck Stuart used cocaine, that he seemed quite interested in young women, that being married made him restless. Reporters began to say that his story didn't pass the "smell test." There was the strange route that Stuart took when he left the hospital, the busy intersection where the assailant was supposed to have jumped into the car and forced the couple to drive to a deserted area, the fact that the gunman allegedly thought Stuart was a cop—and shot his *wife* in the head first.

And then of course came the unbelievable denouement. Charles Stuart's brother went to the police and said that he had met his brother on the darkened street and taken a gun from Chuck (Carol Stuart was dying on the seat beside him) that he (the brother) then flung into the Charles River. As the story spread, as the finger of guilt increasingly pointed to him, Charles Stuart drove to the Tobin Bridge high above Boston Harbor, parked his car, and hurled himself into the water. The perfect husband and distraught father, it turns out, coldly planned his pregnant wife's murder and chose what he thought was the perfect scenario for getting away with it—to blame a faceless black man.

It is chilling to think how close Charles Stuart did come to getting away with it and how close an innocent man came to life in prison for a homicide he did not commit. (Willie Bennett is in prison for a robbery he did commit, but he did not kill Carol Stuart and her baby.)

The Stuart saga was a story the media was conditioned to run—and readers were conditioned to believe. As Mark Jurkowitz, then *Boston Phoenix* media critic, said, "There is one broad area of media culpability in this story and that is creating the psychological atmosphere in which Stuart's story was believable. . . . In the rush to cover the human side of the drug story, we have created the impression that a big chunk of Boston is an urban war zone populated by drug-crazed people, heavily armed, who are mostly of color and are just waiting to pounce."[3] Statistics back him up. When media analyst Kirk Johnson examined more than three thousand stories by Boston media for a 1987 study, he found that 70 percent of all stories from predominantly black Roxbury and Mattapan concerned either crimes or traffic accidents.[4]

"No particular imagination is required," writes Ellis Cose, the author of *The Rage of a Privileged Class*, "to visualize crime with an African-American face. In every major city in this country, blacks accused of the most heinous offenses routinely stare from the front pages and television screens into Middle America's living room. These chilling, even monstrous images have come to represent, in many minds, the predominant reality of black America."[5]

Harvard law professor Charles Ogletree says, "Ninety-nine percent of black people don't commit crimes, yet we see the images day in and day out and the impression is that they're all committing crimes." Los Angeles Police Chief Willie Williams echoes the complaint, noting that a recent *Newsweek* cover on Generation X had only one black on the cover, and he was wearing an undershirt and a gang kerchief: "The message is that you have to fear African-Americans, that you have to fear my 27- and 25-year-old sons."[6]

No one denies that black crime is a major problem in America and that young black men are involved in violence that puts lives—especially black ones—at risk. But most criminals are not black, and fewer than 1 percent of African Americans are criminals. You'd never know that from the barrage of words and images that assails us each day in the media. Robert Entman, associate professor of communications at Northwestern University, studied television news in 1993 and 1994 and found that "the choices TV journalists make appear to feed racial stereotypes, encouraging white hostility and fear of African Americans. TV news, especially local news, paints a picture of blacks as violent and threatening towards whites . . . continually causing problems for the law-abiding, tax paying majority." His study of the three dominant network affiliates in Chicago uncovered these disturbing facts:

- The threat of violence to humans took up about nine of the fourteen minutes devoted to news coverage in a standard half-hour broadcast.
- Black defendants are more likely than white ones to be depicted in mug shots, with no name appearing on the screen, making them seem part of an "undifferentiated group." White defendants were more frequently identified by name and shown in video and photos other than their mug shots, enabling them to retain their individual identities.
- Black suspects are significantly more likely to be shown in police custody, making blacks seem more dangerous than whites.
- White "law enforcers" appear on television twelve times more than black ones, a much greater ratio of white to black than actually exists in law enforcement.
- Television news devoted 450 minutes to white "Good Samaritans" and only 33 minutes to black people performing good deeds.

"The racial stereotypes fostered by the obsession of television news with black crime is heightening racial tension in the U.S.," Entman writes.[7]

When I was growing up in Washington, D.C., the city's poor black neighborhoods had plenty of crime; I was acutely aware of the problem because my father was in law enforcement. My neighbors may have had a sense of unease from stories about people who were attacked in downtown Washington, but they were not bombarded night after night with images of crime. People who grew up in white America underestimate the amount of crime that was around when they were young, because they didn't see it. But now they think crime is everywhere, because they watch it every night in all its bloody horror on the evening news and tabloid TV shows.

Night after night, black men rob, rape, loot, and pillage in the living room. The Demonization of the Black Male is one of the salient features of the American media in the late twentieth century. No wonder a waiting public seemed so ready to lynch Willie Bennett, who became the perfect metaphor for the out-of-control, criminally minded black male.

The demonized black male has given whites a perfect scapegoat. Acel Moore, a *Philadelphia Inquirer* editor, writes, "If you want to divert attention and not be held liable for a criminal act, all you have to do is say a black man did it and you get instant believability."[8]

The Stuart case should have alerted the media. But in 1994, a young Virginia woman named Susan Smith got national attention when she claimed a black man had hijacked her automobile with her two young sons in the back seat. Once again the image of a "murderous black man" sketched by a police artist loomed on TV screens and stared out of newspaper pages. This time police were suspicious, but her neighbors—and millions of Americans—believed her. Some African Americans objected to the coverage, but the big story was the search for the terrible black man. Newspapers were rife with speculation about what he might have done with the children. Why didn't more red flags go up in the press? Why were so many people willing to believe that a black man would steal a car carrying two white babies on a back road in rural South Carolina without seeing the story as—at the very least—problematic? Of course, it wasn't a black man who killed the two little boys. It was Susan Smith herself, who drowned them by letting her car roll into a lake with the two children inside.

Susan Smith wasn't the only Charles Stuart clone. Moore cites a case in which a forty-three-year-old white woman in New Jersey said that a black male intruder had viciously attacked her and her seventy-one-year-old mother; she suffered a hammer blow to the head and her mother was stabbed. A police officer called in an artist to make a drawing of the assailant as the woman described him. Fortunately, neighbors had seen the two women fighting; Granny got the stab wounds from her daughter and wielded a mean hammer herself; the black intruder was a fabrication. But how many black men would have been dragged into custody if neighbors hadn't been aware that the mother-daughter duo were having at each other with the cutlery?[9]

In 1989 another New Jersey woman told police a black male had abducted her child. It turned out that she herself had drowned and dismembered the child.[10] In Chicago in 1992 in a crime similar to the Stuart case, an affluent suburban couple were found bleeding in a parked car. The woman (the mother of four) was brutally stabbed in the face and her husband stabbed in the chest. She never regained consciousness, and the husband told police two young black men had assaulted them in the car while it was parked. Fortunately, he was not as clever as Stuart, having taken out an insurance policy on his wife, which made police suspicious immediately.[11]

Moore says the media's inference that all crime is black crime is feeding most of the legislation to get tough with crime, including the "three strikes and you're out" provisions that send repeat felons to prison for life.[12] But such policies, conceived under the influence of fear and political expedience, are likely to backfire. The prisons may in years to come be clogged with expensive elderly inmates no longer capable of crime, and felons who have committed crimes against property may be taking up jail space while more violent criminals are let go. That's precisely what has happened in some states with mandatory drug sentences. Two-bit drug dealers have been sitting in jail, while rapists walk out the door.

And Les Payne, a *Newsday* editor, points out that the media emphasis on black crime—and the downplaying of white crime—leads to different treatment of criminals by race. Statistics show that whites rarely get the death penalty for killing blacks; blacks killing whites are far more likely to be executed.

For example, Payne says, the young white men who killed sixteen-year-old Yusef Hawkins in Bensonhurst, where Hawkins had gone to attend a party, "noticed only one thing, he was black; he could have been Jamal Payne . . . my son." The teenager was mobbed by a gang of some thirty white youths, then shot in the chest. He had come to the neighborhood at the invitation of a friend.

Only one of the seven men charged in Hawkins's death was held without bail, Payne notes. Bail was also granted to the white men who chased and killed a black man in an earlier slaying in New York's Howard Beach. But the young black men accused in the rape of the Central Park jogger were denied bail. All were terrible, senseless crimes, but the white criminals were treated more leniently than the black ones. "Media stereotypes share the blame for this inequity," Payne told *Los Angeles Times* media critic David Shaw.[13]

Over the whole issue of black crime floats the face of Willie Horton, who, like the Cheshire cat, never seems to quite disappear.

"He was big, he was black. He was every guy you ever crossed the street to avoid, every pair of smoldering eyes you ever looked away from on the bus, subway. He was every person you moved out of the city to avoid, every sound in the night that made you get up and check the locks," Roger Simon writes in *Regardies* magazine.[14]

Willie Horton lingers in the subconscious of every American who ever saw that television ad. How many times do I—knowing better—see a large black man and think instantly of Willie Horton and hurry on with a shiver? He is the symbol of the demonization of the black man, cynically manipulated to serve partisan political ends, and the American news media let it happen. The media were slow to see what was being done, slow to criticize, and by the time they did, the damage was done. Republican political consultant Floyd Brown told reporters, "When we're through, people are going to think Willie Horton is Michael Dukakis' nephew."[15]

And they did. A Lou Harris poll showed that the major factor in the election of George Bush in 1988 was the voters' perception that Dukakis was soft on crime—especially on murderers like Horton. When Kathleen Hall Jamieson, dean of the Annenberg School of Communications at the University of Pennsylvania, ran a series of focus groups about what voters remembered most about the 1988 election, this was what stuck in their minds: that Michael Dukakis had established a revolving door that let convicted murderers like Willie Horton kill again.[16]

Horton, it must be said, is a nasty piece of work. Jailed for armed robbery and murder, he was let out on furlough under a program begun by Republican governor Frank Sargent. Horton fled and later savagely tortured a Maryland couple, slashing the man and raping the woman. But how did Willie Horton become a metaphor for a governor who had in fact one of the best records of managing crime in the United States?

It began with a Republican "nerd squad" doing research on potential Democratic candidates for 1988. Republican operatives needed votes from women, working-class Democrats, and southerners. Or, as some put it, "bubbas and Joe Six-packs and broads," and the "nerds" combed through back issues of newspapers looking for material that might be damaging to Democratic contenders. Horton's name popped up out of the sludge. They tested the Horton story with a focus group of Catholic "Joe Six-packs" in New Jersey. It was magic. Most members of the group had been Dukakis supporters; by the end of the night half had switched to Bush.

The face of Willie Horton became as familiar to Americans as that of a movie star. Again and again it hammered home the message, fed by atavistic fear of the black male, that Dukakis was soft on crime. Not only whites got the visceral message. Black filmmaker Anthony Walton wrote in *New York* magazine, "I thought Willie Horton must be what the wolfpacks I had heard about, but never seen, must be like. I said to myself, 'Something has to be done about these niggers!'"[17]

(Politicians learned a lesson from Willie Horton. When Senator Jesse Helms's reelection bid seemed to be in trouble, Helms began running ads that featured full-face mug-shotlike pictures of his black opponent, Harvey Gantt, in a clear attempt to resurrect the ghost of Horton. Combined with ads suggesting that all blacks wanted handouts, it worked. Gantt was defeated.)[18]

Dukakis had hired more cops, put more drug offenders behind bars, and crime was down 13 percent in Massachusetts. The state had no death penalty, but first-degree murderers faced life sentences without parole. The furlough program begun by Sargent was similar to that of nearly every state—and of the federal system run by the Reagan-Bush administration. Dukakis was far from soft on crime; although a liberal in his politics, he had a pronounced streak of conservative personal attitudes, as do many Greek-Americans, especially when it comes to wrongdoers. The idea that he was soft on crime was as baldfaced a lie as any in the history of American politics. But thanks to the cynicism of political operatives, the power of television, the dread of the black male, and the willingness of the media to look away, one of the most damaging racial stereotypes in American political history was allowed to succeed. Worse, in how many minds does it linger yet?

The press simply reinforced the negative images, Deborah Tannen, linguist and Georgetown University professor, writes in the *Washington Post*. "Journalists reinforced Republican distortions by adapting the terms, like weekend passes and revolving doors. Even the name, Willie, was a Republican reframing of the man who had previously been William."[19]

The frame of the media story was not one of cynical political operatives playing on racial fear and hatred in a perverse way. Stories instead focused on the fact that Dukakis hadn't apologized to Horton's victims, on the merits of furlough programs, on how killers were let out of jail by incompetent prison officials. Some reporters did try to set the record straight, but their efforts were simply background noise against the incessant pounding of the visuals. Dukakis's attempt to refute the lies were doomed, because "every mention of the story occasioned its retelling and the refutations were abstract, whereas the fabricated story was dramatic and memorable," Tannen says.

Those "smoldering eyes" to which Roger Simon alluded hint at sexual threat, the subtext of the Willie Horton ads. American folk culture often has presented black males as hypersexual. The presentation of one particular group in a sexual light—especially an *exclusively* sexual one—is not in our culture a joyous appreciation of lust. Whites have long handed down the myth that blacks possess a great store of carnality. Perhaps the most infamous expression of this notion came from Earl Butz, a Nixon cabinet official, who said that all black men want is loose shoes and a tight vagina—in more colloquial language, of course. Black men are not infrequently referred to as simply sexual animals. There is no little irony in this, because historically in America it was the white men who were the sexual aggressors. The many light-skinned blacks among the slave population in the South were not the result of African field hands coupling with Scarlet O'Hara. The mythology turns history around completely—projecting white behavior onto blacks. But that is what cultural myths often do—create a favorable image of the people who have power.

Whites can have an edge of admiration in their voices when they speak of black sexuality. Even animals can be admired, from afar. But mainly the Myth of Black Carnality is a device to keep blacks in their place, a legacy of slavery, wherein blacks were thought to be a subhuman species only slightly above the beasts of the field. This strain runs strongly through the images of blacks that too many whites hold even today. Would right wingers have called a *white* law professor "a little bit nutty and a little bit slutty," as they did Anita Hill? Indeed, the emphasis on sexuality here seems especially odd, considering that Professor Hill came from a strict Baptist background and appeared to be rather more straitlaced than the average woman of her generation when it came to her reaction to sexual comments by those around her. Yet the right wing disseminated reports that her students found pubic hairs in papers she returned to them, suggested that she spent her time looking through law cases to find pornographic references, and that she was sexually aggressive with men. Although no one could seem further from the image of "black slut" than Anita Hill, the innuendos surfaced anyway. The images of black man as stud and black woman as whore are additional ways to disqualify blacks from the company of "civilized folks."

The specter of uncivilized, out-of-control blacks was a leitmotif of another story in which race was a key issue, the Los Angeles riots. The black-white issues dominated media coverage. When media scholar Erna Smith studied the television coverage of the riots for the Joan Shorenstein

Center at Harvard, she found the frame of the story was consistently one of black versus white tension, even though the approach seriously distorted the reality of the story. "A black-white frame continued to dominate the main coverage. Blacks and whites were centrally featured in over three-quarters of the stories about the Los Angeles riot. Almost all of the most violent rioters seen on TV, such as those assaulting people and burning cars and stores, were black. The American public thus saw the riot as a black uprising—despite the fact that the majority (52 percent of those arrested) were Latino." The networks depicted twice as many blacks as Latinos participating in the riots. But when the Rand Corporation analyzed the arrest records, one researcher concluded, "This wasn't a black riot so much as a minority riot."[20]

More than 50 percent of the victims of the riot appearing on television were white or Korean, so the picture of blacks as rioters and others as victims was widespread. Eighty-eight percent of ordinary residents interviewed, who became, as Smith says, a "Greek chorus of sorts reflecting on the violence of society as a whole" were either black or white: "By their presence or by their words, they invariably placed the events within the context of black-white relations."

It was almost as if television were covering the Watts riots of years before—perhaps because this was a context journalists understood. In any event, the absence of a Latino presence—whether as rioters or "ordinary people-commentators" or as expert or political interviewees—was striking. Smith suggests that the Latino angle "was not more fully explored in the coverage either because (1) it did not fit into the dominant racial story line and therefore journalists did not recognize its significance, or (2) the journalists lacked sufficient reporting strategies and news sources to find ways to report on it except in passing references."

Smith found that the most prominent theme of the television coverage was lawlessness. Social issues such as unemployment, education, poverty, and immigration were far less frequently presented than the issues of lawlessness. And the most violent, most dramatic scenes, like that of the beating of white truck driver Reginald Denny by blacks, were shown over and over again on television. Once again the demonic out-of-control black male was the main image presented by the media, even when that was far from the complete story.

If thoughtful blacks deplore the "face of evil" coverage, they also resent the call—often echoed in the media—that blacks must solve the crime problem before racism can be erased. "These days," writes Ellis Cose, "no serious thinker in the field of criminal justice would propose that the answer to violent crime among whites is for up-and-coming executives to make crime prevention their special mission."

> Nor would anyone propose, for instance, that until the murder rate among twentysomething whites was made to equal that of seventysomething whites, all young whites deserve to be ostracized and scorned. And certainly no reasonable person would argue than since organized crime has historically been run by Italian Americans . . . we should discriminate against all Italian Americans until Italian criminals become part of polite society. Not even bigots would argue that since the Mafia is dominated by Italians, crime is an Italian problem that can only be solved by Italians.[21]

There seems to be no sense, he says, in telling African Americans who have rejected violence that they, personally, are going to be treated like muggers until the black crime rate goes down. "Yet this is what many intellectuals, shopkeepers and self-styled philosophers are telling the black middle class," Cose writes. And this message is being magnified by the media. The Myth of Individualism, coupled with the Myth of the Demonic Black Man, distances whites from any sense of responsibility for the social problems that plague the American black underclass. As Cose writes,

> The problem of crime—and even of violent crime committed by black males—is much too large to be solved by blacks alone. It is all of America's problem. If only because in a mass media age, there is no way to insulate children from the messages the larger media sends. And as long as the dominant message sent to impressionable black boys is that they are expected to turn into savage criminals, nothing will stop substantial numbers of them from doing just that.[22]

13. WAS DAN QUAYLE RIGHT?

Or Did the Media Buy a Pig in a Poke?

@

Children having children. Drive-by shootings. School violence. Troubled teenagers. Bad math scores.

What causes all this? Not poverty. Not a downsizing economy. Not a flood of illegal substances. Not racism.

Family structure is the culprit. Ozzie and Harriet could fix all that ails us. Forget those expensive social programs. All Americans need to do to patch everything up is stay married.

That, in a nutshell, is the message that the right wing has been sounding. "Family values" was a message that failed miserably at the Republican convention in 1992, because American viewers saw a nasty, mean-spirited, exclusionary, smug, hectoring version of that message and rejected it out of hand. Opinion polls show that the big Republican victory in Congress in 1994 was no endorsement of a right-wing social agenda.

But the right has succeeded quite well with the media. More and more often media outlets not identified with the right are repeating the idea that family structure is the main problem in America, that structural flaws in the economy, race, and sex bias, or a changing international marketplace, do not cause our social ills, but the family does. All we need to do is make people shape up, and we will be back in Eden again.

It's a simplistic message, and one that unfortunately plays into a national mood that is punitive, pessimistic, and frightened. Genuine concern for family problems is transmuted into policies that punish and coerce.

Perhaps the high watermark of the success of the "family structure" message came in a 1993 *Atlantic* magazine cover piece that got major national coverage. It bore the sensational title DAN QUAYLE WAS RIGHT, and it leapt immediately into headlines of other newspapers and magazines.[1]

The article was written by Barbara Dafoe Whitehead, and she wrote not as an independent journalist attempting to find out what those in the behavioral sciences believed about such issues as intimacy, divorce, family breakup, and so on but as an advocate of the point of view that family structure is the cause of most social problems.

Now this is perfectly legitimate. I've done it myself. You marshal the facts and arguments you think most persuasive of your point of view, concentrate on those, and try to dissect or belittle the opposition's ammunition. But because of the *Atlantic's* reputation as a bastion of the "liberal establishment," and its tradition of running long, even-handed investigations rather than polemics, many readers may have assumed "Dan Quayle" was such an article.

It wasn't.

Whitehead is affiliated with the Institute for American Values, a group that states that the "two-parent family, based on a lasting, monogamous marriage," is the "most efficacious" one for child rearing and declares that social policy should increase the proportion of children who grow up with two married parents. Although the group says it supports careers for women, a recent newsletter said that quality day care might provide "no net gain at all" for children. And a board member, David Popenoe, writes that academics who support universal day care and believe that children can emerge as happy and productive adults from single-parent families were staging a "counterattack" that "threatened" a consensus on the troubles of the family.[2] Hardly conciliatory words. Although Barbara Whitehead is obviously sincere in her concern for the family, and did not reflect the antifeminist, anti–working woman tone of the far right, her emphasis on family structure—and her downplaying of the role of poverty in America's social ills—dovetails perfectly with the right's agenda.

Historian Stephanie Coontz writes in the *Washington Post*, "When the cover of last month's *Atlantic* magazine proclaimed Dan Quayle was right, one had the sense that the retrenchment was complete. Forget serious battles over restructuring work hours, school schedules, child care policies and urban investment to deal with new economic and family realities. It's smarter just to tell everybody to get married and be better parents." And she noted that "Democrats are happily jumping into bed with the idea that a commitment to two-parent families can solve all our social ills."[3]

The media climbed under the sheets with equal vigor.

HEY, MURPHY BROWN, DAN QUAYLE WAS RIGHT, headlined the *Seattle Times* (April 6, 1993). The *Dallas Morning News* editorialized about ADMITTING DAN QUAYLE WAS RIGHT (March 31, 1993). The *Atlanta Constitution* proclaimed, DAN QUAYLE HAS A POINT (March 28, 1993). William Raspberry of the *Washington Post* praised the article fulsomely, and the *Wall Street Journal*'s Paul Gigot called the article liberating.[4]

Of 184 stories that cited the article in the course of a year, according to NEXIS, most simply accepted its conclusions at face value. Only a handful—fewer than five—bothered to seek out social scientists to see whether they agreed with the article's conclusions about divorce, single mothers, stepfamilies, illegitimacy, and their effect on America's social ills. Had they made the effort, they would have found quite a different picture emerging than the one presented in *Atlantic*.

I've chosen to take a close look at this article because of the almost unprecedented acclaim and acceptance it got in the popular media and the nearly total lack of critical scrutiny of its contents. It's an excellent example of how the media simply accept much information as fact if that information seems to validate popular mythology. It ran in a highly respected publication and gave a skewed picture of what social scientists really believe, carrying an authority that made it far more important than most single articles.

The Whitehead article did not report in anything resembling an even-handed way on the lively controversy in the social sciences, in which "optimists" about new family forms marshal their set of statistics and the "pessimists" trot out theirs. The *Atlantic* gives the impression that by an overwhelming majority social scientists believe that the only functional family form is the two-parent family and that any other family form is pathological and harms both society and the individuals involved. That's simply not true.

Sociologist Paul Amato of the University of Nebraska, who is compiling studies on the topic says, "There's a divergence of opinion. Most social scientists take a middle position. There's a consensus that single parent-hood does, indeed, heighten risks for many children. At the same time, it's true that most kids aren't seriously affected."

How worried should we be about the rising numbers of single-parent families? That depends, Amato told the *Minneapolis Star Tribune*, on "whether you prefer to emphasize a glass that is half full or one that is increasingly empty."[5]

The *Atlantic* article goes for half empty with a vengeance. It offers up a mountain of research—some of it good, much of it flawed. It ignores large studies that do not support the idea that all families but the two-parent one are pathological and concentrates on smaller studies that *do* reflect that position. Whitehead compares apples and oranges and caricatures the positions of those who are more optimistic about single-parent families.

The piece uses statistics in ways that simple common sense reveals as meaningless. For example, Whitehead cites these facts to argue that children from two-parent families do better in school: "North Dakota . . . scores highest on the math proficiency test and second highest on the two-parent family scale. The District of Columbia is second lowest on the math test and lowest in the nation on the two-parent family scale."

The District of Columbia has a huge ghetto population, and it has been called the murder capital of the world; it has a severe drug problem and large pockets of poverty. North Dakota does not. Might these facts have at least a tiny effect on the overall math scores? To suggest that the only meaningful difference between North Dakota and the District of Columbia is the number of two-parent families defies any sort of logic. It is like saying that redheaded children in one family do better on math tests than brunettes in another, thus redheadedness is responsible for math ability. There is no causal relationship between the two sets of facts. (Where was the editor here? Why didn't anybody catch this one?)

This, by the way, is a favorite argument of the right wing, that the single-parent family is the cause of academic decline in America. But in the college classes we teach, my colleagues and I see bright students from happy two-parent families who can't write a coherent sentence. A recent study of writing abilities showed that a meager percentage of eighth graders could make a logical argument.[6] In fact, in the past few decades we have seen a major shift in the way young people get and process information—from a reading culture we've become a visual culture, saturated by television. If you want to find the family member to blame for declines in SAT scores, try the little guy with the big eyes who sits in the living room.

What might be called "voodoo statistics" threads through the Whitehead piece. She cites one study of the link between crime and one-parent families that makes this claim: "The relationship is so strong that controlling for family configuration erases the relationship between race and crime and between low income and crime."

In other words, race and poverty don't cause crime, but the single-parent family does. Quite a few single-parent families live in Wellesley, Massachusetts. Where are the drive-by shootings? How about kids of divorce living in Bel Air? They must be mugging people right and left. Residents of Chevy Chase, Maryland, must be living in terror of the breaking and entering done by the children of divorced lawyers and government officials. The juvenile justice system is just overrun by middle-class kids, right?

Study after study, the Children's Defense Fund (CDF) maintains, refutes the notion that it is family structure—not poverty—that causes children's problems. Whitehead does not cite them. CDF researcher Arloc Sherman told the *Boston Globe*, "As better measures of income and poverty are being developed, studies are finding more and more that children's problems can be explained by poverty. Typically, poverty is at least as important or more important than any other factor. We're universally finding that poverty is very important, and it would just be wrong to say that single-parenthood is the predominant factor."[7] A six-year University of Michigan study, released last year, found that "family income is a far more powerful correlator of a child's IQ at age five than maternal education, ethnicity and growing up in a two-parent family."[8] In other words, if you're affluent, your kids will probably score well on IQ tests, whether you are a single parent or married.

A 1986 study of violence, the CDF says, showed that child abuse by mothers is "a function of poverty, not of family structure. Low income mothers (whether single or married) were consistently 60 percent more likely than higher income mothers to inflict severe violence on their children."[9]

None of this material appears in the "definitive" article by Whitehead. The author also uses thin reeds on which to hang weighty conclusions with which most social scientists would disagree. She announces, "Fatherhood had declined as a norm for men." Her evidence: "In 1976, less than half as many fathers as in 1957 said that providing for children was a life goal."

In fact, as we all know, although fathers who desert or never claim their children are a major problem in the underclass, middle-class fathers tend to be *more* involved with their children than they were fifteen or twenty years ago. In a scientifically well-designed random sample study of three hundred dual-earner couples for the National Institutes of Mental Health, psychologist Rosalind Barnett found fathers much involved with their children. In fact, the problems of children had as much effect on the physical and emotional health of fathers as they did on that of mothers.[10]

To say that the importance of fatherhood has declined defies both scientific research and everyday experience. Books on fathering now fill the racks of bookstores—that certainly was not true when I was a child in the fifties. It is no longer unusual for men to refuse corporate transfers or to switch jobs to have more time with their children. When my husband used to take our kids with him to work from time to time in the 1970s, people thought it odd behavior. Now it is commonplace.

In fact, evidence from the same researchers whom Whitehead cites to make her "decline of fathering" statement (psychologists Joseph Veroff, Elizabeth Douvan, and Richard Kulka, authors of *The Inner American*) prove it to be untrue. When Veroff, Douvan, and Kulka compared fathers in the fifties to fathers in the late seventies, they found the fifties father more focused on work, less involved in the continuous daily interaction of the home. Fifties fathers, they said, were "less emotionally engaged than the mother" with their children and "missed some of the warmth and closeness of the relationship which the mother enjoyed." Fathers in the seventies were more concerned about their relationships with their children and sought to have closer emotional ties with their children. Even divorced fathers in the '70s were more involved with their children than married fathers in the fifties.[11]

Why did fathers give that answer about breadwinning that Whitehead cites? Perhaps they thought that merely breadwinning for their children was no longer a major life goal. The study shows that fathers wanted to be emotionally connected to their kids, not just to be seen as the guy who brings home the bacon. To select that one answer out of context as the basis for a sweeping statement about the decline of fatherhood is misleading.

In a section on divorce Whitehead paints it as unmitigated disaster. She relies largely on the research of psychologist Judith Wallerstein. Wallerstein reported that the children in her study did not "get over" divorce quickly; instead, ten years after the divorce a number of the young men and women appeared to be troubled—drifting, underachieving, and having difficulties forming relationships of their own.[12]

The massive media coverage that greeted this bad news from Wallerstein—including a major article in the *New York Times Magazine*—caused many divorced parents to panic. Psychologist Rosalind Barnett got calls from clients whose children were doing just fine, but their parents wondered if there was some awful damage they simply hadn't been able to detect. Barnett assured them that this was most likely not so.

Why? Because experts in the field have raised serious questions about Wallerstein's research. First of all, it was a small (131 subjects) nonrandom sample of adults in Marin County, California. And most important, the people in the study were drawn mainly from a population of admittedly troubled people who had gone to a divorce therapy clinic to seek help. As historian Stephanie Coontz points out, "Only a third of the sample was deemed to possess adequate psychological functioning prior to the divorce."[13]

If you look at troubled people to start out with, it's not surprising that you find a lot of trouble.

A nonrandom sample such as Wallerstein's can make it difficult to generalize from your work, because you don't know how typical the people you are studying are. A random sample guarantees that your selection has little or no bias. For example, you might pick a town for your study and then invite all the people in the town who fit your criteria to take part in the study. You accept the candidates as they come in, assign them random computer numbers, and select the sample on the basis of the numbers—which Wallerstein did not do. Coontz writes, "More representative samples of children from divorced and intact families have found less dramatic differences in school achievement and school functioning."[14]

Another flaw in the study was that it had no "control group" of children from intact families experiencing difficulties. Would children from intact families in which there was a high level of tension experience the same problems as those in which the parents divorced? There's solid evidence that they would.

One study that Whitehead did not discuss in detail was a study of twenty thousand children in Great Britain and the United States, published in the journal *Science*. It found that psychological problems among children of divorce—especially boys—were not the result of the divorce but arose in the period before the divorce, when the children were growing up in a sharply dysfunctional family. This was the first large-scale study to look at children's adjustment *before* rather than after their parents' separation and divorce. The study followed the children from before birth through the divorce proceedings.[15]

Clinical psychologist Robert Emery of the University of Virginia told the *Los Angeles Times* that the new study "does not mean that divorce isn't difficult. It does mean that we have to be careful about attributing behavioral difficulties in children to the event of a divorce rather than other aspects of family relations."

Emery says that his studies—based on a larger sample than the Wallerstein study—found a much higher level of coping than the California research. He says, "I tend to see children as having a hard time in the short run, but doing OK in the long run."[16]

As noted, the lack of a control group of children from nondivorced parents was a problem with the Wallerstein study. A ten-year-long study done in Sydney, Australia, that *did* have a control group of children in intact marriages found results opposite of the Wallerstein study's. Psychological tests showed roughly identical problems among the children whose parents were still married and those whose parents were divorced. The researchers, Rosemary Dunlop and Alisa Burns of Sydney's Macquerie University, challenged the notion that divorce causes permanent and long-term damage to children.

"I question whether attributing . . . difficulties to divorce is valid," Dunlop told the French wire service Agence France-Presse. "We conducted long interviews with all the children at three stages of their development during a ten-year period and certainly those whose parents had divorced were sad and unhappy about it, but there is no evidence that they were permanently harmed."

They found that children needed a strong and healthy relationship with at least one parent to thrive: "Those who lacked such a relationship were more depressed and had lower self esteem, whether or not their parents were divorced." The researchers said that if children emerge from the trauma of a divorce with a strong relationship with a parent, they are *better* off than if they remained in an intact family in constant upheaval.[17]

Professors Carol Franz and Daniel McClelland of Boston University also found that people who had "warm parenting" as children grew up to be adults able to have long and happy marriages and to develop close friendships. Warm parents held, kissed, and hugged their children often and gave them lots of physical affection and signs that they were liked as people. A "difficult childhood"—including divorce—was not associated with lower social accomplishments in adulthood if warm parenting was available. "I was surprised that the effects of a difficult childhood were not greater," Carol Franz said, because she does believe that childhood troubles can have an influence on later life. But she added, "On the other hand, I believe people are flexible and resilient. There are many things that pull us through."[18]

As for the well-being of children, the level of conflict—not whether the parents stay together—seems to be the important point. The international research team in the U.S.-British study, headed by sociologist Andrew J. Cherlin of Johns Hopkins, concluded that parents should *not* stay together for the sake of the children if severe problems exist in the family. Children in intact marriages that have long-standing intense conflict are worse off than children whose parents divorce.

Cherlin said that in marriages where parents feel merely bored or unfulfilled, divorce might not be better, but when there is intense conflict, "many children would be better if their parents split up."[19]

So the idea that divorce per se will be devastating for children over a long period is simply not supported by the research. Too many other factors—the level of conflict, the availability of a warm parent, the economic situation of that parent—all have an effect on a child's well-being.

But the studies showing the majority of children of divorce facing risks but emerging intact in the long run got barely a notice in the American media. Data base research shows that they were generally ignored, whereas the Wallerstein study and Whitehead's article were the subjects of many articles that assumed the bad news was *all* the news.

NO SURPRISE HERE—DIVORCE IS BAD FOR KIDS, headlined the *Orlando Sentinel.* The writer states as fact that "contrary to myth, most children of divorce do not bounce back," almost the exact words used by Whitehead. A columnist for the *Seattle Times* reports the *Atlantic's* repetition of the Wallerstein research as if no other studies existed. A *Fortune* magazine article gives the larger, better-designed British study one paragraph and devotes the bulk of a long article to studies that report a dismal picture of divorce.[20]

As for the *Atlantic* piece, researchers who disagree with the Wallerstein thesis get scant mention; readers of the article would barely know that most researchers in the field do not agree with the Wallerstein hypothesis. Once again the media's penchant for bad news—and its attachment to the Norman Rockwell myths of the family—does not serve the reader well.

Whitehead acknowledges that divorce must be available "to remove children from families where they are in danger." She adds, "Yet only a minority of divorces grow out of pathological situations; much more common are divorces in families unscarred by physical assault."

But how many of us would want to limit divorce only to cases of physical abuse? Psychological abuse can be even worse. What about the woman whose spouse constantly humiliates and belittles her, calls her a whore and a slut, and says she is no good? How about the man whose wife is a chronic alcoholic, drinks herself blind, and makes the home a battle zone? Or how about the two people who are so incompatible that they argue all the time and make each other—and their children—miserable? What happens when such people stay together "for the sake of the children," as Whitehead suggests they should?

One man I know whose parents lived for years in a state of barely veiled contempt remembers that he thought it was his fault; trapped in the middle, he often prayed for his parents to divorce so he could escape the tension of the house that made it worse than a jail.

Psychologist Jean Baker Miller says that in her practice she is surprised at the number of women who are furious at mothers who never had the nerve to defy or leave controlling or bullying fathers. They are angrier at their mothers than at their fathers—because they felt their mother's passivity never gave them permission to stand up for themselves in their own relationships.[21]

A man I know was married to an alcoholic woman who simply seemed to have no emotional life at all. He describes her as utterly flat, unable to give or receive affection. Divorced, he is trying to give his children that warm loving parent they need. Would staying in that dead marriage have been better for the children? Or would it have given them the idea that no one has the power to change his or her life, no matter how empty and painful it is?

Frank Mott, a researcher at Ohio State University, warns against putting too much blame for social problems on family structure and says that single parenthood "can be used as a proxy for all kinds of environmental factors" that can have an effect on children's well-being. And sociologist Frank Furstenberg of the University of Pennsylvania points out that "marital disruption is not a random event. It occurs disproportionately to already disadvantaged individuals and poorly functioning families."[22]

Whitehead writes with some chagrin that Americans seem to have no appetite for restigmatizing divorce. Maybe because Americans have good sense. They remember the hypocrisy of the days when one parent would invent an affair in order to break up a marriage when the only legal ground was adultery. They remember the days when battered women just stayed and took it, because "nice people" didn't get divorced.

Whitehead writes approvingly of the suggestion that a two-tier divorce law be introduced, making divorce easy for childless couples and difficult for couples with children. In fact, such legislative initiatives are already underway. *U.S. News and World Report* says that two-tier divorce is "one of a battery of weapons being unveiled by pro-family groups in their legal and rhetorical war against divorce. . . . Armed with statistics that link divorce to a trail of economic, psychological and social ills, these crusaders are launching their attacks over the airwaves, in mass mailings, in state legislatures from Washington to Oklahoma and even before the U.S. Supreme Court."[23]

One conservative think tank, the Free Congress Foundation, wants court-appointed lawyers to argue against divorce in every marriage involving children. The late Christopher Lasch, author of *The Culture of Narcissism*, argued for simply forbidding any divorce where minor children are involved.[24]

The specter of a court-appointed attorney arguing that a woman must stay with a husband who demeaned and belittled her—or that a man has to stay shackled to a wife who keeps telling him what a failure and a rotten husband he is—makes my blood run cold. I remember the reality beneath the facade of the happy marriages of the fifties; I remember too many friends whose parents simmered in silent misery, and I know what it did to their children.

But if a media drumbeat, using social science research to "prove" that divorce is terrible for children, grows louder and louder, we could find ourselves suddenly facing legislation that is rigid, punitive, and unbending. Children—in whose name such legislation is enacted—may wind up being the losers in the long run.

Whitehead also writes of divorced parents, "Both mothers and fathers commonly respond to family breakup by investing more heavily in themselves and their own personal and romantic lives."

Not so, according to a major study of adult women by psychologists Rosalind Barnett and Grace Baruch, funded by the National Science Foundation. The study found that for more than any other group of women, the health and well-being of divorced women was closely tied to their children's well-being. If their children were doing well, the women had high self-esteem. When the children had problems, the mothers' well-being dipped as well. The picture that emerged from their study was just the opposite of the one Whitehead posits, of women overinvesting in their personal lives. In fact, divorced women with children tended to obsess about their kids. The study also showed that although the first year after a divorce is difficult for women, after that period a majority of women said they were happier and had more self-respect than they had in their marriage.[25]

Because research shows that maternal well-being has a strong influence on children's emotional health, it can be argued that a happy, self-reliant single mother is better for children than a depressed, unhappy married one. And studies also show that women are more likely to have a drinking problem before a divorce and that divorce reduces the risk of alcohol dependence among women who are problem drinkers.[26]

In her eagerness to make the two-parent family the source of all that is good, and the single-parent family the bane of society, Whitehead overreaches and makes statements that defy reason. For example, she says that families inculcate in their children the traits of independence and initiative. She then goes on to claim: "The erosion of the two-parent family undermines the capacity of families to impart this knowledge; children of long-term welfare dependent single parents are far more likely than others to be dependent themselves."

This exercise in logic is like saying that

Elephants are large.
Some large elephants have mange.
All elephants are mangy.

Few people would argue that parents on welfare may have a hard time passing on traits of independence to their children. But most single parents are *not* on welfare. Will my friend the high school English teacher (who is divorced) have a problem passing on independence to her kids? Or the woman who drives a cab, manages an office, drives a police cruiser, runs a computer, sells real estate? In fact, I could argue that the divorced working woman can teach independence to her children better than the fifties' stay-at-home mother who was supported by a husband. In any event, this is an example of the faulty reasoning that pervades the piece.

Another example of questionable logic comes when Whitehead notes that "several" divorced fathers of children in the Wallerstein study could have contributed to the children's college education but did not.

Whitehead says this "withdrawal of support for college suggests that other customary forms of parental help giving may decline as a result of family breakup" and also that "children from disrupted families may be less likely to help their aging parents."[27]

And then again they could be *more* likely to help if they see a parent as being in trouble. Or just as likely. There is no evidence whatsoever to make a judgment either way. But Whitehead once again doesn't let lack of evidence stand in the way of making a judgment.

The *Atlantic* piece suffers from a tendency to present worst-case scenarios as typical. Whitehead describes "family disruption" for a child this way: separation, divorce, life with a parent and a live-in lover, the remarriage of one or both parents, life in one stepparent family combined with visits to another stepparent family, the breakup of one or both stepparent families.

Now, no one in his or her right mind thinks that two divorces and a string of live-in lovers are good for children. Sometimes it happens, but multiple divorces are not the typical pattern for people who divorce.

Whitehead also lumps all single mothers by choice into the category of selfish hedonists; the only quote from such a woman in the entire piece comes from a letter in the *New York Times*, from a woman who says she knows her decision to have a child is selfish, but she wants to please herself. Indeed, selfish women exist, as do selfish men. But the single professional women I know who have had children without choosing to marry have agonized about the decision and have made sure to provide the emotional and financial support a child would need. A perfect solution? Perhaps not, but this is not a perfect world. Would the children of such women be better off if they had not been born at all? Probably, few would agree.

Single mothers are perhaps the greatest bête noir of the Whitehead article. She blames single motherhood for just about everything that is wrong with the Republic. Of course, few people are enthusiastic about poor, unwed teenagers having children—babies having babies—but again, by heaping too much baggage on family structure, she makes a complex picture seem simple. She quotes extensively from the work of researcher Sara S. McLanahan, an expert on single parents. Readers of the *Atlantic* would have to assume that McLanahan supports Whitehead's conclusions. The reverse is true. McLanahan has publicly decried the effort to, as she says, "demonize single mothers."

She doesn't think Dan Quayle is right; she thinks he's dead wrong to use single parents for political gain and said so in a *New York Times* op-ed piece. She also took a slap at Republican William Bennett and Clinton's Health and Human Services secretary, Donna Shalala, for the same reason.

Although acknowledging that the children of single mothers can have problems, especially if they are poor, McLanahan specifically rejects Whitehead's notions about single parenthood as the cause of most social ills. She says, "The evidence . . . does not show that family disruption is the principal cause of high school failure, poverty, and delinquency. While 19 percent of all children drop out of high school, the dropout rate for children in two-parent families is 13 percent. So the dropout rates would be unacceptably high, even if there were no single-parent families."

McLanahan does not push marriage as a solution to the problem of poor single mothers. She approves of Clinton's plan to give welfare mothers extensive training and good day care so they can get off of welfare in a reasonable time.[28]

The conclusion of the *Atlantic* piece calls, laudably, for more effort to make fathers support their children but supports the dubious idea of making divorce harder. It also suggests changing media messages about illegitimacy and divorce. No mention is made of improved child care—even though studies show that the greatest source of stress for working women is lack of available child care. It does not mention restructuring the corporate culture so that both men and women can respond to family life. Most important, there is no mention of how to deal with the abysmal rise in child poverty among the underclass, except to say people ought to be married. But in a long-term University of Michigan study that has followed five thousand families since 1968, only one-seventh of the children who lapsed into long-term poverty were involved in family breakup. The changing job market accounted for more than half of such cases. Forty percent of America's poor children today live in two-parent homes. In other words, for poor people, being married may increase the odds of escaping poverty somewhat but not much.[29] The United States has the highest child poverty rates of any industrialized nation. Stephanie Coontz says, "A cross-national comparison of poverty rates within different households reveals that different family structures play at best a small part in the higher absolute poverty of American children."[30]

The politics of the family is an unexamined theme throughout the *Atlantic* piece. The "communitarian" movement, of which Whitehead is a part, is more reasonable and milder than the right wing, whose approach to social ills is punitive. But in their zeal to enlist the right in what they see as a new consensus on the family, communitarians are too willing to give away the store. Unfortunately, they often seem naïve about the realities of power politics in the United States. What begins as a seemingly reasonable policy debate often ends up as the harshest sort of punitive legislation directed at the poor, with the right wing leading the charge. When the *Atlantic* says that DAN QUAYLE WAS RIGHT, it validates a right-wing agenda that is punitive and mean spirited. If we begin to identify "family structure" as the main contributor to crime, for example, the result will be more stringent welfare cutoffs, more poor women marrying—and staying with—abusive men. The middle class will not stop getting divorced, nor will it support legislation that will prevent divorce. We couldn't turn the clock back to 1955 even if we wanted to.

Certainly, we ought to encourage people, especially those with children, not to divorce capriciously. But instead of making divorce harder, we ought to support policies that make unwanted pregnancies a rarity. European countries have nowhere near our rate of unwed teenage motherhood, because they vigorously promote and encourage birth control and do not have the terror of adolescent sexuality that permeates the debate in this country. We seem as terrified of adolescents' having sex as we do of their having babies. In fact, the fifties had proportionately more pregnant teenagers than we do today. In those days they got married. And then divorced. The explosion of divorces in my generation was partly the result of the fact that "nice girls" had to get married to have sex. The number of miserable marriages created by that scenario is hard to calculate.

Let us also look at the argument that the two-parent family creates social stability and produces adults who can have stable relationships. The baby boomers were the product of such intact two-parent families. Yet as a generation, when they hit adolescence, the sons and daughters of Ozzie and Harriet and Ward and June Cleaver raised all kinds of hell. They used more drugs than any generation in American history and created a "counterculture" that rejected the materialistic values of their parents and a sexual revolution that had those same parents tearing their hair out. Their refusal to sign up obediently for a war they believed misguided nearly tore the country apart. As adults now they have more divorces and more drug use than any other generation in history.

Does this mean we ought to declare the two-parent family dysfunctional? Of course not. Family structure alone simply doesn't explain what happens in people's lives. Demographics better explains the turmoil of the boomers. Never in our history have so many people been young at the same time, and it threw our entire society into a swivet—at exactly the same moment as the complicated politics of Vietnam were coming to a head.

Just as in the Vietnam era, many complex issues affect the way young people behave today. Drugs and crime among the young are a huge problem. Certainly, with an unemployment rate that equals that of the Great Depression in many urban ghettos, with good jobs at good wages declining, it is not simply "family structure" that makes kids turn to peddling drugs. It may, alas, be an economic decision prodded by market forces.

In any event, poverty and other social ills in America are complex problems and can be solved only with equally complex solutions and the will of the entire population. We desperately need a high-level national dialogue and a deep understanding of the problems that face us. But the media's embrace of the simplistic conclusions offered up by DAN QUAYLE WAS RIGHT does not bode well for the sophistication of the national debate.

14. COMFORTING THE COMFORTABLE

Does News Coverage of the Poor Bolster the Status Quo?

⊚

Sometimes when I am in the middle of a piece on a social issue involving people in trouble—the homeless, or addicted mothers, or the mentally ill, or ghetto teens—a voice that I do not recognize sounds loudly in my head. It says, *These people should not need help.*

The voice is quite authoritative, and my first inclination when I hear it is to believe. I manage to resist that impulse, however, because I know that what the voice says is not true. Of course, people need help; at some point in our lives we all do. But whose voice is that, and why do I hear it, and why does it seem so . . . *right?*

I am hearing, I believe, the voice of cultural myth. And I am not alone. I think many other editors and reporters hear it too. I suspect it is why the coverage of those in need in our society often seems so—passionless. Oh, the stories do get done. We do read about the homeless and babies with acquired immune deficiency syndrome (AIDS) and the ghetto teens wrecked by crack, but I often sense a lack of zeal for such stories. "Garbage can stories" is how one editor described them. They are a duty rather than a passionate concern. Certainly, such stories lack the cliffhanging drama of a Haiti crisis, or the splashy gossip of an S&L scandal, or the thrilling blood-in-the-water scent of a Whitewater or an O. J. Simpson saga. But they are issues that could rip apart the very fabric of the Republic. Why aren't we more turned on by these stories? Why did we, for example, so easily believe Ronald Reagan when he said, oh yes, there's a safety net, it will catch those in need?

One of the biggest unreported stories of the era was the thousands—perhaps millions—of people who fell through the net into the abyss below as we turned away. I know, because my brother was one of them. He had been suffering for years from a severe mental illness—a combination of manic depressive and schizophrenic symptoms—and had been in and out of mental hospitals for fifteen years. In the early eighties he was in a halfway house in Baltimore, doing better than he had in years.

But then the order came down from the administration—cut the disability rolls. My brother's doctors argued that to say that my brother was not disabled—and to cut the funds that allowed him to live a decent life at the halfway house—was both absurd and cruel. There he had continued to improve; his alternative was to shuffle aimlessly through the days on the wards of a state mental hospital. (My parents had already exhausted their lifetime's savings paying for his treatment; they had both died a few years earlier. I chipped in as much money as I could, but I had two young children to help support.)

The doctors' pleas fell on the deaf ears of a bureaucracy. I was able to help my brother get a job that would pay him enough to stay at the house, but he was nowhere near ready for that step, and he was fired. He was sent back to the state hospital where he hanged himself from the shower rod with his belt. He was thirty-eight years old, a kind and loving person. I believe he was murdered—by a society that simply did not care.

There were many like him, but the silence was deafening. If a man walks into a post office and opens fire, killing perhaps a half-dozen people, it's a cover story. But the deaths and human misery caused by the dismantling of the disability rolls—an assault on the most vulnerable among us—happened nearly unnoticed by the media. Homelessness was a story for a while, but now the major issue we cover seems to be hostility toward the homeless. When my husband, *Boston Globe* columnist Alan Lupo, writes about mental patients being pushed out onto the street, hospital closings that displace the handicapped or other issues that affect the dispossessed, he gets little reaction these days. In newsrooms all across the country interest in the powerless and the wretched is waning. The profession whose job it is to "afflict the comfortable and comfort the afflicted" seems little concerned with the latter. Why? I think it was that voice, its volume amplified by a generation of media managers for whom the Depression is something only in the history books, combined with the ideology of the Reagan years that turned it into a mantra: PEOPLE SHOULD NOT NEED HELP.

I began to wonder where that voice came from. It didn't sound like Frank Sinatra, but the lyrics could have been from that anthem to American individualism, "My Way." Americans love that song. Our heroes tend to be "My Way" kind of guys, loners. They are guys in buckskin hacking their way through the wilderness with only squirrels to chat with, or lean-jawed cowpokes driving cattle across miles of range. They are poor boys from foreign shores who got rich by dint of hard work, true grit, and the occasional murderous deed.

We are so fond of the man who does it solo that it is surprising that we didn't edit all but one marine out of the Iwo Jima statue. John Wayne could have put that flag up all by himself.

Sociologist Robert Bellah, who with a team of colleagues examined the American condition in *Habits of the Heart*, writes, "A deep and continuing theme in American literature is the hero who must leave society . . . to find moral good in the wilderness, at sea, or on the margins of settled society."[1] The peculiarly American mythic hero, the cowboy, may do good deeds, but he always rides out of town alone. ("Who was that masked man?") It's as if the myth says that you can be a good person, worthy of admiration and love, only if you resist joining the group.

This is also true of that other quintessentially American hero, the detective, from Sam Spade to Serpico. The detective is a loner, set against the corruption of the group, of society as a whole. Bellah says, "Both the cowboy and the hard-boiled detective tell us something important about American individualism. To serve society, one must be able to stand alone, not needing others, not depending on their judgment."[2]

Alexis de Tocqueville noted that individualism was perhaps the most salient American characteristic. Freed of the Old World's rigid class structures, the New World struggled for its own identity. Independence was its watchword, as in Declaration of *Independence*. Thomas Jefferson worried about both big government and mercantilism—which we now call big business. He thought either might destroy the hardy society of yeoman farmers he believed most conducive to nurturing the republican form of government.

The idea that the individual is good and the group is bad, and that the best of us are those who stand alone, is deeply rooted in American history and thought. The self becomes almost a sacred object in our tradition. As Bellah writes, "The ideal self in its absolute freedom is completely unencumbered." John Locke decreed that the individual came before society and that society was only the voluntary contract of those individuals.

It was Ben Franklin, the archetypal poor boy who made good, who popularized the idea of individuals succeeding on nothing more than their own sweat and merit.

"Plough deep, while sluggards sleep, and you shall have corn to sell and to keep. . . . Early to bed, early to rise, makes a man healthy, wealthy and wise," Poor Richard advises. (Of course, it is never mentioned that behind these lone men ploughing, rising, toiling, and such was usually a woman who raised his kids, darned his socks, and cooked his meals.) But Walt Whitman sang of a different sort of self—the unencumbered one that revels in nature, pleasure, and sensuality. If the yuppies of the 1980s with their fast-track jobs and their Mercedes-Benzes were in the tradition of Franklin, the hippies of the 1960s, smoking pot, making love-not-war, and going back to nature would have been at home on the commune with Whitman. Whether they are earthy and expressive or uptight and money grubbing, "me generations" are not new in America.[3]

By the early nineteenth century, however, Jefferson's fear of a mercantilism that could wreck the Republic nearly became a reality. It was a gilded age ruled by captains of industry who stood high above law, morality, and tradition. Bellah quotes historian James Oliver Robertson: "In the predatory capitalists [that] the age dubbed robber barons, some of the worst fears of republican moralists seemed confirmed; that by releasing untrammeled pursuit of wealth without regards to the pursuit of social justice, industrial capitalism was destroying that fabric of a democratic society, threatening social chaos by pitting class against class."[4]

The first half of the twentieth century saw the struggle to find order in the world that industrialization had created. America with its legacy of individualism would not choose the way of collective authoritarianism; instead, tediously, often violently, Americans carved a balance between private gain and common good. The Depression was the great leveler; it left few untouched, and even those who had plowed deep found that banks had failed and with them all their hopes of corn to sell. With Franklin Roosevelt came government as the bulwark against economic injustice. A whole series of programs designed to protect the lone—and now *weak*—individual against the cold winds of fate was set in place: social security, workers' compensation, federally insured bank deposits—all things we now take for granted. A generation grew up believing that government was the champion of the little guy, protector of the common good, the guardian against the mercantilism gone wild that Jefferson so feared.

But in the years since the New Deal, government has been transformed from the White Knight to the Dark Prince. Newt Gingrich and his antigovernment cadre are perhaps the logical result of years of both government failures and conservative attacks on Washington. The miscalculations of the raid on the Branch Davidian compound at Waco, Texas, led to a mass suicide there and to the terror bombing of the federal building in Oklahoma City by someone apparently convinced that the federal government was some sort of monstrous regime.

That is, of course, a paranoid fantasy, but it has roots in the last thirty years of our history. First was Vietnam, when our government lied about body counts and lights at the end of the tunnel and ersatz naval battles in the Gulf of Tonkin—and the nation nearly tore itself in half. Then came Watergate with the government once again lying, this time about sinister break-ins and missing pieces of tape and documents in burn bags. After that Jimmy Carter campaigned against Washington and all that it stood for. Ronald Reagan of course went much further. His whole political philosophy was based on dismantling government. The Reagan years saw a wholesale federal withdrawal from the programs that created the *real* safety net—like the one that gave my brother safety and dignity. At the same time we got an economic buccaneering unrivaled since the 1920s; the hogs were feeding at the trough, as Reagan's budget director David Stockman put it.

Americans turned to the private sector for salvation; the master's in business administration became the hot new degree, the lure of easy millions drawing young people to Wall Street; American heroes were businesspeople like Lee Iaccoca and Donald Trump. But beneath the rush for private fulfillment was anxiety; Tocqueville could have been writing about the 1980s when he observed, "I have seen the freest and best educated of men in circumstances the happiest to be found in the world; yet it seemed to me that a cloud habitually hung on their brows and they seemed seri-

ous and even sad in their pleasures." The reason? "They never stop thinking of the good things they have not got."[5]

By the nineties it all seemed to be falling apart. The stock market had
crashed, major league Wall Street insiders and junk bond kings had been
sent to jail, and the buccaneers had looted the Department of Housing
and Urban Development and the unregulated s&l institutions to the tune
of a $5,000 bailout bill for every single American. And finally, we could no
longer ignore the homeless in huge numbers who roamed the streets, the
drug problem of plague proportions, and the likelihood that our bridges
would fall down on our heads. Perhaps the final bit of glitter fell from the
glitzy Reagan era when Republican strategist Kevin Phillips argued angrily
that Reagan had presided over the mass transfer of wealth from the middle and lower classes to the very rich. Bill Clinton campaigned for change,
but Americans were not sure what sort of change they wanted; first they
voted for Bill and then for Newt and his gang.

The rush for private gain had left Americans no happier and most of
them poorer. By 1990 the gap between rich and poor was the widest it had
been since 1947. We had a sense of the fabric of society unraveling. But no
one knew how to put it together again. If private gain was hollow, at least
it was secure. The world beyond the self seemed to offer more threat than
promise. And although Americans still wanted to help others, they were
unsure of how to do it, with government out of favor. And they were getting angrier at the poor and the homeless, whose problems seemed to be
worse than ever.

Connected to the American myth of the individual is another myth
that has deep roots in our soil: the moral turpitude of the poor. Your average city editor does not understand, as he moves the story on welfare cuts
into the must-run file for page one, that he is tapping into an old and per-
sistent American tradition. Cotton Mather would have approved. Deep in
the bedrock of Calvinist tradition is the belief that wealth is a sign from
God of virtue. Poverty, on the other hand, is the curse of the Almighty on
evildoers.

When the American sense of endless spaces, endless possibilities, that
still hovers about us like a cloud gets mixed with the Calvinist myth, the
poor are doubly stigmatized. Poor folks obviously didn't rustle up a saddle
and a six-gun to take Horace Greeley's advice to "Go West young man,"
because they are still living in a tenement in Bed-Stuy. That displays a very
un-American lack of initiative, we believe. Not long ago former Reagan
administration official Linda Chavez was on c-span, where she compared

Puerto Ricans unfavorably to Cubans. She blamed the problems of Puerto Ricans on the "fact" that they were able to get welfare in New York and thus didn't strive for greater possibilities. A more logical explanation for the difference in achievement would probably be that the greatest influx of Cubans was middle-class people thrown out of their homeland when Castro came to power. They would have done well wherever they went, whereas most Puerto Ricans who come to the mainland are not middle class and are struggling to make their way up. And in fact when Fidel opened his jails and sent a boatload of lower-class Cubans to the United States, they did not end up owning car dealerships in Miami. The *Marielitos* for the most part did not turn out to be model citizens, and welfare had nothing to do with it.

Add to the myth of individualism the nostalgic glow through which we look at our own history, and there's more bad news for the disadvantaged. A good many of us may be descended from thieves and knaves who got out of the old country a step ahead of the law, but we tend to think of our ancestors as only somewhat less saintly than Francis of Assisi. We really believe that the typical immigrant family arrived on the shores dirt poor, knelt down to kiss the ground, and spent the next twenty years hugging their children, working hard and never cheating, singing the praises of their new land in quaint but broken English, and wound up owning department stores.

So who were the scores of drunks who beat their children, the whores who sold their scabrous bodies for what they could get, the unemployed who died in the streets of dysentery, the thugs who killed people for a few pennies, the hit men for the mob, and those legions who sank out of sight in the swamps of mental illness, despair, drugs, or prison? Nobody in *our* families. Our sanitized picture of the past makes us believe that the poor of today are much worse than the heroic poor of yesterday (who also tended to be *our* color), so we blame them for not living up to our ill-informed fantasies.

The fact is that most poor people are honest, most don't steal or cheat, and welfare fraud, although it certainly exists, is not one of the real budget busters of the day. If you really want to blame somebody, try Granny, who is living longer and making Medicare budgets skyrocket. But people feel a little uncomfortable about smacking Granny in the mouth; it feels much better to rail about the poor folks.

The media often are not far ahead of the rest of us when it comes to knee-jerk reactions about the poor. A good example of this is a page one story in the *Boston Herald*, its headline screaming, WELFARE FRAUD COSTS MASS. MILLIONS![6] And indeed, the story quotes the special investigations unit for the state's Department of Administration and Finance, which had prosecuted cases in which welfare recipients allegedly received some $12 million in illegal benefits.

The story then quotes—at great length—the mayor of a local city who is notorious for getting Brownie points with his constituents by welfare bashing. He relates stories of flagrant abuse—like the welfare mother who loaded up a diaper bag with $5,000 in cash to bail out her jailed boyfriend. True? Maybe. The mayor continues on his soapbox, declaiming, "We have a very loose welfare system in Massachusetts, that's well on its way to bankrupting the Commonwealth!"

By this time readers are ready to leap out of their chairs and go plug any welfare mother they can find. But they would have to read *very* carefully—and to the very end of the story—to learn some other facts:

- Massachusetts at the time had a $1 billion dollar budget for its various welfare programs; the $12 million in fraud represented exactly *1.3 percent* of that total. This deserves a megaheadline? One point three percent?
- The federal government had recently given Massachusetts an award for having one of the *lowest* welfare error rates in the United States.
- Massachusetts did *not* have the wholesale fraud found in other more densely populated areas such as New York City or Newark. And food stamp trafficking—which figured in a large subhead on the story—was not that much of a problem in the state, according to the regional U.S. Inspector General's Office.

In other words, a routine report of an investigation that in fact revealed no sensational findings became a major three-page story with a screaming page one head. White-collar crime in fact poses a much bigger threat to the region's economy than welfare fraud does, but rarely do outraged stories on that issue appear on page one. White-collar crime tends to cause a giant yawn among the readers of newspapers and the consumers of TV news.

The media fall neatly into the snare of the dual mythologies that the poor are evil and that all individuals can transcend their circumstances, no matter how difficult they may be. These lead journalists to ignore the iron straitjacket that poverty places on most people locked in its grip through low self-esteem, few skills, cultural patterns, racism, bad health, and neglect and to focus on individual effort as the only real way up. This disregards the obvious fact that most people locked in the underclass do *not* get out, and to neglect societal solutions while calling for heroic individual effort is to doom most of those in poverty to staying there.

A good example of this is a *Time* story on low achievement among black youth that shows how "objective" reporters give their readers what they think is the real truth—in this case, that blacks have to solve their own problems.

There's almost a formula for writing such a story. First, mention, as the *Time* writer did, the other side of the argument, then knock it down with the back of your hand: "For years, the failure of black students to succeed in white-run schools was attributed in part to institutional racism."[7]

That also takes care of the required racism reference. Now comes the *but*: "But some black educators are reassessing the blame."

Then select the quotes that back up your point of view, in this case from a black teacher who says you can't blame racism when you're talking about a 95 percent black student body. (That quote, of course, ignores the fact that African Americans get messages all their lives from society as a whole, not just from the classroom. It's also short, so it probably does a disservice to the teacher's position on a complex issue.) Then you add another quote, in this case from a black mother who says, "We dropped the ball. Our generation failed to pass on the value of an education."

The thrust of the story—although it mentions in passing such social issues as crack, the flight of the black middle class to the suburbs, and the pressures on the black family—is that this is a problem the black community must remedy on its own. The story says, "As more black administrators reach positions of power in the public school system, the anti-achievement ethic presents a special challenge to them as educators."

And, of course, this is true. It's what the story *doesn't* say that makes it truly one for the '90s. Nowhere is there even a *suggestion* that the broader white society has any obligation to assist in the problem of black underachievement. It does not recognize that as well-paid industrial jobs dry up and low-paying service jobs replace them, an anti-achievement ethic may sadly be a realistic one for many black youngsters. Why dream about what you can't have? The story does not even mention cutbacks in federal funding that have devastated urban schools. That idea used to get tossed into such stories, at least as a token recognition that this is a societal problem. No more. The story presents the dilemma to the white reader in a comfortable way—saying, in effect, that racism is irrelevant and that the problem is an interesting anthropological issue that blacks must deal with and for which whites have no involvement or responsibility. It's a sort of journalism that fits well with a nation in recession, angry about demands made by blacks and other nonwhite minority groups, and fearful about its own economic future.

A major *Newsweek* piece took a different tack, calling for the return of sin—a concept tailor-made to let the affluent breathe easier. If teenage pregnancy, alcoholism, and ghetto crime can be attributed to the misdeeds of sinful wretches, not only can we feel morally superior, but we don't have to do anything about them. A cover piece titled HEY, I'M TERRIFIC! had good words for sin and sneered at the concept of low self-esteem as the root of many social ills.[8] Unfortunately, the piece not only skewered the pop psychology feel-good snake oil peddled on talk shows and in best-selling books but lumped them together with real efforts to deal with problems that often affect the poor.

The *Newsweek* story scoffed at Jesse Jackson's mantra I AM SOMEBODY as "minimalist," used a quote from a critic—"pettifoggery"—to dismiss a study linking teenage pregnancy and low self-esteem, and held up to subtle ridicule a California State task force that suggested that self-esteem could be a powerful vaccine against social ills. But perhaps the most striking paragraph is one that questions the right of the state to even try to enhance self-esteem among its children and adults: "It is one thing for the state to discourage welfare dependency, for instance, by requiring recipients to get jobs. It is a big—and thus far unexamined—step for the state to do the same thing by tinkering directly with citizen's psyches."

This is neoyuppie thought in its essence and a sentence that could hardly have been written by anybody who has been poor—or near it. The idea that programs to help enhance the self-image of poor teenage mothers or drug addicts or ghetto kids are more intrusive than force-marching welfare mothers off to dead-end jobs is an interesting view of civil liberties. The workfare programs most states come up with usually offer no day care, no training, and no future. And because most welfare recipients are women with young children, these are the people who are affected. But the story dovetails perfectly with a growing attitude among the middle class that efforts to help those in poverty are misguided, whereas draconian measures are perfectly okay.

Today black conservatives who oppose affirmative action or other special government programs become instant media stars: they get newspaper

columns, magazine cover stories, guest appearances on television shows—
they become household words. Is this because they are so brilliant, so
witty, so urbane? Indeed, some of them are, but it would be naïve to suggest that this is the main reason they are so eagerly taken up by the white
media. In a time of dwindling resources these people are indeed reassuring
to affluent whites with their message that blacks must reject the "victim
mentality" fastened upon them by liberals who rant too much about
racism. They argue that blacks must be more like whites and climb the ladder by their own hard work and success, clean up their own neighborhoods, save their own children from despair, and not rely on white
America for help.

This argument is immediate. It fits in perfectly with the myth of
American individualism. For example, the presentation by the Bush
administration of Clarence Thomas as the perfect self-made man who
pulled himself up by his bootstraps is one way to frame that story—which
much of the media simply bought at face value. But Thomas, born dirt
poor in Georgia, might have wound up in a low-level job like so many
other poor black American men—if it had not been for the intervention
of his grandfather who raised and encouraged him and a group of caring
nuns in a Catholic boarding school who nourished his talent and self-
esteem. An "affirmative action" scholarship to college helped him on the
trail that led to Yale Law School and the federal bench.

But Thomas seems not to realize how fortunate he was, compared to
other members of his family. At a meeting of black conservatives in San
Francisco, Thomas cited his sister Emma Martin as an example of everything that is wrong with liberals and the welfare system: "She gets mad
when the mailman is late with her welfare check, that's how dependent she
is. What's worse is that her kids feel entitled to the check too. They have
no motivation for doing better or getting out of that situation."

Thanks to her brother, Emma Martin became a public example of the
evils of welfare. I heard that story and believed it, until I learned it was
not exactly the truth. It was a scenario perfectly suited to neoconservative white attitudes: the self-made black man and the dependent, lazy
welfare woman.

But if the self-made man frame wasn't right, neither was the schematic
of the lazy welfare woman. Jack E. White writes in *Time*:

> Thomas' version of his sister's plight was seriously distorted. In fact, she was
> not getting welfare checks when he singled her out, but working double

shifts at a nursing home for slightly more than $2 an hour. Over the years she has been forced from time to time to accept public assistance—once after she walked out of a troubled marriage and most recently to care for an ailing aunt. But even while on welfare, Martin continued to work part time, picking crab meat at a factory near her home. She eventually weaned herself from the dole entirely by taking two part-time jobs. When asked about how she feels about her brother's attempt to portray her as a welfare queen, Martin replies with a shrug. She comes across as a far too gentle and forgiving person to hold a grudge.[9]

Even when a poor person has had an admirable life, he or she can get blamed for simply being poor. Clarence Thomas gave tacit support to the mythology of the "good" poor (himself) and the "bad" poor—his sister—by his public comments. I suspect that most people will remember the headline stories in which he disparaged his sister—and not the follow-up stories that showed her to be an admirable and hard-working woman. That doesn't fit our picture of the poor.

But the go-it-alone argument made by black conservatives has some practical value in tough times. It could be argued that blacks have to feel empowered to succeed on their own, because there's not going to be much money or much help coming from white America anyway. However, the conservative black attitude not only lets the rest of society off the hook for ills that affect all of us, but if other blacks internalize this attitude, it might serve only to replace the so-called victim mentality with a deep sense of guilt. If blacks believe they have to do it alone, and then they fail or face obstacles, they could bear a huge burden of personal guilt and failure.

Black conservatives often seem to hold a special contempt for the dispossessed of their race. Harvard psychiatrist Alvin Poussaint explains this phenomenon by saying that some blacks can unconsciously accept all the negative images that whites project on their race, then scurry to distance themselves from such images.[10] *Time*'s Jack White writes,

Denying that luck, family support and other factors, including affirmative action, maybe have helped them . . . [they] con themselves into believing they have made it solely because they are exceptionally gifted individuals who are innately superior to less fortunate members of their race. They often exhibit disdain for poor blacks, especially those who are on welfare or have given birth to a child out of wedlock. They believe that if more blacks were "like me"—intelligent instead of stupid, hard-working instead of lazy, educated instead of ignorant, morally upright instead of slatternly—racial progress would be assured.[11]

(Clarence Thomas and his sister seem a perfect example of this syndrome.)

Admittedly, it's a tricky business, confronting the evils of racism or sexism without internalizing the notion that because of them you are powerless, recognizing the obstacles but at the same time believing that your own talents and resiliency can get you through. Traps are at both extremes: paralyzing depression on the one hand, arrogance and lack of compassion on the other. Scholar and essayist Cornell West writes that if liberals have sometimes leaned too heavily on the idea that racism is the sole cause of the predicament of the black poor, black conservatives peddle the idea that "moral breakdown" created by the welfare state has caused all the problems. (And the mainstream media chant this idea like a mantra.) Although black conservatives are stars in the white media, their arguments, West notes, are much less convincing to other blacks, who see that creating more jobs for poor people is not in the economic game plan of the downsizing private sector, and moral rectitude won't change that.[12] And how many blacks are going to be Supreme Court justices or Ivy League academics?

New York University professor Derrick Bell says,

> For white people who both deny racism and see a heavy dose of the Horatio Alger myth as the answer to blacks' problems, how sweet it must be when a black person stands in a public place and condemns as slothful and unambitious those blacks who are not making it. Whites eagerly embrace black conservatives' homilies to self help, however grossly unrealistic such messages are in an economy where millions, white as well as black, are unemployed, and more important, in one where racial discrimination in the workplace is as vicious (if less obvious) than it was when employers posted signs "no negras need apply."[13]

Black superstars play much the same role as Superwomen—giving out the dual messages that people do not need help and that only the superhuman individual can actually succeed. By showcasing conservative blacks who are high achievers—and at the same time presenting the image of most blacks as muggers, carjackers, or rapists, the media give the message that deserving black people will do just fine on their own and the others aren't worth helping anyway because of their moral degradation.

At the same time competitive pressures in the news business—and the social class of reporters—often lead to articles catering to white suburbanites, much desired by advertisers. Joseph Lelyveld, now executive editor of the *New York Times*, says, "There's a dirty little secret in all newspapers. The advertisers we cater to are not thrilled when you sign up a bunch of readers in some poverty area for home delivery." He thinks such attitudes may have seeped into the newsroom, especially in the eighties: "There was a time when this paper could have been accused of abandoning certain kinds of readers. We had bumpy times in which it seems to me there was a kind of weariness with poverty issues, city issues. We didn't seem particularly committed to coverage of minorities, especially in our own area. We used to give more coverage to Zimbabwe than the Bronx."[14]

Alan Lupo, my husband, not long ago was standing in a corridor at Boston City Hospital, his finger gripped by a wanly smiling two-year-old in the failure-to-thrive clinic. It was a place, he noted, that few reporters ever visit. He reflected on the time when he started in the business, when many reporters came from poor and working-class backgrounds, and such scenes as a poor two-year-old were not alien to their eyes. Now, he notes, few journalists understand such things in their gut, and fewer still think of such issues as worthy of their time. Editors and reporters come from the middle and upper classes and are more intrigued by issues that affect those groups. The urban crisis was a major story when he was a young reporter, because the cities were burning. The smell of smoke is gone, and he wonders if it won't take a relighting of the fires to send reporters back to the mean streets in any numbers or to get editors "turned on" by such issues.[15]

The poor are indeed very different than you and I. They are evil, and they deserve what they get. It's a belief that's as American as apple pie, and the media unknowingly keep it firmly anchored in place.

15. THE WAR ON WELFARE

How the Media Scapegoat
Poor Women

My journalism career has stretched from the War on Poverty to the war on welfare. I watch the latter with the sense of having stepped through the looking glass. "Curiouser and curiouser," I want to say.

In my thirty years of observing the media I have rarely seen such whole-sale scapegoating of a portion of the population as what's being done to welfare mothers. One story I covered as a young reporter was the saga of one Joseph McD. Mitchell, who gained the national spotlight in the early sixties as city manager of Newburgh, New York, with his own personal war on welfare. Claiming that loafers and chiselers were taking taxpayers' money, he made the halt, the lame, and the blind line up outside his office to be inspected. The national media descended and found that all those "able-bodied loafers" did not in fact exist. Mitchell went on to ignominy and later surfaced working for the White Citizens Council, a racist national organization.

Today Joe Mitchell would be in the mainstream. The picture of the poor—welfare mothers in particular—that has emerged from the media as I write has been one that is so savage, so lacking in compassion, that it takes my breath away. I first started covering people on welfare when I did my master's thesis on the struggles of drug addicts in Harlem. I met a lot of welfare mothers—some of them were feisty, funny, tough, loving. Some were depressed, slothful, had given up. They were, I found, just like the rest of us. Only poorer.

The news media of course have sporadically gone on welfare-bashing sprees. It is almost a rite in the city room, like Groundhog Day stories. The "welfare queen" story was traditionally dear to the hearts of city editors across the land; it made their green eyeshades quiver. They were—and still are—elated when a reporter stumbles on some sharp cookie who lives in a five-story walk-up on rent control but has three color TVs, a VCR, and a Cuisinart, because she's on the welfare rolls as Selma Blatz, Jane Washington, *and* Mary Smith, and her dog Herman and cat Fonzie are listed as her kids. Bannered across page one, the story will raise the choler of average Americans as they gulp down their morning coffee. We find something infuriating about somebody who is poor and has the audacity to cheat the system. Insider trading, on the other hand, has an aura of glamour. So what if white-collar crooks make off with millions, and the welfare queen bilks us out of a couple of thou? *She's* the one we'd like to throttle. This always puzzles me; the $22 billion a year it costs for Aid to Families with Dependent Children and food stamps is *$128 billion less* than the S&L bailout is costing.[1] The money we are spending to clean up the mess caused by white-collar crooks could pay for welfare in all fifty states for seven years. Where is the national outrage? Nonexistent. But we hate welfare mothers.

Radio talk show hosts speak of "welfare sluts" and "whores," and one columnist for the *Boston Herald* calls welfare mothers "the Gimmie Girls." The venom that flows from one right-wing radio show to another is stunning. And the mainstream press has fallen into line. *Time* magazine, in a 1994 cover piece titled THE WAR ON WELFARE MOTHERS, cheerfully lobs another shell against the very same victims. The story opens with a police raid on a Chicago apartment, where nineteen children lived in wretched squalor. Some were malnourished, some had been abused, and all were living in incredible stench and filth. This was a story, by the way, that had gotten national play—with film—on all the networks. Of course, most mothers on welfare don't live this way, but this image became one of the horror stories that would linger in the minds of people already quite willing to believe that this scene was typical.

Time then said in its own editorial voice: "The Chicago story was a classic example of how a big-hearted, deep-pocketed government ends up subsidizing disaster. In all, the six mothers who lived in filth were collecting $5,496 a month in welfare payments. The system will keep on paying such women as long as they keep having children."[2]

Note the frame set up around the story: bad mothers and indulgent big government. But what if the welfare story were presented instead with this anecdote: A woman with a little boy with a learning disorder walks her child to school every day through dangerous and drug-infested streets. He's doing so well in a special program that he's getting *A*s in school. Food stamps, welfare, a lunch program, and a loving mother are giving him a chance at life.

Or what about the woman married to an alcoholic—who ran off and hasn't been seen in years—who finished her college degree, and is now a productive citizen, supporting her three kids?

I know both women. Are they not examples of a big-hearted, deep-pocketed government subsidizing *success*, not disaster? Women like the ones in the Chicago apartment certainly exist, but they are much less typical than the two women I know. But these two don't fit the media's appetite for conflict, disaster, and—these days—moral outrage.

Then there was the welfare mother in Boston who scalded her little boy's arms with boiling oil and Drano; a terrible act, and she deserved to be punished. But her story was a media sensation, making headlines in the newspaper and lead stories on the evening news. Once again, she was seen as the embodiment of "welfare" simply because of the massive coverage. *Boston Globe* columnist Jeff Jacoby wrote, "Might life on welfare have something to so with what kind of a mother Clarabel Ventura turned out to be?" He answers his own question in the affirmative, noting that the Massachusetts Department of Social Services reports that the cities and towns with the worst cases of child abuse and neglect were the towns that had the most welfare recipients.[3]

Interesting logic—what might be called the guilt-by-association statistical method. If I live in New York city, home to many murderers, does it mean I am inclined to murder? The cities and towns with the worst abuse cases also tend to be the poorest areas, where families are under the greatest stress. It stands to reason such areas have more problems than, say, Wellesley.

But in recent years Boston has seen a rash of stories about white middle-class men who have abused children, and experts say that such abuse is not simply a problem of the poor. Could someone then say that life in the middle class has something to do with what kind of fathers these abusers turned out to be? There has been a rash of scandalous stories of pedophilia by Catholic priests. Might we say that the priesthood causes child abuse?

Also, child abuse in more affluent families tends not to get reported, even when it is severe. No social workers are poking around middle-class homes. One of my students was buried alive by her mother when she was three as a punishment. She was put in a box with a tube that led up to the air. Her family was not on welfare.

When you read through media stories, again and again you see extensive coverage of worst case scenarios of misbehavior by welfare mothers, whereas you see the responsible behavior and day-to-day struggles of most welfare mothers only in occasional features. Headlines present welfare as a crisis: UNWED MOTHER PROBLEM AFFECTS US ALL (*Phoenix Gazette*, July 26, 1994), WELFARE MAMA: NO MORE SUBSIDIES FOR WANTONNESS (*San Diego Union*, November 23, 1993), THE VICIOUS CYCLE (*Time*, June 20, 1994), and on and on.

The media have swallowed without a second look the argument of the right that welfare is a moral issue, that welfare created a "culture of dependency." Mortimer Zuckerman writes in *U.S. News and World Report*, "When Americans look at welfare, they see a program that has created a culture of dependency, especially in the inner city. The welfare culture must be shattered. The obligation to work must replace the right to income maintenance as the organizing principle of welfare policy."[4]

We are in the land of the Red Queen. The *obligation* to work? Women on welfare can't find jobs that will pay them enough to afford food and child care for their children. Unemployment in many urban ghettos has reached rates not seen since the Great Depression. As I write, my state, Massachusetts, has passed one of the most restrictive welfare plans in the nation, including a cutoff for women receiving Aid to Families Dependent Children (AFDC) if they don't have a job after two years. Meanwhile, a number of my students, finishing four years of education at an elite university, are complaining that *they* can't find jobs. My daughter's friends, in their early twenties and college educated, are working at jobs that high school graduates would have turned their noses up at in my day. Laid-off white middle managers are unemployed or fighting for low-paying jobs that they once would have scorned. All around us the world economy is reshaping itself like some giant kaleidoscope, and forces beyond the power of *nations* to control—much less ghetto teenagers—swirl about us and we take no heed. Critic Jeremy Rifkin writes of "The End of Work," and Harvard economist Juliet Schor suggests that we may have to go to the four-day work week so substantial numbers of Americans can at least have jobs.

It's as if we are standing on a beach with a huge tidal wave looming above us, and we are arguing about how much sand we will be allowed to put in our pails. One great victory of the right has been to shift the debate about welfare from social policy to personal morality.

Why are we singling out welfare mothers for censure when the entire nation is facing an economic shift that may rival the move to industry from farming in its effect on our lives? How did we get to this state of affairs? Through a combination of history, myth, a well-financed campaign of the right, and the willingness of the media to simply accept the framework of the discussion in moral—rather than economic and political—terms. The entire debate seems to be taking place with an almost religious fervor. And welfare mothers are especially vulnerable targets. First, they have no political power, so no politician has anything to fear from whipping up anger against them. Second, the idea that they are "lazy whores" is another riff on the Calvinist idea that the poor are evil. If you are female, being poor *and* sexual is a double stigma. And third, the ground under welfare mothers has shifted dramatically. Not long ago all good women were supposed to be at home, caring for their children. So if welfare mothers were poor, that was bad, but at least they were home with their children, which was good. They got at least a modicum of social approval. But now, with most nonpoor women in the workforce, often struggling to juggle home and family, support for the idea of subsidizing poor women to stay home with their children has eroded.

The welfare system as we know it had many problems, but it did keep mothers and children together, not in workhouses or orphanages or on the streets. The welfare system evolved partly because of growing public horror at the appalling conditions children endured in the industrial age. Irish and German girls in the nineteenth century often went into domestic work at the age of eleven or twelve; other immigrants went into sweatshops where children as young as six labored from sunup to sunset under dreadful conditions. Children made up 23 percent of factory workers in southern mills. At the turn of the century 20 percent of children were in orphanages because their parents had cast them out, couldn't afford them, or abused them. More children were poor than were well fed.[5]

Fathers had no legal obligation to support their children, and a great many children lived in poverty. The problem of today's latchkey children seems mild by comparison to that era. City streets were filled with thousands of urchins, many of them homeless, who stole or lived by their wits. "Not only were they the products of inhuman flaws in the American economic order, but they also symbolized the collapse of the family," one historian notes.[6] Dealers sold children candy laced with liquor, and young boys often used the pennies they earned to pop into a local saloon for a drink. Street gangs stole and fought, and police could do little to stop them. In big cities some neighborhoods were so violent that police feared even to enter them. Some fights between rival gangs went on for days.

On the whole the welfare system gave temporary respite to women while they got their lives together. Indeed, it did help to create a cadre of families that spent generations on welfare, but what would have happened to such people in prewelfare days? They, and their children, might simply have been the ones who sank into disease, alcoholism, or the penal system, never to surface. Is that a better fate than life on the dole?

In any event, the idea that the answer to issues of poverty is for all welfare mothers to find jobs that make them self-supporting is one both liberals and conservatives could applaud. But is it feasible?

"Welfare mothers are going to have to work!" say the politicians. "Yes indeed!" say the media. But as scholars and long-time researchers on poverty Frances Fox Piven and Richard Cloward write, "There is no economically and politically practical way to replace welfare with work at a time when the labor market is saturated with people looking for jobs."[7]

Unemployment has been steadily climbing—from 4.5 percent in 1959 to 7.2 percent in 1990, for example. Thirty million workers are in "contingent work"—part-time or temporary work with no benefits. Eighteen percent of full-time workers, or 14.4 million, have incomes that put them below the poverty line. As companies downsize, millions of people are losing their jobs; our manufacturing base is almost gone. Hundreds of thousands of ex-steelworkers, ex-car makers, ex-machinists are out of work. "Low employment riddles the economy," Piven and Cloward say. One in seven full-time jobs in the United States pays $11,500 a year, roughly $2,000 below the poverty line for a family of four. "There is no reason to think that AFDC mothers can become self-sufficient when growing millions of currently employed workers cannot."[8]

And American workers are competing with low-wage workers in Mexico, Taiwan, Singapore, and a growing number of underdeveloped countries. British industrialist James Goldsmith wonders about the effect of free global trade between developed high-wage economies and low-wage undeveloped ones. He believes the balance will tip so far toward capital and away from labor that some developed countries will face long-term chaos and destabilization.[9]

Workfare is such a buzzword these days that we are rushing to march welfare mothers out to any job available. Massachusetts's welfare plan decrees that if women can't find such jobs, they must do volunteer work. Governor William Weld suggested they could lift crates in food pantries. Is a woman really better off lifting crates than taking care of her young children? Perhaps—if she had good quality day care and some skills training so that she was not simply exploited as cheap labor. And someone has to supervise and schedule all these "volunteers." That could wind up costing even more than the system we have.

Workfare could exacerbate the political problems of the dependent poor. "What are displaced heavy-industry workers to think of the free education and job training benefits that welfare mothers would receive from liberal workfare benefits?" asks social historian Michael Katz in his book *The Undeserving Poor.*[10] Workfare could heighten tensions between the working poor and women on welfare. Worse, it could flood the labor market with low-wage workers and depress the wages of those already working at or near the minimum wage. In any event, workfare is a complex issue with many ramifications for the economy. It is not just a quick fix for politicians eager to appease constituents made furious at welfare mothers by the media's attacks—and by an economy that seems to be creating few jobs even as it improves.

On top of that, studies show that the inability to find adequate child care is a major source of stress for employed families. There is nowhere near enough good child care for people who are already working. Are we ready to spend the billions of our tax dollars it will take to care for the children of poor women? The electorate wants to slash taxes and cut funding for schools its own children attend. Will we really fund day care for welfare mothers? (Maybe we could just pay off the street gangs, and let the drug runners take care of the kids between deals. Let the kids count the drug money—it will improve their math skills.) Ten years down the road, will we be dealing with more homelessness, more drug addicts, more street crime—because of welfare "reforms"?

The uncomfortable truth is that we may be entering a period in the postindustrial economy in which we simply have more people than jobs. As Katz asks, "Is the American deification of work a constructive response to post-industrial society? Is work really available for all who want it? . . . The American economy increasingly will have more workers than it needs, even to raise productivity and remain competitive in world markets."[11]

This is a question few politicians want to tackle: the globalizing of the marketplace, the incredible efficiency of new technologies like robotics, and the streamlining of corporations, which have already put millions of Americans out of work. The need for unskilled labor that made it possible for many immigrants to work their way out of poverty has vanished. How then do we deal with this growing problem of surplus people? Plenty of middle managers who are quite "moral," who are dedicated to the work ethic, are out on the street. They didn't take drugs, have children out of wedlock, or loaf on street corners. But they are unemployed. Most welfare mothers are poor women who are trying to eke out a half-decent life for themselves and their children in a society in which they have become economic outsiders, unable to find work even when they desperately want it. Their children are one of the few joys in their lives. Yes, some are hopeless junkies or slothful and ignorant people, just like their more affluent sisters, but most are not. To stigmatize them for a world economy they are powerless to control is the cruelest of acts.

But cruelty is never far from poverty.

We would like to think that the welfare system comes only out of our kind hearts. Historically, this doesn't seem to be the case. Piven and Cloward argue that, historically, poor relief has been an instrument of social control of the workforce, mainly to prevent disorders. Until about the sixteenth century, almsgiving was a private matter in Europe and considered good for the soul; the poor were considered unfortunate but not morally evil. Organized relief systems began in the midst of the disturbances that broke out during the long transition from feudalism to capitalism. Food riots erupted in Lyons, France, in 1529 with looting and theft, and a few years later mobs of starving peasants overran the town. A relief system was set up, a list of the needy was determined by a house-to-house survey, and town fathers "did not take so much pride in their charity as in their aspiration to make Lyons a 'vision of peace.'"[12]

In England the threat of social disorder created by the disruption of a changing marketplace was the incentive that replaced parish almsgiving with a nationwide system of relief. Those who did not have a document authorizing begging—but begged anyway—were whipped publicly until the blood ran. As factories replaced the old agricultural economy, the English textile industry used pauper children from poorhouses, some only five years old, as factory workers. British poorhouses were so awful that they served as a brake on worker revolt. Piven and Cloward say the threat of the poorhouse terrorized the impoverished masses: "The workhouse was designed to spur people to contrive ways of supporting themselves by their own industry, to offer themselves to any employer at any terms. It did this by making pariahs of those who could not support themselves. They served as an object lesson, a means of celebrating the virtues of work by the terrible lesson of their agony."

The expansion in the welfare rolls in the 1960s, Piven and Cloward argue, was a result of fear of unrest following the civil rights movement, combined with greater sophistication and organization in the cities that helped poor people understand and actually get benefits for which they were eligible. Without it, they argue, the victims of agricultural modernization and unemployment in the cities would have remained perilously close to starvation—as they did in the late 1940s and the 1950s.

But the ahistorical bent of the news media allows ideas that no social scientist takes seriously to be transmuted into "fact" in the news columns. Take, for example, the idea that the welfare programs of the sixties created the black underclass. This underclass has been a feature of the American landscape since the great migration to the cities began. American cities have had a turbulent history. Race riots like those in Detroit during World War II may not be remembered by many Americans today, but they were deadly and violent. In 1959 the national poverty rate among African Americans was three times that of whites.[13] (And if current members of the underclass seem more firmly fastened to the bottom of American society than ever, it is not their morality that is the problem but the massive changes in the American economy.) My father was the head of the parole board in the District of Columbia in the 1950s, and he could have told you a great deal about the black underclass. In fact, most of the crime in the District was committed by the poor black graduates of the area's reform schools, the National Training School in particular. There was no dearth of poverty, crime, or illegitimacy in the world my father encountered every day. JFK once complained to an aide about the issue of black mothers having children out of wedlock, and this was in the early sixties. The notion that a black underclass was created by welfare and appeared magically in the seventies is historical nonsense.

But the right-wing version of history is often reported as fact, as in this *Boston Globe* story on growing illegitimacy among whites: "The surge in this fatherless tier of poor white Americans, analysts said, vividly resembles the development of the black underclass 30 years ago, beginning with the rampant growth in young, single-parent households and eventually descending toward a culture of poverty and violence largely supported by government programs."[14]

There in a nutshell is the right-wing take on history—with which few historians would agree. As a journalist, I was covering poverty before there *was* a war on poverty, and discussions about the black underclass and what we ought to do about it were common. It is a mystery to me how I was covering it before it existed, but there I was.

The "culture of poverty" notion, by the way, was developed by sociologist Oscar Lewis, who studied poor families in the sixties, *before* the large-scale social programs of the War on Poverty. In fact, Lewis found that one of the few cultures in which he did not find the hopelessness and despair of the "culture of poverty" was in Cuba, where massive government programs of education and health care and jobs had changed the nature of the life of the peasants. (Today, of course, with no money from the Soviet Union, and an oppressive dictatorship, Cuba is sliding toward chaos and despair.) In any event, the idea that government programs are at the root of the growth of the underclass is utter nonsense. Lewis also noted that many poor people don't think about the future much because it is too uncertain and that women often don't marry the fathers of their children because the men have no jobs and are irresponsible.[15] This is as true in the slums of Rio or Hong Kong or Kenya as it is in Bed-Stuy.

Welfare is often cited in the media as the *cause* of the growth in single-parent families. This argument does not withstand serious scrutiny. A major study on hunger, poverty, and nutrition, released by Tufts University in 1994, says, "The political wisdom about the relation between welfare, single parent families and poverty is out of step with scientific knowledge. That key political leaders could be contemplating a major shift in federal policy—based on incorrect information—is alarming." The increase of single-parent families, the study points out, has been mainly among those who are not poor.[16]

The trend in welfare benefits between 1960 and 1990 does not match the trend in single motherhood, writes researcher Sara McLanahan. Welfare and single motherhood both increased dramatically during the 1960s and early 1970s. After 1974, however, welfare benefits declined—the value of cash assistance plus food stamps fell 26 percent between 1972 and 1992—but single motherhood continued to rise.[17]

Increases in welfare certainly don't explain why women with college educations increasingly experience divorce and give birth out of wedlock. (McLanahan's ten-year study, by the way, showed that welfare women have lower birthrates than women in the general population.)

Even though all other Western countries have much more generous payments for single mothers than the United States does, the prevalence of single motherhood is much lower elsewhere. If "welfare" motivated births, certainly this would not be the case. In the United States women on welfare in states that offer the highest benefits have the lowest birthrates.[18]

Of course, it is impossible to talk about the war on welfare without getting into the thorny area of sex. The image of the black woman as whore is a subtext of the war on welfare. What enrages many people is the idea that tax dollars are subsidizing black sexuality. In some stories the notion is right out there—like the *San Diego Union* headline about "wantonness." But often it is just below the surface. Although young white women from good families are commonly sexually active, they are rarely viewed as "sluts" and "whores." But if an educated, upper-middle-class black woman like Anita Hill can't escape the sexual innuendo, how much harder is it for poor black women?

But what really is causing illegitimacy?

A combination of factors. A major issue is the decline of men's earning power relative to women's. After World War II and through the sixties a strong economy and the availability of good jobs for men made marriage for women much more attractive than remaining single. But the disappearance of factory jobs in the 1970s hit men and women at the lowest rung of the ladder especially hard. Low-skilled men who can't play the breadwinner role often shy away from marriage out of fear of failure. "Welfare may have played a part in making single motherhood more attractive than marriage for women with the least skills and education," says McLanahan, "but only because low-skilled men were having such a hard time and received no help from the government."[19]

The notion that cutting off welfare would be a miracle cure for the upward spiral of out-of-wedlock births is being repeated again and again in the media—but there is no evidence for it. In fact, sixty-seven prominent academics, among them scholars most familiar with the issues of welfare and poverty, signed a joint statement in 1994 saying just that. They charged that statements by conservative guru Charles Murray, who claims that illegitimate births would be halved by cutting welfare, was a speculation that was "irresponsible science," according to their spokesman, University of Michigan economist Sheldon Danziger.[20] In fact, ending welfare would create a "profound implosion" in America's inner cities and could spark chaos that could spill over the whole nation, says Elijah Anderson, a sociologist who has worked for years in inner-city neighborhoods.[21]

Academics say that conservatives and the news media distort their work by making claims about welfare for which they have no evidence. For example, Anderson takes columnist Charles Krauthammer to task for misuse of his work.

"Krauthammer cites my research in one inner city neighborhood," Anderson says; his research shows that welfare does indeed provide economic support for women with illegitimate babies. "This is one consideration in the sexual game that leads to illegitimacy." But, he says, when Krauthammer argues that if you take away welfare, you take away the motivation for having illegitimate babies, the logic is flawed and simplistic: "It ignores all the other considerations bearing down on adolescents."

Because young men can't get jobs that make them self-reliant—the traditional mark of manhood—Anderson writes, "They emphasize sexual prowess as a sign of manhood with babies as evidence. A sexual game emerges as girls are lured by the (usually older) boys' promises of love and marriage." The girls submit and end up seduced and abandoned.

What is happening, Anderson days, is that the alienation and despair in the inner city create a nihilism "born of a lack of hope and an ability to form a positive view of the future. So, many of the young men I got to know don't get married because they don't feel they can 'play house.' What they mean is they can't play the roles of men in families in the way they would like."

Anderson points out that drugs have moved into this vacuum as one of the only sources of revenue available. Welfare in fact is one of the few *legal* revenue sources around. Ending welfare would "destroy an important source of capital in the community. If welfare suddenly ceased to exist, many people would . . . be driven to desperate measures. Cities would become almost unlivable. Illegitimacy rates would rise, not diminish," as kin networks crumbled and chaos became more intense. "When a sense of the future exists, we will see more responsible behavior, sexual and otherwise," Anderson says. Without it people collapse into the pleasures of the moment, and to hell with thinking about the future.

Today Anderson sees a world much more desperate than the one he knew hanging out on street corners in South Bend as a kid in the fifties. His father, with only a fourth-grade education, worked in the Studebaker plant. "What my dad did was set his kids up for middle-class lives," he says. The white owner of a typewriter store gave Anderson a job that would lead him to college. Both influences that shaped his life—his father's stable industrial job and his own job at the small store—have disappeared from today's urban landscape.

While men's declining economic power, the growing independence of women, and changing social mores have combined to create the rise of illegitimacy, ironically another factor has been America's stubborn puritanism. The concerted effort to see sexuality as a moral issue has helped illegitimate births in the United States to soar, whereas European societies, which have seen roughly the same changes in sexual mores, do not have the problem. "Only in the United states is abstinence the aim of public policy," writes Katz.[22] America's high adolescent birthrates reflect both government policy and cultural attitudes. The American adolescent pregnancy rate soars above those of Western Europe, twice as high as in many countries. In Europe aggressive promotion of contraception and easy access to abortion have kept the rates low. In the United States, although we have decried the rise in illegitimacy, we have at the same time made it nearly inevitable by actively blocking the availability of contraception in high schools and making pregnant teenagers get permission from judges or go out of state to get an abortion.

At the same time, the ever-present media bombard kids with messages about the desirability of sex and sell everything from toothpaste to cars with sexual messages. However, condom ads are not permitted on television. Our moralistic attitude about sexuality on the one hand—combined with relentless promotion of sexuality on the other—combine to make the United States the Western world's leader in children having children.

Columnist George Will speaks of reviving the "stigma" against illegitimacy and says the decline of the stigma since the 1960s is surely related to the increased number out-of-wedlock births.[23] But we can no more bring back the culture of the 1950s than we can bring back the whalebone corset or "Banned in Boston." The past wasn't all that pure, anyway. As I noted earlier, in pre–Revolutionary War Concord, Massachusetts, fully one-third of births were out of wedlock. And there is no record of any of these women collecting food stamps.

The new moralism of the right, picked up by the media, suggests that marriage will solve all our social ills. To talk of marriage without examining the structural, social, and economic factors involved is absurd, but that is the framework in which the media debate about welfare mothers has been cast.

Do we really want to encourage the pregnant fifteen-year-old to marry her sixteen-year-old drug dealer boyfriend so the toddler can get caught in the crossfire? To push marriage as some sort of miracle cure-all for the ills of the underclass makes no sense. Yet the media ring with the claim that marriage would lift women out of poverty. That might be true for white women, who often *become* poor when their marriages break up, but most black women already were poor before they divorced or had an illegitimate child. With men's wages plummeting, with black male unemployment stratospheric, the idea that marriage would automatically lift women out of poverty seems a will-o'-the-wisp.

The Moynihan report on the black family, published in the sixties, is often cited by conservatives who claim that single-parent families are the cause of all our woes. But, Katz notes, the Moynihan report was in part based on an assumption that today seems out of date: "Ours is a society which presumes male leadership in private and public affairs," wrote Daniel Patrick Moynihan, now a senator from New York. "A subculture, such as that of the Negro American, in which this is not the pattern is placed at a distinct advantage."[24]

Society no longer assumes male leadership in public and private, and few would argue that a professional woman could not create a decent life for herself and her children.

Critics also noted that Moynihan ignored the issue of class and would have found similar patterns among poor whites, had he looked. Moynihan's vision of the "pathology" of the female-headed family at the time may have been partly a vision of the white upper class. Scientists like Lee Rainwater and Carol Stack, who actually looked at female-headed black families, found a stable kinship of mothers, grandmothers, aunts, and other female relatives among black women who headed families and who raised boys who were able to contract successful marriages.[25]

This was very much what I learned as I talked with families (many on welfare) wrestling with drug addiction in Harlem thirty years ago. When the addict simply couldn't cope, grandmothers, aunts, or other kin simply stepped in to help with children. But three decades later in inner-city Boston my experience was quite different. The drug epidemic had become far worse, and kin networks seemed to be extremely tenuous. In one apartment the grandmother, the mother, and the daughter were all addicted to crack. There seemed far more despair and hopelessness, more guns, much more lethal violence among young men. Anyone who thinks a few wedding rings will change this is living in Fantasyland.

In any event, what massive coverage of the Moynihan report virtually ignored was his argument that unemployment was a major issue. He said that the "wage structure" needed to be addressed, that housing desegregation kept blacks isolated from the wider society, that narcotics addiction stunted chances for advancement. Only a program of national action could begin to undo the problems, Moynihan declared, rightly.

Unfortunately, both his poor choice of words, which seemed to be an attack on a black family struggling to survive, and the fury of African Americans who saw only the attack and not the call for action, made the Moynihan report a storm center of controversy. "The ironic outcome of Moynihan's report, therefore, was to sweep the black family off the agenda of policy research and to hasten the culture of poverty's amputation from its liberal origins," writes Katz. "The idea of such a culture, however, did not disappear. Instead, it became a conservative rationalization for cutting welfare."[26]

Senator Moynihan himself wants nothing to do with drastic welfare reforms: "You let loose a lot of forces when you say 'end welfare as we know it,' which is why I never said any such thing. We may look back and say, 'What in the name of God have we done?'"[27]

The war on welfare makes good political sound bites, snappy headlines, and fast food for hungry ideologues. But it is a war that threatens to give us a Pyrrhic victory. Poorly designed programs, created in haste and anger, that could have serious economic effects in a rapidly changing society could promote social discord and intensify racial and class divisions. As Pogo says, we could find that we have met the enemy—and he is *us*.

16. THE CALL OF THE WILD

Are Journalists a Slavering Pack?

It makes for high drama: the stag, blooded and faltering, plunges onward through the reddening snow. But the wolves are upon him, a silvered pack, relentless in the cold glare of the moon. Rolling back their dark lips to reveal the white sudden flash of fang, foaming and savage, the pack brings the stag shuddering to earth.

It is a popular—and overly romantic—view of the news media, but one that is not entirely lacking in truth. Richard Nixon must have seen flecks of foam during the final days of his presidency. There is some irony in the fact that from a bungled second-rate burglary grew deeds so dark they threatened to pull asunder the credibility of the United States government. An attorney general perjured himself, a president lied, and a veritable goody basket of felonies and misdemeanors was offered around. But if Nixon had just gone on TV and said, "A couple of lowlifes and a CIA spook got caught jimmying the lock on the Democratic National Committee. It was a dumb trick, nothing I'd approve, and I'm sorry," it would have all blown over. After all, he got away with the Checkers speech, with the most maudlin lines since Peter Pan asked for applause to resurrect Tinker Bell. (One good shave and a tan, and Nixon might even have outshone JFK at the debate.) But Nixon believed so in the ferocity of the journalistic pack that in the end he took actions almost sure to unleash it.

Yes, the media can be the wolf pack, going for the jugular; Bill Clinton gets bitten regularly. Vince Foster spoke of the murderous climate of Washington before the Clinton aide drove to a wooded area and shot himself. When it comes to personal scandal, the press is perhaps more voracious than at any time since the wild days of the 1920s, when sensational trials, murders, kidnappings, and all varieties of True Crime screamed from the front pages. Tabloid journalism has moved into the mainstream, pursuing sources with money and the chance of a brief fling at fame, and its centrifugal force has whirled the mainstream media much closer to its brand of sensationalism. At the same time worried editors see statistics on shrinking readership and move away from coverage of serious public policy issues. People are bored with government? Then let's give them more O.J., more celebrities, more ersatz trends. The scandal stories have the virtue of being titillating and demand little in the way of thought from readers. But although the pack will follow the scent of scandal at a moment's notice, the idea that the press is constantly aggressive, constantly on the prowl, guarding against corruption, malfeasance, and sheer incompetence is more illusion than reality. A more apt animal metaphor than the wolf pack might be Garfield—fat, cynical, slovenly, hanging on the screen door by his toenails for lack of anything better to do, thinking *Bored, Bored. Bored. I'm so bored I could* scream!

When the press does act in a pack, the species is more often *Sardinius canned* than *lupus*. It is packed together in a small space, eyes glazed, and—to say the least—uncomprehending. The news media are more often passive than predatory, the pads on their paws more accustomed to carpet than the frozen pack ice. Oh, yes, the beast has fangs, but if you scratch its tummy and make nice, it is more likely to purr.

The image the press likes to present of itself is of the more tough, aggressive variety; the public remembers such pictures as Mike Wallace, camera crew trotting behind, doing one of his "ambush interviews" or newsmen and newswomen sniffing about for conflict of interest in Whitewater or badgering members of Congress about misusing the congressional post office or trailing a cabinet official who appears to have engaged in questionable financial deals. Perhaps the quintessential "gotcha" story was *All the President's Men*, Bob Woodward and Carl Bernstein defeating the White House.

What few people may remember about the latter, however, is that for a long time the *Washington Post* was a pariah in the press corps for staying with the story. The paper was accused of being suckered by two inexperienced reporters on a trail to nowhere or of engaging in a vendetta against the administration. The popular myth of Watergate is of the wolf pack getting its prey, but in fact the cover-up came close to succeeding; at one point John Mitchell gloated that publisher of the *Post* "Katie Graham's gonna get her tit caught in a big, fat wringer." As it turned out, it was a tender part of *his* anatomy that wound up in the wringer, but who knows how many other cover-ups have gone like clockwork? The pack didn't assemble until there was a lot of blood.

A few years after Watergate I was invited to speak to the New York Broadcasters Association. Much to my surprise, a majority of delegates were still furious with Dan Rather for being impolite to Nixon. If was almost as if he had spat at the king. These were the people who controlled the flickering images on the tube, and they were still siding with Power—even when it had been dethroned.

The general public sees the media as both predatory and powerful. But while the pack is in a feeding frenzy on an obvious target, other meatier game roams free, because the pack doesn't lunge until a fair amount of blood already has been spilled. Indeed, the press is always powerful, but sometimes this power is simply the enormous force of inertia, just sitting there, a forty-ton boulder, keeping the status quo in place.

Stronger than the scoop mentality is the delicious comfort of running with the bunch. It's like the strategy of some marathoners—get too far behind, and you're hopelessly out of it; too far ahead, you could trip. Your best shot is just staying with the pack.

I like to explain to my journalism students that "news" is cyclical, like the phases of the moon, and I make them a little drawing:

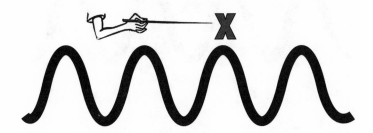

When you approach editors with story ideas, I say, *here* is where you want to be:

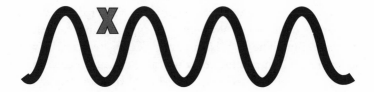

The story is not so new that the editor has never heard of it; she might have gotten a snippet at a cocktail party or seen a tiny news item someplace. It's fresh—but not utterly unheard of. But if you are here

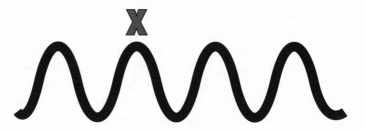

you are probably already too late. The story may have been assigned. And if you're here

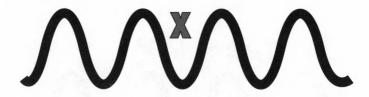

Deadsville. The story has already been on the cover of *Time*. You would think that an ideal place to be on the story would be where nobody's ever heard of it; when it is really fresh and new:

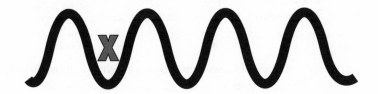

Wrong. This is the level of the most acute discomfort for editors, because the story has not yet entered the media maelstrom. News that's *really* new is the most distrusted. And if it challenges the conventional wisdom about the way things are—or ought to be—it is even more suspect.

For example, in the early seventies I was assigned by the *New York Times Magazine* to write a piece on Vietnam veterans. It was a subject I didn't know much about, so I approached it with few preconceptions. What I found was an enormous well of rage and pain toward a country that sent them off to a war it then disavowed, that most of their friends, neighbors, and family had come to despise. My story, written in a fairly straightforward and reportorial way, reflected that rage. I did use some poems I had found in a collection put out by a veterans' group, because they seemed to express so well the feelings of many vets. This one, for example, describes the "flashback" experience:

Streets quiet and wet
Green bags of garbage and leaves
Neatly placed by the road.
Abruptly another scene pierces my mind
Other green bags are remembered
Neatly placed by the road
Green bags made from ponchos
Bags with legs sticking out the bottoms
A nightmare awaiting the Man from Glad.[1]

At the time the *Times* was the site of a generational battle between senior editors who had hawkishly cheered the war as a patriotic duty and younger ones who had sided more with the protesters. Word came back to me; the poems would have to go. Too emotional.

Reluctantly, I complied. I thought the poems captured the quality of the vets' experience with great clarity and passion. But I edited out the poetry and sent the revised version to my editor. Word came back again: *still* too emotional.

I pointed out that none of these emotions was mine. I simply reported what I saw and heard. Few people wanted to touch the edge of that rage, however—especially those senior editors. My story ran elsewhere—and the veterans' rage stayed underground until it burst out later with explosive force.

But that was then, you say, and this is now. Alas, I have had similar experiences all along the way and quite recently too. It happens in particular with stories about feminism, race, gays, peace issues, environmental racism, human rights. This experience, of being regarded with suspicion, is quite familiar to all journalists who are exploring stories that are on the edge, that are foreign to middle-class editors' sensibilities or that run counter to some societal expectation. When sexual harassment first surfaced as a story, many editors not only didn't jump on the bandwagon, they questioned whether it was a story at all. In an article I wrote, I interviewed two single mothers who worked as bar waitresses to stay off welfare. One editor with whom I was working did not think their tales of continual harassment were legitimate, because of the place they had chosen to work. Didn't women who worked in a bar *ask* for it? And if it upset them so, couldn't they have gotten jobs as domestics?

That one nearly left me speechless. This was an affluent male with a good job who probably had never scrubbed a toilet in his life. Did he have any idea what domestics do all day? And what they are paid? A bar waitress can pick up good money in tips; that's why the women were there. It wasn't because they loved getting pinched on the thigh by drunks every night.

This sort of reaction isn't uncommon when the story is about emerging stories such as rape, or heterosexual AIDS, or the fact that working women are not dropping dead of heart attacks. The same mechanism was operating against reporters who wrote in the sixties that we were not winning the war in Vietnam. The entire *Time* bureau in Saigon resigned one day when reporters found out their stories were being rewritten in New York to give a picture exactly opposite of what they were reporting. So eager were editors not to jump on the story—to believe that the war was a patriotic crusade that we were winning—that they borrowed a page from Orwell and simply rewrote history to make it more agreeable.

I once interviewed Clark Clifford, after he had left the job of secretary of defense under Lyndon Johnson, and he told me that his first trip to Vietnam convinced him the war was an utter disaster. I asked him why it was so clear to him, when so very many other smart people could not see what was happening. He said that so many people's careers had become so entwined with the war that they were seeing not reality but what they hoped to be true. He felt that many were not lying but deceiving themselves—believing that if they could just hang on, they would see the proverbial light at the end of the tunnel. Things would come out all right, and history would speak well of them.

It is not surprising that many Big Stories are not broken by Big Names in Journalism. In Vietnam then-young reporters like David Halberstam and Neil Sheehan and Frances FitzGerald could see that the body counts were a charade and the war was a disaster. Seymour Hersh was working for a small news service when he broke the story on the My Lai massacre; Woodward and Bernstein were rookies on the metro section when they broke Watergate. The Big Foot reporters were dining at the homes of bureaucrats in Georgetown, not freezing their asses in underground parking garages.

And that's another reason that the pack doesn't form more often; it's not really hungry. Usually, journalists don't want to rip out the throats of powerful people; we are too busy going to their parties and drinking their booze. (When politicians are high in public approval ratings, it's amazing how good their press clippings are. The press adores winners.)

Make no mistake about it: being around power has a definite glow to it. Careers get made that way. The perception of having access to the powerful means that you get assigned to stories that other people don't, that editors are more than a tad more respectful, and that when the job just above yours opens up, you have a shot at it when some other less-well-connected journalist does not. I remember one reporter who ran a small bureau from a minuscule office next to mine in the National Press Building for a string of Texas dailies during the Kennedy administration—and who had been friendly with Vice President Lyndon Johnson back in Texas. A few days after the assassination, when Johnson came to power, the reporter suddenly had a syndicated column. It is always that way. Today "Friends of Bill" have access that other reporters can't get. If Newt

Gingrich continues to be one of the most powerful men in Washington, he may still be dodging the occasional brickbat, but he will find himself transformed in the press from mean little assassin into respected power broker. (Newt seems to be his own worst enemy, though, always slipping into guerrilla mode; he is so used to snarling that he may not be able to get the hang of the amiability that Ronald Reagan used so well, nor the self-deprecating good humor that John Kennedy brought to his encounters with the press.)

Being on the inside not only can do wonders for your career but *feels* great. All those schmucks out there can't go where *you* can. (I will admit it: I used to let my wallet hang open when I was paying at the supermarket counter so people could see my White House press pass. The looks of envy from supermarket clerks made me so toasty warm. Of course, it was stupid, but I did it anyway.)

Journalist and critic Hodding Carter III observes of the national press corps, "They spend so much of their time with the Philistines that they hardly notice they have been shorn, perhaps because they offer themselves up to the shears so eagerly. They move in packs with the affluent and powerful to Washington (just doing their job, of course), then swarm with them every summer to every agreeable spot on the eastern seaboard between Canada and New Jersey." And he notes that when they get to the level of being asked to appear on a TV panel show, even the least well paid of them "makes at least six times more than the average American family."[2]

This does not make a journalist a member of the Red Brigades, eager to overthrow the system—or even to criticize it very loudly. Carter writes, "The truth is that there is not a hell of a lot of sympathy among the leading figures of national journalism for outsiders, losers, nonconformists or seriously provocative political figures and causes. The ideological spread of what is published regularly moves from A to E, with A being anchored on the right and E barely making it to center left. . . . We have a national press that does not so much question the national consensus as reflect it."

And *Washington Post* media critic Howard Kurtz notes, "The seductions of power are everywhere." He writes of reporters' taking free trips with Donald Trump, watching a Redskins game from the box of the owner, dining privately at the White House:

> One of the big crises in the Capitol unfolded last year when the Clinton administration's new ethics rules threatened to shut down the White House Correspondents dinner, the Gridiron dinner, and other black-tie affairs at

which reporters hobnob with officials. There was an almost audible sigh of relief among media people when high-level negotiations produced a face-saving compromise. Gradually, almost imperceptibly, this sort of high-level schmoozing and socializing can change one's outlook. Soon, the little perquisites and luxuries that are part of the expense account life no longer seem unusual.[3]

Although the news media made a big deal of Clinton's fancy "runway" haircut from Christophe, Kurtz notes that several reporters he knows regularly drop by Christophe's pricey Washington shop for a trim.

If ever the media were in their Garfield mode, it was during the Reagan years, when a constellation of factors came together—as if by some gravitational pull of an unseen planet—to defang the pack. The Reagan years saw a massive transfer of wealth from the lower and middle classes to the upper classes. In retrospect we learned of the looting of the Department of Housing and Urban Development in those years as well as a frenzy of speculation with monies from deregulated s&ls. How did the press not notice? Writer Mark Hertsgaard notes that "upon Reagan's Ascension to power, the media quickly settled into a posture of accommodating passivity from which they never completely arose."[4]

What were the factors that produced this semistupor? First, a president who was a professional actor, a uniquely salable product, who could not only go over the heads of the media directly to the public via television but whose coating of "Teflon" discouraged journalistic snarls. And perhaps more than any president in recent memory, Reagan was shielded from the media by his managers, while they buffed his image to a burnished hue. What most Americans will probably remember about the president and the press is Reagan walking to his chopper, shouting one-liners to a reporter who is trying to scream over the whirling rotors.

We rarely saw Reagan when he was not scripted, packaged, and cued by the TelePrompter. And in that situation he was very, very good. The public relations superstructure that surrounded Reagan was savvy and knew the quirks of the media the way the old family doctor used to know his patient's coughs and crotchets. Hertsgaard quotes one Reagan operative as saying, "The media will take what we feed them. As long as you come in there every day, hand them a well-packaged, premasticated story in the format they want, they'll go away." Give the pack a little Gravy Train, and it won't lust for red meat.

This manipulation fed perfectly into the TV-dominated media of the '80s, Hertsgaard points out, and with the fact that reporters who wanted to slaver at least a *bit* "reported to superiors whose individual and collective self-interest mitigated against strong or consistent criticism of a government as pro-corporate as Reagan's."

Never before in the modern media era had all those factors come together so perfectly. Two decades earlier John Kennedy had understood that TV was the medium of the future and would compliment reporters, who admired his élan and his wit and his smarts, on their stories (so long as they were favorable). But their bosses didn't really go for the liberal domestic agenda of the Kennedy administration, so the press was often quite critical. Media bosses did like Nixon's probusiness stance, but reporters couldn't stand his paranoia and his inability to be comfortable with the press. (One of my favorite Nixon photos is of him trying to be Kennedy casual by walking along the shoreline—but he was still wearing his suit.)

The Nixon years brought out the pack instincts to a fare-thee-well—at least after the blood started to flow. Jimmy Carter had neither the policies that pleased corporate America nor the warm rapport with the media that would have made him a popular favorite. George Bush wasn't popular enough to overcome the thud in the economy. Bill Clinton hasn't been able to get past voters' suspicion that he's always changing his mind.

But the machinery of manipulation all came together with Reagan. When it came to criticism by the press, the silence was deafening. David Broder of the *Washington Post* writes: "Virtually every reporter in Washington knew that Reagan had only a fleeting interest in the day-to-day policies and operation of government. But too many of us convinced ourselves that it made no difference, that it was enough to be lucky and popular."[5]

And former *Washington Post* editor Ben Bradlee told Hertsgaard, "The return to deference was part of that subconscious feeling we had. . . . You know, initially, after Watergate, the public was saying, about the press, 'OK, guys, now that's enough, that's enough.' . . . I think we were sensitive to that criticism much more than we should have been, and we did ease off."[6]

Bill Clinton made a big mistake when he came into office with a crew that knew how to campaign but that seemed to view the Washington press corps as the enemy. Clinton's minions restricted access and refused to give the media the perks they required; instead of scratching tummies, the White House was more than a tad scornful of the press. These were young people who just won an election by going over the heads of the Big Feet to such places as *Arsenio*, and they were just a bit cocky. But of course, governing is a lot different from running, and you need the media day by day to tell your story in the frame *you* choose, if possible. The Clinton media operation was helped for a time by bringing in old pro David Gergen, but it has never quite been able to get it right. Stumbles over such issues as gays in the military, health care, and appointees who didn't pay taxes for their household help gave the impression that the White House was not a powerful juggernaut but a bush league operation. And of course, Clinton faces a vicious and unrelenting campaign of vilification from the right, a level of attack that never assailed Reagan or Bush.

Indeed, competitive pressures are driving all forms of media these days, but they are driving the pack not to high-minded defense of the Republic and punishment of malefactors but to *novelty*—to strive to come up with something "new." And because editors don't cotton to anything that is *really* new—so new it hasn't made the story meetings or even the gossip around the water cooler—this often means that writers strain to come up with a "take" or an "angle" that seems innovative and that can be enhanced with catchy headlines and graphics. The need for a compelling narrative too often drives the story these days. The "high concept" headline comes first, the facts and figures second.

Hillary Clinton as Superbitch! Hillary as Saint! Whitewater as the New Watergate! Welfare Mothers as Sluts! The Family in Crisis! Women a Mess! Inferior Black Brains! I've talked to respected journalists who say they are tearing their hair out to find the spin on the story that will make editors nod their heads. These days the wolf pack—in search of a sexy new angle on an old story or a personal scandal—will rush right past somebody who is looting the treasury. Investigative reporting is at a low ebb, because it is expensive, and because baseless suits can put a real dent in a publication's cash flow. The sound and the fury of the press as it stalks a key figure in a sexy murder trial or thunders after some hapless official who wrote checks to his mistress with what should have been the kids' milk money give the public the idea that the media are vigilant, when they are merely following the crowd to the most obvious place. And as the media get more and more fragmented, as the competition for readers' time and attention becomes ever more frantic and crowded with players, the most serious, most complex stories will tend to get elbowed out by the glitzy, the "new," and the scandalous.

The laziness of pack journalism allows cultural stereotypes to multiply like bacteria on the locker-room floor. It is dangerous to be too far out in front or too far behind. Being in the middle of the pack is comfortable, risk free, and—too often—rewarded. Journalists have to show more willingness to break free of the pack, to cover new and little-trodden turf, to risk the snickers and even the scorn of their colleagues and editors when the story they are pursuing is not trendy or in line with the conventional political wisdom of the moment.

Despite all the pressures that help to render the press toothless except in certain high-profile cases, the image of the media as the ever-ravenous wolf pack has great staying power. Will the pack gather and run once again, when the moon is bright and cold and the prey is dripping blood? Probably. But don't sit up nights waiting to hear the howling at the moon. It will come intermittently, and the prey will be obvious and easy to spot. Your best bet, if you'd really like a glimpse of the press at work, is just to put the Friskies out on the porch.

NOTES

1. Totem and Taboo: The Culture of the News Media

Unless otherwise noted, all newspaper, magazine, and scholarly articles cited can be found in NEXIS.

1. George Gerbner, Michael Morgan, and Nancy Signorielli, *Living with Television* (Hillsdale, N.J.: Erlbaum, 1986), pp. 17–40.

2. James Alan Fox, "A Nation with Peril on Its Mind," *Los Angeles Times*, February 14, 1994.

3. Readership figures come from Media Watch, the watchdog group based at University of California at Los Angeles, 1990.

4. Erna Smith, "Transmitting Race: The Los Angeles Riots in Television News" (paper prepared for Joan Shorenstein

Center for Press, Politics, and Public Policy, Harvard University, research paper R-11, May 1994).

5. Cited in Jonathan Alter, "Is the Press Fair to Ferraro?" *Newsweek*, September 24, 1984.

6. Ibid.

7. Theodore L. Glasser, "Objectivity Precludes Responsibility," *Quill*, February 1984, p. 15.

8. Evelyn Fox Keller, "Feminism as an Analytic Tool for the Study of Science," *Academe* (September–October 1983): 15–16.

9. Glasser, "Objectivity."

10. Howard Kurtz, "When the Press Outclasses the Public," *Columbia Journalism Review*, June 1994.

11. Herbert Gans, *People, Plans, and Policies* (New York: Columbia University Press, 1993), p. xvix.

12. Michael Katz, *The Undeserving Poor* (New York: Pantheon, 1989), p. 5.

13. Ibid., p. 152.

2. Put the Blame on Eve, Boys: The Devil Made Her Do It—Or Maybe It Was Just Her Tiny Brain

1. Sherry Ortner, "Is Female to Male as Nature Is to Culture?" *Feminist Studies* (October 1978).

2. Vivian Gornick, "Woman as Outsider," in Vivian Gornick and Barbara K. Moran, eds., *Woman in Sexist Society* (New York: Basic Books, 1971), p. 137.

3. Ibid., p. 143.

4. Quoted in Edwin Schur, *Labeling Women Deviant* (New York: Random House, 1984).

5. "Breaking Silence," *People*, November 11, 1991.

6. Steven Jay Gould, *The Mismeasure of Man* (New York: Norton, 1981).

7. Ibid.

8. Quoted in Anne Eisenberg, "Women and the Discourse of Science," *Scientific American* (July 1992).

9. Paula J. Caplan and Jeremy B. Caplan, *Thinking Critically About Research on Sex and Gender* (New York: HarperCollins, 1994).

10. Ibid.

11. Camilla P. Benbow and Julian C. Stanley, "Sex Differences in Mathematical Ability: Fact or Artifact?" *Science* 210 (1980).

12. "Do Males Have a Math Gene?" *Newsweek*, December 15, 1980; "At Mathematical Thinking, Boys Outperform Girls," *Washington Post*, December 5, 1980; "The Gender Factor in Math," *Time*, December 15, 1980; "Are Boys Better at Math?" *New York Times*, December 7, 1980.

13. Edith H. Luchins with Richard Levin, "Women and the Pursuit of a Career in Mathematics," *Christian Science Monitor*, May 27, 1981.

14. "Bias in the Schools Still 'Cheating' Girls, Authors Find," *Houston Chronicle*, June 26, 1994.

15. Quoted in Anne Fausto-Sterling, *Myths of Gender: Biological Theories About Men and Women* (New York: Basic Books, 1985).

16. Lynn Fox, "Sex Differences Among the Mathematically Precocious," *Science* 224 (1984).

17. Luchins, "Women and the Pursuit of a Career."

18. K. C. Cole, "Hers," *New York Times*, December 3, 1981.

19. Luchins, "Women and the Pursuit of a Career."

20. Quoted in Susan Baxter, "The Last Word on Gender Differences," *Psychology Today*, March 1994.

21. Caplan and Caplan, *Thinking Critically.*

22. Evelyn Fox Keller, *Reflections on Gender and Science* (New Haven, Conn.: Yale University Press, 1985).

23. Allison Bass, "America's Failing Grades," *Boston Globe*, February 20, 1989.

24. Fausto-Sterling, *Myths of Gender.*

25. Baxter, "Last Word."

26. Caplan and Caplan, *Thinking Critically.*

27. Ibid.

28. Ibid.

29. "Closing the Gap," *Newsweek*, April 11, 1988.

30. Bass, "America's Failing Grades," p. 33.

31. "Closing the Gap," *Newsweek.*

32. Bass, "America's Failing Grades."

33. Keller, *Reflections on Gender.*

34. Recounted in Jon Beckwith and John Durdin, "Girls, Boys, and Math," *Biology as Destiny*, Sociobiology Study Group, 1984.

3. Unruly Bodies: Is It PMS, or Just the Wrong Side of Her Brain?

1. Carol Tavris, *The Mismeasure of Woman* (New York: Touchstone, Simon & Schuster, 1992), p. 132. (The story of the judge, A. Andrew Haulk, originally was reported by the *Los Angeles Times*, May 10, 1990.)

2. Paula J. Caplan and Jeremy B. Caplan, *Thinking Critically About Research on Sex and Gender* (New York: HarperCollins, 1994).

3. Tavris, *Mismeasure*, p. 147.

4. Ibid., p. 149.

5. Ibid.

6. Ibid., p. 150.

7. "Vicious Cycle: The Politics of Periods," *Washington Post*, July 8, 1993.

8. "Guns and Dolls," *Newsweek*, May 28, 1990.

9. Quoted in "Vicious Cycle," *Washington Post.*

10. Harriet C. Lerner, *Women in Therapy* (New York: Harper and Row, 1989).

11. "PMS: Misogynist Propganda?" *Sassy*, December 1992, p. 66.

12. Tavris, *Mismeasure*, p. 151.

13. Ibid., p. 152.

14. Caplan and Caplan, *Thinking Critically.*

15. Reported in Anne Fausto-Sterling, *Myths of Gender: Biological Theories About Men and Women* (New York: Basic Books, 1985).

16. Tavris, *Mismeasure*, p. 44.

17. Ruth Bleier, "Sex Differences Research: Science or Belief?" in Ruth Bleier, ed., *Feminist Approaches to Science* (New York: Pergamon, 1988).

18. Tavris, *Mismeasure*, p. 44.

19. R. C. Lewontin, Steven Rose, and Leon Kamin, *Not in our Genes* (New York: Pantheon, 1984).

20. Tavris, *Mismeasure*, p. 49.

21. Ibid., p. 48.

22. Fausto-Sterling, *Myths of Gender*.

23. Bleier's argument with *Science* is recounted in Tavris, *Mismeasure*, pp. 50–51.

24. Naomi Weisstein, "Tired of Arguing About Biological Inferiority?" *Ms.*, November 1982.

25. "Subtle but Intriguing Differences Found in the Brain Anatomy of Men and Women," *New York Times*, April 11, 1989.

26. Fausto-Sterling, *Myths of Gender*.

27. Ibid.

28. "Guns and Dolls," *Newsweek*, May 28, 1990.

29. "Old Chestnut, New Thoughts," *Economist*, December 26, 1992.

30. "The Brain: His and Hers," *Discover*, April 1, 1981.

31. Bleier, "Sex Differences Research."

4. Dragon Ladies: Give Women Power, and Who Knows What Will Happen

1. Marilyn French, *Beyond Power* (New York: Ballantine Books, 1985).

2. Edwin Schur, *Labeling Women Deviant* (New York: Random House, 1984).

3. Dorothy Dinnerstein, *The Mermaid and the Minotaur* (New York: Harper/Colophon, 1977).

4. Schur, *Labeling Women*.

5. "The Hillary Factor," *Time*, September 14, 1992, p. 30.

6. Barbara Bonham, Letter to the Editor, *Lawrence* (Massachusetts) *Eagle Tribune*, October 15, 1993, in regard to a Scripps Howard News Service column about the Bobbitts that the *Lawrence* (Massachusetts) *Eagle Tribune* printed on September 30, 1993.

7. Dinnerstein, *Mermaid*.

8. French, *Beyond Power*.

9. Cited in Carol Hymowitz and Michaele Weissman, *A History of Women in America* (New York: Bantam, 1981), p. 36.

10. Caryl Rivers, "The Specter of a Dragon Lady," *Boston Globe*, August 11, 1988.

11. Geraldine Ferraro with Linda Bird Francke, *My Story* (New York: Bantam Books, 1985), p. 209.

12. Susan Faludi, *Backlash* (New York: Crown, 1991), p. 277.

13. Ibid., p. 209.

14. Bernice Buresh, "Innovations in Reporting on Women and Public Policy" (proposal prepared for Joan Shorenstein Barone Center for Press, Politics, and Public Policy, Harvard University, May 1989), p. 5.

15. Katherine Corcoran, "Pilloried Clinton," *Washington Journalism Review*, January–February 1993, notes the *New York Times* story. Karlyn Kohrs Campbell, "Shadowboxing with Stereotypes: The Press, the Public, and the Candidates' Wives," (paper prepared for Joan Shorenstein Barone Center for Press, Politics, and Public Policy, Harvard University, research paper R-9, July 1993), p. 7, notes the comparisons with Glenn

Close's portrayal and the *Wizard of Oz* character; Don Feder, "Hillary's America's Own Eva Peron," *Boston Herald*, April 1, 1992.

16. "The Hillary Factor," *Time*, September 14, 1992, p. 30.

17. Ibid.

18. Campbell, "Shadowboxing," p. 8.

19. Cited in Corcoran, "Pilloried Clinton," p. 19.

20. Quoted in Campbell, "Shadowboxing," pp. 6–7.

21. P. J. O'Rourke, "Collective Guilt," *American Spectator*, November 1993.

22. Corcoran, "Pilloried Clinton," cites *U.S. News and World Report*. "What Hillary Problem?" *Spy*, February 1993; "The Trouble with Bill and Hillary," *Maclean's*, April 11, 1994.

23. Patricia J. Williams, "Attack of the Fifty-Foot First Lady," *Village Voice*, January 26, 1993, p. 35.

24. Quoted in Susan Douglas, "Pundit Watch: Feminism and Radicalism," *Progressive*, February 1993.

25. Michael Barone, "Is She a Liability to Feminism?" *U.S. News and World Report*, March 21, 1994.

26. Mickey Kaus, "Thinking of Hillary," *New Republic*, February 15, 1993.

27. A. M. Rosenthal, "The First Ladyship," *New York Times*, March 11, 1994.

28. Kaus, "Thinking of Hillary."

29. Jonathan Rowe, "The View of You from the Hill," *Columbia Journalism Review*, August 1994.

30. Michael Kelly, "Saint Hillary," *New York Times Magazine*, May 23, 1993.

31. Ellen Hume, "Reliable Sources," cnn, March 20, 1994.

32. Williams, "Attack," p. 38.

5. Vanishing Acts: How Good News About Working Women Disappears

1. Susan Faludi, *Backlash* (New York: Crown, 1991), p. 71.

2. Ibid.

3. "You Can't Do Everything," *USA Today*, March 10, 1989; "Mommy Career Track Sets Off a Furor," *New York Times*, March 8, 1989; "Pressed for Success, Women Careerists Are Cheating Themselves," *Washington Post*, May 14, 1989; "Women Discovering They're at Risk for Heart Attacks," Gannett News Service, March 12, 1991.

4. "N.Y. Times Initiating a Media Crusade to Orient Us back to Home Again," *Media Report to Women* 9 (2) (March–April 1983).

5. United Press International, "Majority of American Working Women Under Stress," March 27, 1991; "Working Women Stressed Out," Reuters, March 27, 1991; "Female Managers Face Super Stress," *Chicago Tribune*, May 8, 1989; *Business Week*, September 26, 1988; "Are You Headed for Overload?" *Redbook*, June 1990; "A Gender at Risk," *National Journal*, April 28, 1989.

6. Meyer Freidman and Ray H. Rosenman, *Type A Behavior and Your Heart* (New York: Alfred A. Knopf, 1974).

7. S. Haynes and M. Feinleib, "Women, Work, and Coronary Heart Disease: Prospective Findings from the Framingham Heart Study," *American Journal of Public Health* 70 (1980): 133–41.

8. "Women Discovering They're at Risk," Gannett News Service.

9. Rosalind C. Barnett and Caryl Rivers, "The Myth of the Miserable Working Woman," *Working Woman*, February 1992, p. 65.

10. Elaine Wethington and Ronald Kessler, "Employment, Parental Responsibility, and Psychological Distress," *Journal of Family Issues* (December 1989).

11. Faludi, *Backlash*, p. 89.

12. Barnett and Rivers, "Myth."

13. Sandra Scarr, Deborah Phillips, and Kathleen McCartney, "Working Mothers and Their Families," *American Psychologist* (November 1989).

14. Wethington and Kessler, "Employment."

15. Ibid.

16. "Are These Women Old Maids?" *People*, March 31, 1986.

17. Katha Pollitt, "Being Wedded Is Not Always Bliss," *The Nation*, September 20, 1986, p. 239.

18. Ibid.

19. Edwin Schur, *Labeling Women Deviant* (New York: Random House, 1984).

20. *Orlando Sentinel*, April 22, 1994; *Atlanta Constitution*, May 2, 1994; *Ebony*, May 1994.

21. "The Ever-Present Problem of Absent Parents," *Guardian*, April 12, 1994; *Independent*, May 5, 1994.

22. "Home but Not Alone," *Newsday*, January 5, 1994.

23. "Mommy vs. Mommy," *Newsweek*, June 4, 1990.

24. The Caplans tell this story in Paula J. Caplan and Jeremy B. Caplan, *Thinking Critically About Research on Sex and Gender* (New York: HarperCollins, 1994).

25. *Washington Monthly*, 1982; *New York Times*, November 18, 1982.

26. "Can Your Career Hurt Your Kids? Yes, Say Many Experts," *Fortune*, May 20, 1991.

27. Lois Hoffman, "Effects of Maternal Employment in the Two-Parent Family," *American Psychologist* (44) (1989): 283–92.

28. "Spock, Brazelton and Now . . . Penelope Leach," *New York Times Magazine*, April 10, 1994.

29. Grace Baruch, Rosalind Barnett, and Caryl Rivers, *Lifeprints* (New York: McGraw-Hill, 1983).

30. Cited in Robert Karen, "Becoming Attached," *Atlantic*, February 1990.

31. "Spock, Brazelton," *New York Times Magazine*.

32. Faye J. Crosby, *Juggling* (New York: Free Press, 1991).

33. Scarr, Phillips, and McCartney, "Working Mothers."

34. Cynthia Longfellow and Deborah Belle, "Sources of Stress for Children" (paper presented at the National Conference of Social Stress Research, Durham, N.C., October 11, 1982).

35. Ann Oakley, cited in "Women: Paid-Unpaid Work and Stress," Canadian Advisory Council on the Status of Women, March 1989.

36. "A Change of Place," *Barron's*, March 21, 1994, p. 34.

37. Ibid.

38. Staff economist, U.S. Bureau of Labor Statistics, interview by author, March 12, 1995 (telephone).

39. "Middle Class Debt Is Seen as Hurdle to Economic Gains," *New York Times*, March 28, 1994.

40. "More Women Choose to Stay Home," *Christian Science Monitor*, May 24, 1994.

41. "The Return of the Single Breadwinner," *Chicago Sun-Times*, June 28, 1994; "Number of Stay-at-Home Moms on the Rise," *Courier Journal* (Louisville, Ky.), June 26, 1994; "Mothers Jilt Jobs for Homes, Families," Gannett News Service, June 20, 1994.

6. Monkey Business: Why the Media Love Our Primate Cousins

1. Nancy Tanner and Adrienne Zihlman, "Women in Evolution, Part 1: Innovation and Selection in Human Origins," *Signs: Journal of Women in Culture and Society* 1 (3) (1976).

2. Robert Bly, *Iron John* (Reading, Mass.: Addison-Wesley, 1990).

3. Robin Compton, "Old Bones Shatter Old Myths," *Biology as Destiny*, The Sociobiology Study Group, Science for the People, 1984.

4. Donna Haraway, *Primate Visions: Gender Race and Nature in the World of Modern Science* (New York: Rutledge, 1989).

5. Ellen Ruppel Shell, "Flesh and Bone," *Discover*, December 1991, p. 39.

6. Haraway, *Primate Visions*.

7. Adrienne Zihlman, "Sex, Sexes, and Sexism in Human Origins," *Yearbook of Physical Anthropology* 30 (1987): 12.

8. "Apes in the Office: It's a Jungle in There," *Chicago Tribune*, March 18, 1985.

9. "Irven deVore: Anthropologist Interview," *Omni*, June 1993.

10. "Encountering the Simple Truth of the Caveman," *Dallas Morning News*, November 4, 1992.

11. Zihlman, "Sex, Sexes, and Sexism," pp. 11–19.

12. Tim Hackler, "Is Anatomy Destiny?" *Cosmopolitan*, November, 1982, p. 219.

13. Naomi Weisstein, "Tired of Arguing About Biological Inferiority?" *Ms.*, November 1982, p. 41.

14. Cited in Haraway, *Primate Visions*.

15. "Racism, Murder, Genocide—They're in Our Genes," Reuters Library Report, July 28, 1992.

16. Compton, "Old Bones," p. 46.

17. Ibid.

18. Cited in Weisstein, "Tired of Arguing," p. 46.

19. Compton, "Old Bones," p. 47.

20. Ibid.

21. Shell, "Flesh and Bone."

22. Tanner and Zihlman, "Women in Evolution."

23. Sally Linton, "Woman the Gatherer: Male Bias in Anthropology," in S. E. Jacob, ed., *Women in Cross-Cultural Perspectives* (Urbana: University of Illinois Press, 1971).

24. Haraway, *Primate Visions*.

25. Ibid.

26. Cited in Haraway, *Primate Vision*.

27. Zihlman, "Sex, Sexes, and Sexism."

28. Haraway, *Primate Visions*.

29. Marcelo Gomes, "The Walking Way," *Omni*, January 1993.

30. Nancy Tanner, *On Becoming Human* (London: Cambridge University Press, 1981).

31. Marilyn French, *Beyond Power* (New York: Ballantine, 1985).

32. Weisstein, "Tired of Arguing," p. 46.

33. John Pfeiffer, "Did Woman Make Man?" *New York Times*, August 30, 1981.

34. Zihlman, "Sex, Sexes, and Sexism."

35. Mary Maxwell West and Melvin J. Konner, "The Role of the Father: An Anthropological Perspective," in Michael E. Lamb, ed., *The Role of the Father in Child Development* (New York: Wiley, 1976).

36. Eleanor Leacock, "Women's Status in Egalitarian Society: Implications for Social Evolution" *Current Anthropology* 19 (1978).

37. Weisstein, "Tired of Arguing," p. 85.

38. Sarah Blaffer Hrdy, *The Woman That Never Evolved* (Cambridge, Mass.: Harvard University Press, 1983).

39. Robert Wright, quoted in Steven Pinker, "Is There a Gene for Compassion?" *New York Times Book Review*, September 25, 1944, p. 3.

40. Scott Sleek, "Struggles for Equality Lead to More Divorce," *American Psychological Association Monitor* (October 1994): 20.

7. Born to Be Bad: The Fault, Dear Brutus, Is in Our Genes

1. Richard Herrnstein, "Deep Waters in the Gene Pool," *Independent*, November 13, 1994.

2. Stephen J. Gould, "Curveball," *New Yorker*, November 28, 1994.

3. Ibid.

4. Richard Lewontin, "Another Biological Determinism," *Biology as Destiny*, The Sociobiology Study Group, Science for the People, 1984, p. 4.

5. Jonathan Beckwith, "The Origins of Crime," *Technology Review* (February–March 1983).

6. "Born Bad? New Research Points to a Biological Role in Criminality," *American Health*, November 1993.

7. "Seeking the Roots of Violence," *Time*, April 19, 1993.

8. "Born Bad?" *American Health*.

9. Richard Hernnstein, "I.Q.," *Atlantic*, September 1971, pp. 43–64.

10. Quoted in "Seeking the Roots," *Time*.

11. "Researchers Link Gene to Aggression," *Los Angeles Times*, October 22, 1993.

12. Leon Kamin, paper presented at the Science and Journalism Conference, Harvard School of Public Health, Boston, April 19, 1986.

13. "Researchers Link Gene," *Los Angeles Times*.

14. Natalie Angier, "Gene Tie to Male Violence Is Studied," *New York Times*, October 22, 1993.

15. "How Brain's Chemistry Unleashes Violence," *Chicago Tribune*, December 13, 1993.

16. Steven Rose, "Mean Gene Streak," *Guardian*, June 2, 1994.

17. Ibid.

18. "New Storm Brews on Whether Crime Has Roots in Genes," *New York Times*, September 15, 1992.

19. Ibid.

20. "How Brain's Chemistry Unleashes Violence," *Chicago Tribune*.

21. "New Study of Adopted Danes Suggests Genetic Link to Crime," *Boston Globe*, January 8, 1982.

22. "Fear Clouds Search for Genetic Roots of Violence," *Los Angeles Times*, December 30, 1993.

23. "The Genetics of Bad Behavior," *Newsweek*, November 1, 1993.

24. "Evidence Found for a Possible Aggression Gene," *Science*, June 18, 1993; "Old Chestnut, New Thoughts," *Economist*, December 26, 1992.

25. "Fear Clouds Search," *Los Angeles Times*.

26. "Buchanan Note Probed," *Newsday*, January 5, 1992.

8. Flash—Feminism Is Still Dead: But It's Bad for You, Anyhow

1. Susan J. Douglas, *Where the Girls Are* (New York: Times Books, 1994). I found Douglas's work invaluable in retracing the history of press coverage of the women's movement. See especially pp. 163–65, 168–69, and 171.

2. Susan Faludi, *Backlash* (New York: Crown, 1991), p. 80.

3. Ibid.

4. Ibid., p. 76.

5. Cited in Karlyn Kohrs Campbell, "Shadowboxing with Stereotypes: The Press, the Public, and the Candidates' Wives" (paper prepared for Joan Shorenstein Barone Center for Press, Politics, and Public Policy, Harvard University, research paper R-9, July 1993), p. 9.

6. Murray Kempton, "Beware a 'Sober' Media," *Newsday*, July 1, 1994.

7. "Don't View Men as the Enemy," *Dallas Morning News*, June 25, 1994.

8. Christina Hoff Sommers, *Who Stole Feminism: How Women Have Betrayed Women* (New York: Simon & Schuster, 1994).

9. Laura Flanders, "The Stolen Feminism Hoax," *Extra*, September–October 1994.

10. Cited in Flanders, "Stolen Feminism Hoax."

11. Ibid.

12. Ibid.

13. "Gender Battles in the Civil War," *Kirkus Reviews*, July 1, 1994.

14. "Along Comes Disney with Its Version of 'Real' America," *St. Petersburg Times*, June 28, 1994; "Author's Twisted Theory Ties Athletics to Abuse," *Buffalo News*, July 18, 1994.

15. Evelyn Trapp Goodrick, "Different Voices: Selected Women Editorial Page Editors Discuss Their Work" (paper presented to the Commission on the Status of Women, Association for Education in Journalism and Mass Communication, August 1992), p. 9.

16. Georgie Anne Geyer, "The Threat Around Us, " *Memphis Commercial Appeal*, March 12, 1994.

17. John Leo, "Skirmishes in the Topless War," *U.S. News and World Report*, July 25, 1994.

18. "Can Do Is Byword of New Chief of County Bar," *Cleveland Plain Dealer*, July 3, 1994.

19. Claudia Wallis, "Onward, Women!" *Time*, December 4, 1989.

20. Richard Cohen, "Demagoguing the Family," *Washington Post*, July 5, 1994.

21. Eleanor Clift, "The Year of the Smear: Feminazi," *Newsweek*, July 11, 1994.

22. Douglas, *Where the Girls Are*, p. 294.

9. Thought Police, Tribes, and Victims: The Media and Multiculturalism

1. David Gates, "White Male Paranoia," *Newsweek*, March 29, 1993.

2. Cited in Ted Pease, "Race and Resentment in the Newsroom: Perceptions of Minority Journalists at U.S. Newspapers" (paper submitted to the Minorities and Communication Division, Association for Education in Journalism and Mass Communications, March 1992).

3. *Boston Republic*, 1880, cited in Alan Lupo, *Liberty's Chosen Home* (Boston: Little, Brown, 1977).

4. Pat Buchanan, "American Values Are Drowned in Rising Tide of Immigrants," *Boston Herald*, August 18, 1991.

5. Irving Kristol, "The Tragic Error of Affirmative Action," *Wall Street Journal*, August 1, 1994; Thomas Sowell, "Multiculturalism Is a Media Delusion," *Arizona Republic*, December 2, 1993; William Bennett on *This Week with David Brinkley*, ABC, May 5, 1991; Charles Krauthammer, quoted in *Seattle Times*, January 7, 1991; Arthur Schlesinger, quoted in "Divided We Stand," *Los Angeles Times*, April 13, 1993.

6. Max Lerner, "Having Helped Save the World, Has America Lost its Own Way?" *New York Post*, July 14, 1990.

7. Joe Klein, "The Threat of Tribalism," *Newsweek*, March 14, 1994.

8. Ibid.

9. Richard Bernstein, "The Arts Catch up with a Society in Disarray," *New York Times*, September 2, 1990.

10. Ibid.

11. Quoted in "Divided We Stand," *Los Angeles Times*.

12. John Leo, "Tribalism in the Newsroom," *U.S. News and World Report*, December 6, 1993.

13. "Thought Police," *Newsweek*, December 24, 1990.

14. Todd Gitlin, "On the Virtues of a Loose Canon," in Patricia Aufderheide, ed., *Beyond PC* (St. Paul, Minn.: Graywolf Press, 1992), p. 186.

15. "Diversity: Colleges Struggle with Separatism," (New Orleans) *Times-Picayune*, March 27, 1994; "Asian Infux at Cal Stirs Questions," *San Francisco Chronicle*, April 10, 1992; Bernstein, "The Arts Catch Up."

16. "Platform: Diversity," *Los Angeles Times*, January 4, 1992.

17. "Separate Ethnic Worlds Grow on Campus," *New York Times*, May 18, 1991; Bernstein, "The Arts Catch Up."

18. "Campus Racial Lines May be Blurring," *Boston Globe*, April 5, 1994.

19. Ibid.

20. Ibid.

21. Gitlin, "Virtues of a Loose Canon," p. 186.

22. The Harvard case is described in detail in Jon Weiner, "What Happened at Harvard," in Aufderheide, *Beyond PC*, pp. 98–105.

23. The SUNY case is reported in detail in David Beers, "What Happened at SUNY" in Aufderheide, *Beyond PC*, pp. 108–12.

24. The Houston case is detailed in Linda Brodsky and Shelli Fowler, "What Happened to English 306?" in Aufderheide, *Beyond PC*, pp. 114–17.

25. Beers, "What Happened at SUNY," p. 111.

26. Bernstein, "The Arts Catch Up."

27. Arthur Austin, "They're Turning Juries into Social Workers," *Cleveland Plain Dealer*, February 26, 1994.

28. "Lies of the Mind," *Time*, November 29, 1993.

29. Mike Males, "Recovered Memory: Child Abuse and Media Escapism," *Extra*, September–October 1994.

30. Ibid.

31. "The Date Rape Debate," *Newsday*, October 13, 1993.

10. Quota Queens Meet Affirmative Discrimination: When Fairness Comes Under Fire

1. Cited in Mercedes Lynn DeUriarte, "Exploring (and Exploding) the Media Prism," *Media Studies Journal* 8 (3) (Summer 1994): 170.

2. "Men's Group Sees Bias in Day for Daughters," *Chicago Sun-Times*, April 26, 1994; "Affirmative Discrimination," *Sacramento Bee*, November 19, 1993; "Political Debates Disrupt the Arts in Fulton County," *Atlanta Constitution*, June 5, 1993; CNN news reports, July 31, l994, NEXIS.

3. James Kilpatrick, "When Women's Rights Result in Wrongs," *St. Louis Post-Dispatch*, April 15, 1991; "Reverse Discrimination Is Widespread and Legal," *Houston Chronicle*, April 16, 1995.

4. David Gates, "White Male Paranoia," *Newsweek*, March 29, 1993.

5. Ibid.

6. Ibid.

7. Ellis Cose, "To the Victors, Few Spoils," *Newsweek*, March 29, 1993.

8. Gates, "White Male Paranoia."

9. Cornell West, *Race Matters* (New York: Vintage Books, 1994), p. 95.

10. "Class Privilege," *Boston Globe*, September 18, 1992, p. 1.

11. Ibid.

12. Ted Pease, "Race and Resentment in the Newsroom: Perceptions of Minority Journalists at U.S. Newspapers" (paper submitted to the Minorities and Communication Division, Association for Education in Journalism and Mass Communications, March 1992), p. 1; Ted Pease and J. Frazier Smith, "The Newsroom Barometer: Job Satisfaction and Racial Diversity in U.S. Daily Newspapers," Ohio Journalism Monograph series, Bush Research Center of the E. W. Scripps School of Journalism, Ohio University.

13. Pease, "Race and Resentment," p. 9.

14. Ibid., p. 4

15. Ibid., p. 15.

16. Ibid., p. 18.

17. Cited in Laurel Leff, "From Legal Scholar to Quota Queen: What Happens When Politics Pulls the Press into the Groves of Academe?" *Columbia Journalism Review*, September 1993.

18. Cited in Leff, "Legal Scholar to Quota Queen."

19. Ibid.

20. Patrick Buchanan, *Crossfire*, June 2, 1993.

21. "Media Spreads Lies and More Lies," *Arizona Republic*, June 24, 1993.

22. "Gotcha Journalism Takes No Prisoners," *Editor & Publisher*, April 23, 1994.

23. Leff, "Legal Scholar to Quota Queen."

24. "So Long, Lani," *Newsweek*, June 14, 1993.

25. "Gotcha Journalism," *Editor & Publisher*.

26. "The Plain Truth About Lani Guinier," *St. Louis Post-Dispatch*, April 17, 1994.

27. "Lani Guinier Won't Be Backing Down," *Dallas Morning News*, June 15, 1994.

11. Strangers Among Us: Zoo Stories and Ice Queens

1. David Shaw, "Negative News and Nothing Else," *Los Angeles Times*, December 11, 1990.

2. Ibid.

3. National Association of Black Journalists, *Kerner Plus 20* (Reston, Va.: National Association of Black Journalists, March 1988), p. 12.

4. Cited in "Adding Color to Coverage of the News," *St. Petersburg Times*, July 25, 1994.

5. Ibid.

6. Shaw, "Negative News."

7. Susan Trausch, "Protest Greets *Post* Magazine Story" *Boston Globe*, November 30, 1986.

8. Manning Marable, "Reconciling Race and Reality, *Media Studies Journal* 8 (3) (Summer 1994): 15.

9. Asian American Journalists Association (AAJA), *Project Zinger* (Washington, D.C.: Asian American Journalists Association, August 29, 1992).

10. Ibid., p. 23.

11. William Wong, "Covering the Invisible Model Minority," *Media Studies Journal* 8 (3) (Summer 1994): 55.

12. Elena Tajima Creef, "Model Minorities and Monstrous Selves," *Visual Anthropology Review* 9 (1) (Spring 1993): 143.

13. Ibid.

14. Ibid.

15. Ibid.

16. Cited in AAJA, *Project Zinger*, p. 11.

17. Ibid.

18. Shaw, "Negative News."

19. Cited in Shaw, "Negative News."

20. Ibid.

21. Ibid.

22. "Hispanic Activist Group Takes Swipe at Media," *Houston Chronicle*, July 22, 1994.

23. Cited in "Adding Color to the Coverage," *St. Petersburg Times*.

24. Jorge Quiroga, "Hispanic Voices: Is the Press Listening?" (paper prepared for Joan Shorenstein Center for Press, Politics, and Public Policy, Harvard University, discussion paper D-18, January 1995), p. 13.

25. "Racial Stereotyping and the Media," *Editor & Publisher*, August 6, 1994.

26. "Hispanic Activist Group," *Houston Chronicle*.

27. Cited in "Racial Stereotyping," *Editor & Publisher*.

28. Mike Barnicle, "All I Am Is Cold," *Boston Globe*, January 29, 1994.

12. The Color of Evil Is Black: The Media Demonize the Black Male

1. "An American Tragedy," *Time*, June 27, 1994.

2. "A Dark Night of the Soul in Boston," *People*, November 13, 1989.

3. Quoted in "A Stuart Legacy," *Boston Globe*, October 23, 1990.

4. Cited in "Study: Media in Boston Reinforce Racism by News Coverage," *Boston Globe*, January 28, 1987.

5. Ellis Cose, *The Rage of a Privileged Class* (New York: HarperCollins, 1993).

6. Ogletree and Williams are quoted in David Savage, "Minority Journalists Assail Crime Stories," *Los Angeles Times*, July 29, 1994.

7. Robert Entman, "African Americans According to TV News," *Media Studies Journal* 8 (3) (Summer 1995): 31, 32.

8. Quoted in "Crime Through Unclouded Eyes," *Times-Picayune*, March 25, 1994.

9. Ibid.

10. Ibid.

11. "Once a Victim, Now a Suspect," *Chicago Tribune*, April 28, 1992.

12. "Crime Through Unclouded Eyes," *Times-Picayune*.

13. David Shaw, "Negative News and Nothing Else," *Los Angeles Times*, December 11, 1990.

14. Roger Simon, "Willie, We Too Much Knew You," *Regardies*, October 1990.

15. Ibid.

16. Cited in Deborah Tannen, "The Unholy Alliance: Politics, Advertising, and the News," *Washington Post*, September 13, 1992.

17. Cited in Simon, "Willie."

18. Ibid.

19. Tannen, "The Unholy Alliance."

20. Erna Smith, "Transmitting Race: The Los Angeles Riot in Television News," (paper prepared for the Joan Shorenstein Barone Center for Press, Politics, and Public Policy, Harvard University, research paper R-11, May 1994), p. 6.

21. Cose, *Rage*.

22. Ibid.

13. Was Dan Quayle Right? Or Did the Media Buy a Pig in a Poke?

1. Barbara Dafoe Whitehead, "Dan Quayle Was Right," *Atlantic*, April 1993.

2. David Popenoe, "Family Affairs," *Institute for American Values* 6 (1 & 2) (Winter 1994): 9.

3. Stephanie Coontz, "Dan Quayle Is Still Wrong," *Washington Post*, May 9, 1993.

4. William Raspberry (*Washington Post*, April 5, 1993) and Paul Gigot *(Wall Street Journal*, April 9, 1993) are cited in *Institute for American Values* (1 and 2) Winter 1994: 9.

5. Steve Berga, "Valuing the Family: A Perspective," *Minneapolis Star Tribune*, June 6, 1993.

6. Cited in "U.S. Kids Need Right Stuff," *USA Today*, June 8, 1994.

7. Arloc Sherman, interview by Alan Lupo, May 25, 1994 (telephone).

8. Ibid.

9. Ibid.

10. As detailed in the forthcoming Rosalind Barnett and Caryl Rivers, *She Works, He Works . . . and the New American Family Works* (San Francisco: HarperCollins, 1996).

11. Joseph Veroff, Elizabeth Douvan, and Richard Kulka, *The Inner American* (New York: Basic Books, 1981).

12. Judith Wallerstein and Sandra Blakeslee, *Second Chances: Men, Women, and Children a Decade After Divorce* (New York: Simon & Schuster, 1991).

13. Stephanie Coontz, *The Way We Never Were: American Families and the Nostalgia Trap* (New York: Basic Books, 1992), p. 222.

14. Ibid.

15. Andrew J. Cherlin, Frank F. Furstenberg, P. Lindsay Chase-Lansdale, Kathleen Kiernan, Philip K. Robins, Donna Ruane Morrison, and Julien O. Tietler, "Longitudinal Studies on Effects of Divorce on Children in Great Britain and the United States," *Science*, June 7, 1991. Data are from the National Child Development Study of 17,414 women who gave birth in England, Scotland, and Wales in March 1958 and from the National Study of Children, which began in 1976 in the United States with a survey of 2,279 randomly chosen children aged seven to eleven.

16. "Study Disputes Divorce as Cause of Child's Problems," *Los Angeles Times*, June 7, 1991.

17. "Children Are Not Crippled by Divorce, Says Australian Study," Agence France-Presse, May 17, 1993.

18. Quoted in "Does Parenting Make a Difference?" *Families Today* (supplement to *Boston University Today*), September 21–27, 1992.

19. Cherlin et al., "Longitudinal Studies."

20. "No Surprise Here—Divorce Is Bad for Kids," *Orlando Sentinel*, March 29, 1993; "Hey, Murphy Brown, Dan Quayle Was Right," *Seattle Times*, April 2, 1993; "The American Family," *Fortune*, August 19, 1992.

21. Jean Baker Miller, interview by author, ca. 1991 (telephone).

22. Quoted in Berga, "Valuing the Family."

23. "Wedding Bands Made of Steel," *U.S. News and World Report*, April 6, 1991.

24. Ibid.

25. Grace Baruch, Rosalind Barnett, and Caryl Rivers, *Lifeprints* (New York: McGraw-Hill, 1983).

26. Coontz, *The Way We Never Were*, p. 223.

27. Whitehead, "Dan Quayle Was Right."

28. Sara S. McLanahan, "The Consequences of Single Motherhood," *American Prospect* (Summer 1994): Sara S. McLanahan with Irwin Garfinkle, "Welfare Is No Incentive," *New York Times*, July 29, 1994.

29. Cited in Coontz, *The Way We Never Were*, p. 259.

30. Ibid.

14. Comforting the Comfortable: Does News Coverage of the Poor Bolster the Status Quo?

1. Robert Bellah, Richard Madsen, William M. Sullivan, Ann Swidler, and Steven M. Tipton, *Habits of the Heart* (Berkeley: University of California Press, 1985), p. 144.

2. Ibid., p. 146.

3. Bellah et al. draw the connection between Franklin and Whitman as seminal figures in the development of the American sense of individualism, pp. 32–33.

4. Ibid., p. 43.

5. Alexis de Tocqueville, *Democracy in America* (1835–1839; reprint, New York: Doubleday Anchor Books, 1969).

6. "Welfare Fraud Costs Mass. Millions!" *Boston Herald*, July 15, 1990.

7. "The Hidden Hurdle,' *Time*, March 16, 1992.

8. "Hey, I'm Terrific!" *Newsweek*, February 17, 1992.

9. Jack E. White, "The Pain of Being Black," *Time*, September 16, 1991.

10. Ibid.

11. Ibid.

12. Cornell West, *Race Matters* (New York: Random House, 1994), pp. 73–90.

13. Derrick Bell, *Faces at the Bottom of the Well* (New York: Basic Books, 1992), p. 5.

14. David Shaw, "Negative News and Nothing Else," *Los Angeles Times*, December 31.

15. Alan Lupo, conversation with author, April 1994, Winthrop, Mass.

15. The War on Welfare: How the Media Scapegoat Poor Women

1. "Reforming Welfare," *Boston Globe*, May 17, 1994.

2. "The War on Welfare Mothers," *Time*, June 20, 1994.

3. Jeff Jacoby, "A Blunt, Ugly Truth: There Is a Connection Between Abuse and Welfare," *Boston Globe*, March 8, 1997.

4. Mortimer Zuckerman, "Starting Work as We Knew It," *U.S. News and World Report*, July 4, 1994.

5. Stephanie Coontz, *The Way We Never Were: American Families and the Nostalgia Trap* (New York: Basic, 1992), p. 11.

6. Perry R. Duis, *The Saloon: Public Drinking in Chicago and Boston, 1880–1920* (Urbana: University of Illinois Press, 1983), p. 100.

7. Frances Fox Piven and Richard Cloward, *Regulating the Poor* (New York: Vintage Books, 1993), p. 395.

8. Ibid., p. 390.

9. "Billionaire Sees Free Trade as a No Win Situation," *St. Louis Post-Dispatch*, August 7, 1994.

10. Michael B. Katz, *The Undeserving Poor* (New York: Pantheon, 1989), p. 231.

11. Ibid., p. 163.

12. Piven and Cloward, *Regulating the Poor*, p. 9.

13. Katz, *The Undeserving Poor*, p. 26.

14. "Sharp Rise in Births to Unmarried Whites Stirs Welfare Worries," *Boston Globe*, January 3, 1994.

15. Cited in Katz, *The Undeserving Poor*, pp. 17–21.

16. Alan Lupo, "Don't Let Facts Spoil Welfare Debate," *Boston Globe*, February 19, 1995.

17. Sara S. McLanahan, "The Consequences of Single Motherhood," *American Prospect* (Summer 1994): 49–55.

18. Ibid., p. 53.

19. Ibid., p. 54.

20. "Academics Say Welfare Cutoff Won't Reduce Illegitimate Births," *Boston Herald,* June 24, 1994.

21. Quoted in "Abolishing Welfare Would Only Hurt Inner Cities," *Houston Chronicle,* January 10, 1994.

22. Katz, *The Undeserving Poor,* p. 218.

23. George Will, "The Two-Parent Solution," *Boston Globe* , June 20, 1994.

24. Katz, *The Undeserving Poor,* p. 26.

25. Cited in Katz, *The Undeserving Poor,* p. 49.

26. Ibid.

27. Quoted in "In Welfare Debate, It's Not How But Why," *New York Times,* May 8, 1994.

16. The Call of the Wild: Are Journalists a Slavering Pack?

1. Charles Purcell, "The Walk," *Winning Hearts and Minds* (New York: McGraw-Hill, 1972).

2. Hodding Carter III, "Journalistic Pundits Move in the Right Circles," *Wall Street Journal,* August 16, 1984.

3. Howard Kurtz, "When the Press Outclasses the Public," *Columbia Journalism Review,* June 1994.

4. Mark Hertsgaard, "How Reagan Manipulated a Passive Press," *Boston Globe,* November 21, 1988, Focus section.

5. Quoted in Hertsgaard, "How Reagan Manipulated."

6. Ibid.

INDEX